Praise for *Sustainagility*

"Every person who worries about how we will be able to afford new, greener technologies should read this book: much of it will pay for itself."
Maud Olofsson, Deputy Prime Minister of Sweden and Minister for Enterprise and Energy

"Vital handbook for life and business in the 21st century."
Philip DesAutels, Director, Microsoft

"Smart recommendations for action both from business and consumer point of view. Every official dealing with sustainable energy should use this book as a reservoir of ideas in decision making."
Valdis Dombrovskis, Prime Minister of Latvia

"*Sustainagility* contains vital messages for all business leaders. Practical ways to reduce carbon footprint, save energy and other resources. The book is also a brilliant guide to new investment opportunities."
Brian Souter, CEO, Stagecoach Plc

"This book will change how you see the future. Every business leader should read it. Full of new ideas, business opportunities, and practical insights about solving many of the world's greatest challenges in a profitable way."
Sir Peter Vardy, former Chairman of Vardy Group Plc

"An optimistic, innovative yet technologically realistic vision of the future, which breaks from the luddites and doom merchants."
Professor Edmund King, President of the Automobile Association

"Excellent book that talks about actions and solutions. A good practical view of future challenges."
Frank Appel, CEO Deutsche Post DHL

"No nation, however large or small, wealthy of poor, can escape the impact of climate change."
Barack Obama, US President

"Global greenhouse gas emissions could be cut by about 40 per cent by 2030 at a cost of less than half a per cent of global GDP. I will say it again: the cost of inaction is far higher than the cost of action."
Prime Minister Fredrik Reinfeldt, Prime Minister of Sweden and President of the European Union

"If we falter, the earth itself will be at risk."
Gordon Brown, UK Prime Minister

"Failure to reach broad agreement would be morally inexcusable, economically short-sighted and politically unwise."
Ban Ki-moon, UN Secretary General

"The time has passed for diplomatic tinkering, for narrow bargaining. The time has come for courage, mobilization and collective ambition."
Nicolas Sarkozy, President of France

SUSTAINAGILITY

Definitions

Agility: fit and flexible, ability to move at high speed in response to change.

Mental agility: ability to think rapidly, enjoy new situations and form new ideas.

Sustainagility: ability to solve complex sustainability challenges in a profitable way, with rapidly evolving business innovations, applications, methods, products and processes, adapted to changing situations.

SUSTAINAGILITY

How smart innovation and agile
companies will help protect our future

PATRICK DIXON

JOHAN GORECKI

KoganPage

LONDON PHILADELPHIA NEW DELHI

First published in Great Britain and the United States in 2010 by Kogan Page Limited

120 Pentonville Road	525 South 4th Street, #241	4737/23 Ansari Road
London N1 9JN	Philadelphia PA 19147	Daryaganj
United Kingdom	USA	New Delhi 110002
www.koganpage.com		India

© Patrick Dixon and Johan Gorecki, 2010

The right of Patrick Dixon and Johan Gorecki to be identified as the authors of this work has been asserted by them in accordance with the Copyright, Designs and Patents Act 1988.

ISBN   978 0 7494 6083 9
E-ISBN   978 0 7494 6084 6

British Library Cataloguing-in-Publication Data

A CIP record for this book is available from the British Library.

Library of Congress Cataloging-in-Publication Data

Dixon, Patrick.
    Sustainagility : how smart innovation and agile companies will help protect our future / Patrick Dixon, Johan Gorecki.
        p. cm.
    Includes bibliographical references and index.
    ISBN 978-0-7494-6083-9 – ISBN 978-0-7494-6084-6 (ebook)   1. Sustainable development.
2. Technological innovations–Environmental aspects.   3. Social responsibility of business.
4. Recycling (Waste, etc.)   I. Gorecki, Johan.   II. Title.
    HC79.E5D59 2010
    338.9'27–dc22
                                                                                2010004984

Typeset by Graphicraft Limited, Hong Kong
Printed and bound in Great Britain by MPG Books Ltd, Bodmin, Cornwall

CONTENTS

ACKNOWLEDGEMENTS

We are deeply grateful to the large number of people who have helped us develop *Sustainagility*, have made comments and suggestions and inspired us along the way. In particular we would like to thank: Simon Blanchflower, Hazel Vinson, Sheila Dixon, Rejin Ibrahim, Fabian Levihn, Annelie Andersson, Carl Norlin, Magnus Lindell, Anders Modig, Bertil Rosquist, Jerry Ralowski, Gustav Brandberg, Anders Forsbom, Philip DesAutels, Carl-Harald Andersson, Brian Donnellan, Andreas Nilsson, Mattias Ohlson, Howard Kunreuther, Bernd Korves, Christine Cox, Helen Savill and Jon Finch, Publishing Director at Kogan Page. We are also grateful for comments and insights from many different workshops, seminars, forums and conferences where we have had the opportunity to debate these issues and explore green tech innovations. We welcome any comments, thoughts, corrections and suggestions on issues related to *Sustainagility*, which we will use to improve and update the next edition.

Note on carbon dioxide equivalence

Throughout this book we talk about carbon dioxide emissions, but other gases (methane for example) can also have a warming effect in the atmosphere. To simplify the text we refer to carbon dioxide emissions as a shorthand for a range of carbon-containing gases, and their equivalent impact, as if these gases were all carbon dioxide.

ABOUT THE AUTHORS

PATRICK DIXON is one of the world's leading futurists, and has been ranked as one of the 20 most influential business thinkers alive today (Thinkers 50, 2005). He speaks to many thousands of business leaders every year about *Sustainagility* issues including lifestyle trends, climate change, future energy needs, corporate image, growth of emerging markets, transport trends, leadership, innovation and agile organizations – identifying risks and maximizing opportunities. His clients include Microsoft, Google, Hewlett Packard, Nokia, AT&T, Siemens, Ford, Airbus, KLM/Air France, ExxonMobil, BP and Shell. Chairman of Global Change Ltd, and Fellow, Centre for Management Development, London Business School, author of 12 other books including *Futurewise* and *Building a Better Business*, he has spoken to audiences in over 50 nations, and presents at more than 40 corporate events a year, to audiences of up to 4,500 a time. His websites have been visited by over 12 million different people with 2 million video views.
Contact: patrickdixon@globalchange.com, +44 7768 511 390, http://www.globalchange.com.

JOHAN GORECKI is the founder/owner and CEO of Globe Forum, which is an internationally recognized marketplace for sustainable innovation, bringing together innovators, investors, multinationals and entrepreneurs. Globe Forum holds sustainability forums in European cities. He is also the founder of Globe Awards, for sustainability innovations. As an entrepreneur, Johan worked with the founding team of Skype, the world's leading IP telephone company, and he worked with the international entertainment broadcasting group Modern Times Group (MTG).
Contact: johan.gorecki@globeforum.com, +46 8 586 199 00, http://www.globeforum.com.

INTRODUCTION:
FUTURE SCENE

UN President Interview, 20 May 2040,
CNN World Report

UN President Rikard Bersgstrom with Sara Lewis, Presenter, World Report

Q: Looking back from your appointment as President of the United Nations in May 2031 to your retirement today, what is the one outstanding issue that has dominated your attention?

Sustainability and climate threats – no question. And how to meet the daily needs of the 9.1 billion people alive today. The drought across much of Northern and Southern Africa from 2031 to 2035 was a terrible disaster, killing over 3.7 million. The catastrophic flooding of Bangladesh in 2036, with monsoon and rising sea levels, which drowned at least 235,000. The Water War between Uganda, Sudan and Egypt over the control of the Nile, which continues. The sharp rise of energy prices three years ago and their subsequent collapse in January.

Q: Looking back over the last 30 years, what progress have we made?

The pace of innovation in green tech has been astonishing. Back in 2010, few realized the scale, speed and low cost at which it would deliver, mostly paying for itself in less than 10 years. The 2015 Istanbul Accord was an important step, committing our world to reduce CO_2 emissions 60 per cent by 2040 and 80 per cent by 2050...

Q: But disappointing? Total cuts in CO_2 by 2038 were only 52 per cent...

Global wind power is rising 1 per cent every eight weeks. Every week at least two large coal, gas or oil power plants are closing down. Twenty-three per cent of EU electricity now comes from solar-powered turbines in the Sahara desert, while the United States gets 17 per cent of power from its own deserts. Cars, trucks, trains and planes are together using 78 per cent less fuel per kilometre than they were 25 years ago, mainly with electric vehicles, and biowaste fuel for aviation. Global manufacturers have reduced carbon use 72 per cent per unit of production since 2000. We are on track for 80 per cent reduction in CO_2 emissions by 2050 compared to 1995.

Q: Are we in time?

The greatest threats are to come. Sea levels rose more in the last decade than in the previous 30 years. More methane has escaped from permafrost in the last five than in the previous 50.

Q: The greatest controversy?

Nuclear. It was almost inevitable with over 450 new power stations completed from 2020 to 2035 that there would be an accident, and the Tilsternlen explosion reminded us we need to treat the technology with great caution. However, nuclear power has given us 21 per cent of the fall we have seen in carbon emissions over the last 10 years. The fusion projects in France, China and Japan are entering phase-two trials, and with full-scale global investment we may yet develop a new, safer and uranium-free nuclear age. But it may of course be overtaken by the massive growth and falling costs of wind and solar power together with other renewables.

Q: *What about worries over genetically modified food?*

Despite scare stories about the safety of some recently introduced crops and livestock, I think people will come to see that the risk is very small compared to benefits in higher food production, especially in the poorest nations. A total ban would trigger the worst food crisis our world has ever seen.

Q: *What are you most concerned about?*

Water shortages remain one of our most urgent challenges, as well as coping with severe storms and flooding. Low-cost desalination can help cities near coasts, but hundreds of thousands of square miles of land in the poorest of nations are turning to desert, threatening the lives of over 650 million people, destabilizing entire regions. This is our greatest technical, moral and political challenge. It will require new infrastructure on a scale never seen before. The only alternative would be the relocation of entire people groups on a vast scale, often from one country to another. This is impossible to imagine by any peaceful means and would create many moral issues.

Q: *What are you most excited about?*

First, back in 2010, people wondered if we could power the world sustainably, worried about oil running out and so on. Now our world is rapidly phasing out carbon as a fuel, and at the same time proven reserves have continued to grow.

Second, the 'Green Farm' programmes across Africa are producing four times the amount of food than the continent did back in 2010 (apart from the recent droughts in north and south).

Third, I am encouraged by tens of millions of smaller innovations made by ordinary people, collaborating often in virtual communities to solve common problems, for the sake of humankind, maybe starting profitable businesses at the same time.

But *most* of all I am encouraged by a new spirit of partnership that has united our world. Common threats have forced nations to work together, which gives me great hope for the future.

CHAPTER ONE
TAKE HOLD OF
THE FUTURE

Solving the greatest sustainability challenge,
which is the cost of changing how we live

12 January 2010, 2.31 am, −23°C, Muskeg River Mine, Alberta

The earth shakes and trembles under glaring floodlights as 80 tons of brown, oily sand thunder from a giant digger into the back of one of the largest dump trucks in the world.

Caterpillar 797B trucks have four jumbo wheels as tall as small houses, and lumber day and night across the uneven mine floor, each carrying over 400 tons of earth, in which there is 12,000 gallons of thick oil – around 30 gallons per ton. Their engines take colossal strain. One violent change of gear and the huge machine could be out of action. One burst tyre – and the waiting list for a replacement can be up to 18 months.

Our world uses 44,000 gallons of oil every second – so if these Canadian sands were all our oil, those same trucks would need to mine 1,500 tons of sand a second, 90,000 tons a minute, or 5.4 million tons of sand an hour.

They are certainly digging fast. Vast 1,450 ton shovels are eating away tens of thousands of square miles of the surface of Alberta, in search of more black gold. An ancient forest the size of Greece, or Bangladesh or Florida, is being destroyed in the world's largest open pit mining operation. Over 54,000 square miles of wild, virgin landscape will be consumed in the next few years – and much of its native wildlife. All to get at hidden oil reserves that are greater than all the rest of the world's put together – apart from Venezuela, which has even more oil sand of its own.

Some of these sands are only a few metres down, and can be mined by stripping the surface of trees, vegetation, soil and surface rock. Others are over 250 metres down – too deep to dig. But you can inject them with steam or hot water to melt the sticky bitumen out of the sand.

Either method uses vast amounts of energy – up to 25 per cent of all the carbon extracted is needed just to keep the machines going. And water too: over five gallons per gallon of oil, all of it grossly contaminated, stored in toxic lakes so large that they can be seen from space. These sands could produce over 3 million barrels of oil a day by 2015 – but at what price?

As diggers and trucks churn their way across the horizon, they are followed by giant land-fillers, to try to repair the damage, and then by tree planters.

Machines give us power to destroy at breathtaking speed. A single driver, sitting in a heated cab 30 feet above the Alaska sands, can dig 5,000 tons an hour – or 100,000 times faster than by hand.

But the oil beneath has gone forever.

Future generations will be shocked at how fast we burnt the surface of the earth, as well as vast stores of ancient fossil fuels below. They will be astonished that we *burnt 500 billion tons of carbon in 250 years* – and were about to burn *another 250 billion tons in the next 20 years*.

They will try to understand how we allowed the earth's human population to treble from 3 to 6 to 9 billion, from 1960 to 2000 to 2050.

They will learn that there were 1 billion children growing up *at the same time* in 2010.

We cut and burn rainforest the size of 30 football pitches every minute – 40 square miles a day, destroying 10 million tons of plants and animals. As a result, eight more species of plants and animals are lost forever every hour – extinct.

Size of the problem

We can continue our rape of the planet, or work together to save our future.

Our planet cannot possibly go on delivering the relentless, destructive economic growth that every nation seeks, as things stand today. We would need all the resources of two or three earths if the lifestyles of all those in emerging nations were the same as in wealthy nations.

> We are consuming the world's resources 20 per cent faster than they can recover – whether fish in the sea, groundwater levels or forest trees.

Some say the answer is to *consume less*, buy less or do less. While that message may work with a few, it will not save our future – at least not in time. Of 9 billion people alive by 2050, at least 7.5 billion will be in Asia and Africa, most of whom will have known great poverty. They will expect to consume more, buy more and do more than their parents ever did.

Others say the main problem is *over-population* and the answer is birth control, but family size is already falling fast in most of the world, as incomes rise.[1] Birth control is important and gives choices to women, but the greater challenge is supporting future lifestyle growth, rather than preventing more babies from being born.

More than 2 billion people will migrate to cities over the next 40 years, leaving their mud huts and other traditional dwellings. They will aspire to middle class lifestyles, and many will achieve them. But unless action is taken, most will end up in over-crowded slums with open sewers, toxic water and fumes, and will be vulnerable to disease, flooding, drought, hunger and despair.

Despite all these urgent and complex challenges, we believe that most of the human race *will* have a *great* future, even with more than 9 billion people living on earth at the same time. This book explains why and how, what is likely to be done, and actions that each of us can take in our business, homes and wider world.

At *some* point it will become clear to almost all humankind that the crisis we face is so serious, so severe and so immense, that massive action

> Levels of CO_2 in the atmosphere are 40 per cent higher than 200 years ago. Our world warmed 0.74 per cent °C in the last 100 years, mostly since 1970.

must be taken now, with a level of commitment that we have only ever seen before in a world war. We are being forced to act, *not* because we are certain of terrible catastrophes, but because such actions are the only insurance we have to reduce the risk of them happening.

That is why governments will introduce huge numbers of new taxes, regulations, laws and subsidies. Old business habits will land managers in prison. Old, lazy and careless lifestyles will be fined. Old products will be taken away, and every molecule in them will be recycled into something better. Old political voices will be silenced or ignored. Old antisocial freedoms will be removed – even perhaps the democratic right to vote for policies that destroy the planet.

Force of a hurricane

Four major events combined with the force of a tornado to focus the attention of global leaders:

1 *Growing worries about climate change*, linked in many people's minds with severe weather such as Hurricane Katrina in 2005, and publication of new climate studies in 2007–09, warning of severe risks from carbon emissions.

2 *Sharp fuel price rises in 2008*, driven by growth in emerging economies. Prices doubled to $147 a barrel in 12 months, fell to $35 in the credit crisis, and rose to $80 by early 2010. Just nine years earlier, the price had been $17. There were also concerns about falling oil reserves and vulnerability to future shocks.

3 *Soaring food prices in 2008* – wheat prices jumped 140 per cent in 10 months, with food riots in 33 nations. Food shortages added to worries about consumption of other resources, including water.

4 *Global economic collapse in 2008–09* followed by $3 trillion of government stimulus, of which many billions were allocated to green technology.

Energy prices and climate change often get more attention than other sustainability issues, but all the problems above are complex and interlinked.

Leaders of wealthy nations began to listen to warnings about their need to cut their own emissions by 40 per cent (1990–2020), to reduce the risk of the world warming up by more than 2°C. Governments from more than 100 countries gathered in Copenhagen in December 2009 to debate what to do, but the result was confusion, apart from a general commitment to keep global warming to no more than 2°C above pre-industrial levels by 2050.

One nation's cut can become another's rise. China's soaring emissions are partly because countries like the United States and the UK are buying a huge range of goods from China that they used to make themselves (using carbon-based energy).[2] China now produces 24 per cent of all global emissions, set to double by 2025.[3] China announced in Copenhagen that it was prepared to cut the amount of carbon used per unit of production by 40–45 per cent by

2020; India announced a target to cut by 20 to 25 per cent, Brazil by 39 per cent and South Africa by 34 per cent.

Changes in CO_2 emissions per person 1990–2007 (per cent):

China +138	Italy +8
India +79	Canada +5
Middle East +49	France 0
Australia +38	United States −1
Argentina +33	EU −4
Brazil +30	Sweden −5
Mexico +17	Poland −11
Japan +16	UK −12
World +10	Germany −13

World Energy Outlook Report by the International Energy Agency, 2009

Future shaped by passion

You may be totally convinced that the worst warnings about our future climate are correct, or that the risks have been exaggerated.

Some people have claimed that the earth is cooling, and think there is a conspiracy to deceive the world on global warming. There are natural variations within decades and between them, which make it almost impossible to interpret complex global data reliably over less than 10–20 years (a mere flash of geological time). The first decade of the third millennium was the hottest recorded on average since 1880 (UK Met Office, 4 December 2009).

The truth is that our planet has seen huge ice ages and warming: climate change on a scale that dwarfs any projections we have seen for man-made climate change. The mechanisms for these mega-shifts are poorly understood. Nor do we know where we are in relation to the next 'natural' mega-shift that may hit us. However, the recent, accelerating rise in CO_2 is a fact, as is the accelerating rise in fossil fuel emissions, and the warming ability of CO_2 gas is well understood.

Climate change scientists have given us a wide range of views about how much warmer our world could be by 2050; the height of the sea by 2100; shortages of key resources by 2060 and so on, if we do nothing, The consensus is that we are heading for disaster if we carry on this way for another 60, 40 or even maybe just 20 years.

But if we wait 30 years to see which of their many predictions are turning out to be most accurate, we may be far too late to prevent an uncontrollable spiral of events with the power to destroy our world as we know it.

However, here is another truth: if you want to know how the world is likely to change in the next *decade*, you have to look at *emotion* rather than at scientific forecasts for 2050. *Even if you think the climate warnings are wrong*, the fact is that *most* people are worried enough to force business and government to immediate action, and their emotions are getting stronger.

Every year 13,000 square miles of ancient Arctic ice melts and crumbles into the sea, on average (2.5 per cent per decade, 1979–2009). That's more than 400,000 square miles over the last 30 years – almost twice the size of France.[4]

The Arctic sea could be free of ice in summer within 20 years.[5]

Look closely at shifts in public mood and plot their likely direction. What we are seeing is growing anxiety about the problems, but also growing concern about the costs of dealing with them. Those emotions will drive the technologies, markets and business strategies in every chapter of this book.

Cost is the number one issue

As we will see, we already have *all* the basic technologies, methods, products and processes we need to solve global warming, feed the world, provide health for all, conserve scarce resources, rebuild rainforests and secure the future of our planet. New methods will be even better, but the main problem now is *not* lack of technology, nor lack of political will, nor careless consumers. The central issue is *cost*.

If green ways of doing things were cheaper and easier than non-green, no force on earth could possibly prevent the stampede of humankind to make it happen.

Market forces and agile, innovative business will bring almost all the changes we so urgently need, so long as people know what can be done, the price is right, and governments act together in a responsible way. The greater the cost-savings, the faster it will happen.

Most green tech is profitable if oil prices stay above $75 a barrel – profits may more than double with every additional $25 above that basic ceiling.

So green tech companies are making a big bet on the future price of energy.

And one of the greatest market forces will be the price of oil. The higher the price of oil (within limits of what the global economy can stand without another crash), the faster those green tech revolutions will happen.

Market forces can encourage sustainable choices

Some people prefer to focus on inter-governmental treaties, global regulations, new tax penalties and incentives, persuading others to change lifestyles, stricter industry standards and so on. All these things are vital, but far more than these will be needed to change the future fast enough.

Yes it is true that market pressures have led to many evils – for example the destruction of rainforests where land owners earn more by cutting trees to herd cattle, or grow biofuels, than by caring for the ecosystem. As we will see, market forces need to be directed, harnessed and focused by inter-government action, and then allowed to drive the revolution.

The $40 trillion green tech boom

Many people have tried to work out the global bill to deal with climate change as just one part of concerns about a sustainable future. In our view, such estimates often ignore the speed of innovation, the impact of technologies paid for out of energy savings, and the effect of natural cycles of replacement. Total spending on green tech could exceed $40 trillion over the next 30 years, but much of this will be paid for in costs we will plan for as part of normal life, or will be paid for directly out of energy savings and other cost reductions.

For example, most central heating boilers in homes will need replacing by 2020, most cars by 2030 and most coal-fired power stations by 2040. Electrical goods have a normal lifespan of less than 15 years, or as little as five in the case of computers and mobile phones. In every case, the models replacing them are likely to be much more energy efficient.

Therefore, normal cycles of renewal will automatically transform much of our world's energy production and use by 2030 at zero additional cost. But 2030 could be too late: we need to accelerate the process now. One important way to do that is to renew or replace more quickly, with the additional cost paid by future savings in energy bills.

More than a billion people will be short of fresh water by 2050, on current trends. Some countries could be turned to desert. At the same time, many urban areas will be hit by freak storms and flash floods, costing billions a year in reconstruction.

The Stern Report estimated that the necessary global action could cost an *additional* 1 per cent of global economic activity (GWP),[6] or *$600 billion* of the $60 trillion global economy.[7] To compare, the US government spent more than twice that amount in the 2008–09 crisis, and $1,400 billion is spent each year by the world's armed forces, as insurance policies to protect national security.[8]

One per cent of GWP is only the same as the world economy stalling for three months, before carrying on for the next three decades at 'normal' rates of growth. The OECD's own calculations are that $10.5 trillion more needs to be spent by 2030 than we would do otherwise – less than half the Stern Report figure.[9] The cost of doing nothing could be much, much greater – and is impossible to calculate. For example, how do you place a value on millions of lives that could be lost through more severe drought, flooding, disease and other challenges?

It is possible that all such estimates may underestimate the *real* size of the challenge. They are all based on the same aim, which is to stabilize CO_2 in the atmosphere at 450 parts per million – today's level is 380ppm. But no one knows what a safe level really is: 450 ppm could be severe enough to set in train a long sequence of unstoppable events, such as release of CO_2 from frozen tundra as it melts.

There is also uncertainty about the speed at which CO_2 is going to rise in the next few years of global economic growth. The Global Carbon Project estimated in 2009 that there had been a 29 per cent increase in global CO_2 emissions from fossil fuels from 2000 to 2008 – or 3 per cent increase a year, mainly related to the economic boom in China. That would place emissions at the top end of the worst-case scenarios in the UN Intergovernmental Panel on Climate Change report of 2007 on which most discussions about climate change are still based.[10]

Over the next 40 years, we will welcome 4 billion new babies into the world, but attend only 2 billion funerals. That's 50 million more people every year, on average – almost the size of the populations of the UK, France, or Italy.

We may debate the *additional* costs to society to reach sustainability, particularly in carbon use, but as we will see, most of the $40 trillion green tech boom will be using normal patterns of spending to do things better, especially in energy production and use.

We have all the tools we need

Let us take a brief look at existing green tech for power generation, then at what is available now to radically alter energy consumption.

Generation of (almost) carbon-free power

We are about to see a huge shake-up in the way the world generates electricity, which is mainly today by burning fossil fuels but shifting fast to renewable power. The first step is to replace old turbines that run on steam heated by fossil fuels. New models can increase output per ton of carbon by 5–10 per cent or more.

Wind turbines are already very efficient, well able to produce up to 20 per cent of electricity in many nations with some subsidies, and have *theoretical capacity to provide 40 times all the world's electricity demands* – if storage and transmission problems could be solved in an affordable way (and they will be).[11] Expect hundreds of new schemes like the £100 billion UK wind farm programme, reported in *The Sunday Times* on 3 January 2010, aiming to provide 33 per cent of UK power from wind by 2020.

Solar power could supply all the electricity for many nations.[12] Huge arrays of mirrors are being built in deserts, using sunlight to heat water or hydrogen, and drive turbines. Power will be carried several thousand miles without major losses, on high voltage DC cables. In theory, the whole of Europe could be powered in this way from the Sahara desert, while the United States could be 100 per cent solar-powered from a desert area 91 miles long by 91 miles wide,[13] if we find a way to store enough power for use at night (we will do so). Every home can become a power generator using photovoltaic cells, with prices falling by 10 per cent a year or more.

Carbon capture is an important technology: it is already possible to capture every molecule of CO_2 coming out of the vast chimney of a coal-fired power station.[14] A simpler and cheaper method is being used now to capture 95 per cent of CO_2. The methods will improve, and costs will fall, but even now such systems could run for about 20 per cent extra on a domestic electricity bill.[15] That is only the same as a 1 per cent price increase, year on year for 20 years – a negligible impact on consumers, as our consumption will fall over the same period through things like energy saving light bulbs.

Global emissions of greenhouse gases are around 47 billion tons of CO_2-equivalent. To give ourselves a 50 per cent chance of avoiding a rise in global temperatures of more than 2°C, many scientists think we need to reduce emissions to 44 billion tons in 2020, 35 billion in 2030 and much less than 20 billion by 2050.[16]

There are hundreds of places around the world where carbon capture could be installed right now – near sites that are suitable to store gas (usually places that have successfully contained natural gas for millions of years). We need to be confident that the CO_2 will stay underground in each site, and more research is needed, but we can be almost certain that carbon storage will happen on a significant scale in many parts of the world, despite concerns. Governments are committed to it, and oil companies have been pumping CO_2 underground for many years. (For more see pages 41–44.)

Then there is nuclear energy. France already produces 80 per cent of power this way. That means eight out of 10 miles driven by electric cars in Paris are nuclear powered. Our world is set for a huge nuclear boom, with hundreds of new reactors by 2030, many in China. The efficiency of old reactors is being improved with new turbines, and new reactors will use less fuel. There is enough uranium in seawater to generate all the power we will need for 5 million years. That will depend on existing extraction methods becoming cheap enough, or uranium prices rising far enough.[17]

Yes there will be big future costs from decommissioning and waste, and worries about accidents, but few additional worries about nuclear proliferation or abuse of nuclear material by terrorist groups, so long as new nuclear plants are in countries that already have them, and that control security well. In the much longer term, fusion reactors may yet provide almost unlimited nuclear power with much less risk or radioactive waste.[18]

Hydroelectric dams provide almost 20 per cent of global electric power, and often do so at a price that is less than wind or solar or any other non-carbon generator. There are tens of thousands of ideal locations for small-scale water-driven turbines, which could supply almost all the energy needed by towns or villages, with minimal damage to wild life or other disruption. Dams also help conserve water, but are very controversial, attacked for disrupting local ecology, displacing millions of people and impacting the livelihoods of people downstream. (For more on the ethics of dams, see pages 130–33.)

Need for courageous decisions now

So we have the technology, and finance is often available (and will be increasingly so). We need to get on with it, but there is still a huge risk that nothing will happen. It is almost impossible to get permission for any major generating project without getting blocked for months or years by protests and arguments about the relative merits of different solutions. Delays in getting planning permission are one of the greatest challenges in meeting deadlines for curbing emissions. We see this with wind, solar, tidal barrages, nuclear, carbon capture and so on. Where do you build these things? How many? What will be the local impact?

We are faced with very tough choices that need to be made urgently and with courage. Sadly it will be *impossible* to act fast enough on global emissions by 2030 without also influencing other aspects of the environment, sometimes in a profound way. We have to balance two or more 'evils', for example to choose between more renewable wind power and an unspoiled view. Public debate is vital to establish where such balance should lie, but final decisions must not be delayed beyond a reasonable period, so that sufficient size and range of projects can proceed in time.

> **Four legitimate questions**
>
> 1 Percentage of CO_2 increase due to human activity?
>
> 2 Percentage of global warming due to increased CO_2?
>
> 3 Cost of reducing CO_2 emissions significantly?
>
> 4 Cost of alternative coping mechanisms?

Steps taken today to reduce our emissions are an insurance policy to help reduce future risks, the size of which remains uncertain.[19] Such steps also help conserve supplies of oil, gas and coal for future generations.

Consumption – how to save over 30–40 per cent at zero cost

Table 1.1 shows a few examples from hundreds of ways that green technology can pay for itself by reducing consumption; assuming oil prices are at least $75 a barrel. All of these products already exist.

These examples could easily save 30–40 per cent of global energy, effectively at zero cost, since they all repay their entire investment costs in a short time. Further innovation will mean even shorter payback periods, smaller capital outlay, faster adoption and many more ways to make savings. And many other actions cost nothing at all: something as simple as turning down the heating or air conditioning by a single degree centigrade can save 10 per cent of energy use in buildings.

And as we have seen, if upgrades happen as part of the natural cycle of replacement, there may be no *additional* capital cost of 'going green' – for example replacing a broken down, fuel-hungry car with a diesel-electric hybrid. In such cases, the payback period is zero, and the owner is earning money within hours.

TABLE 1.1   *A few ways to save 30–40% of today's global CO_2 emissions at 'zero' cost*

Technology	% Energy saving	% Cut global energy use	Payback period	Speed of introduction	Book Chapter
Low energy street lamps	60	3	4 years	1–10 years	6
Aviation efficiencies (multiple)	35	1.5	3–10 years	1–15 years	5
Vehicles – next generation combustion engines/electric	35–70	10–20	5 years	1–15 years	5
Building controls (eg office heating systems)	30–40	4–5.5	4 years	1–15 years	6
Insulating homes better	5–50	6–8	3–15 years	1–15 years	6
Heat pumps	25–50	6–8	10–15 years	1–25 years	6

**30–40%
saved of all energy**

'Carrying on as we have been risks a rise in global average temperature of 5°C or more, to levels our planet has not seen for more than 30 million years. Humans, who have only been here for 200,000 years, have never experienced global average temperatures on this scale.'[20]

Lord Stern, Chair Grantham Institute on Climate Change

In addition to revolutionizing power generation and consumption, we also know how to protect and restore forests, which account for 20 per cent of global emissions: pay local people and forest owners to manage trees – one of the most cost-effective ways to control global emissions.[21] Make sure *intact* forests have greater commercial value than if converted to pasture or crop-growing. Monitor on the ground as well as from space.[22]

In practice, these things can be hard to achieve, but remarkable progress has been made in protecting forests in some locations.[23]

When we put together the revolution in electricity production, with reductions in consumption, plus reduced emissions from forests, we begin to see how our world can easily achieve 50–60 per cent cuts in carbon emissions at almost zero additional cost to what we would have spent anyway over 20 years, just using technology that is already available. However, without further innovation and lower costs, many of these changes are unlikely to take place on a global scale before 2020–2030.

There is more to sustainability than energy. We are already seeing water and food shortages, despite the fact that the tools and knowledge exist to enable our world to grow far more food, using the same amount of land. We can also manage water much more effectively. Africa could grow four times as much if the continent saw a green revolution like the one that swept across India in the 1970s, banishing famine in that country.[24] Larger farms, more fertilizers, stronger crop varieties, better management of water; Africa will have its green revolution – the only question is how soon.

There is another factor: we are only at the very beginning of the green tech revolution. Almost *all* the most exciting technologies we can expect to be using in 2050 have yet to be discovered or invented. So how can we accelerate the pace of change?

Scale up to get costs down

The fastest way to increase the use of green tech globally is to lower costs, and the fastest way to lower costs is to increase scale, as costs usually fall with larger volumes, as shown in Figure 1.1. The easiest way to encourage this is to pass a new regulation. For example, the EU announced phasing out sales of incandescent light bulbs in Europe. Manufacturers then increased

FIGURE 1.1   *How price falls as sales rise of green tech*

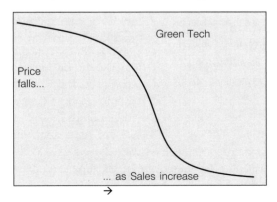

output and invested more in better alternatives. As a result, low energy light-bulbs are far cheaper and better than they were, and are more attractive for people to buy in other nations where there is no legal requirement.

A second way to increase sales is to subsidize the costs to customers. Germany led the way on solar cells by forcing electricity companies to buy surplus electricity from households at 57.4 cents per kilowatt hour for 20 years (three times domestic retail price and eight times industrial price).[25] Sales boomed, as millions of people started to see their homes as micro-power-stations. German companies benefitted, and by 2008 almost half the world's installed solar-voltaic cells were in Germany.

The German government had single-handedly attached a turbo-charged rocket to the solar cell industry, forcing the pace of innovation, pushing manufacturers to invest in huge factories.

The most powerful decisions can cost almost nothing

The genius of what the German government did is that it only took a stroke of a pen to sign into law, and cost them nothing. Governments have a habit of making agile decisions when it comes to regulations that are cost-neutral, easy to carry out and enforce, popular with voters and make sense in the medium term. Because it is such an easy decision for other EU governments to take, we can expect more to follow soon. Spain and the UK have already done so.

Another example that could be scaled up rapidly is heat pumps for new buildings. These are like fridge motors, pushing heat in and out of homes, connected to pipes underground. They save up to 50 per cent of energy costs a year.[26] It costs very little to include heat pumps in new homes, and they pay for themselves in 10–15 years. They also add to the capital value, so their purchase price is also effectively zero.

Many green innovations pay for themselves in less than five years – and save money after that, so the true cost is less than zero, assuming you can borrow the money to do it, or have the cash yourself.

Seventy per cent of new homes in some parts of Sweden have heat pumps, but sales are almost unknown in most other parts of the world. What would it take for a country like the UK to pass a new regulation requiring 50 per cent of all new homes in large developments to use heat pumps?

We have seen that the pace of green tech is bound to accelerate. Even with what we have today, and at today's prices, we can well afford to take giant, rapid steps towards sustainability.

Governments will interfere in energy markets

Governments have always interfered in energy markets, with subsidies to coal mining or nuclear energy for example. The EU's largest power companies have set a goal to make their electricity carbon-free by 2050, but the *big* issue to watch is EU-wide changes to energy subsidies.

Sweden reduced carbon emissions by 7 per cent while growing economic output by 40 per cent from 1993–2008. Sweden is aiming to cut CO_2 emissions by 40 per cent by 2020, compared to 1990[27] while the G8 nations have announced their aim to cut 80 per cent of those to 1990.[28, 29]

California has already passed laws requiring the State to reduce emissions to 1990 levels by 2020, and requiring emissions by new cars to fall by 30 per cent from 2008 to 2016.[30] More than 218 US cities have adopted similar local programmes to reduce emissions.[31]

China will dominate global exports of green tech

China will build green tech on a vast scale. For example, the world's largest solar power plant is being built in Mongolia, by First Solar. The country already generates 20 per cent of power from dams, is ramping up investment in wind and solar, and is trying to scale back the growth in coal power, partly to reduce air pollution.[32] China burns 43 per cent of all the coal in the world, and its consumption rose 7 per cent in 2008 despite the downturn.[33] China is struggling to keep pace with electricity demand and builds huge numbers of power stations every year, so it has the opportunity to introduce green tech more rapidly than Europe or the United States.

Part of China's motivation is energy security, with half of its oil and some coal from imports. That is why China signed energy deals with Brazil, Venezuela, Russia and Kazakhstan. (The United States is also worried about threats to national security from dependency on foreign oil,[34] while the EU is vulnerable to cuts in Russian gas supplies.)

Most of the world's megacities are in coastal areas and likely to be hit by rising sea levels, caused by water expansion as temperatures rise, plus melting of ice. We could see tidal surges half a metre to a metre higher than today.

But China also seeks a large share in the global green tech boom. The country is the world leader in small-scale hydropower with over 43,000 plants in use, generating up to 28 megawatts of peak output, and is also the world's largest manufacturer of equipment for the power industry.[35]

Annual spend of $500 billion on green innovation

In 2008 $155 billion was spent on clean energy.[36] Investment in solar power was growing at 250 per cent a year from 2004 until the credit crunch – over $30 billion of new money every 12 months.[37] Investment fell steeply in 2009. For example, BP cut spending on green tech from $1.4 billion to around $750 million in 2008–09. Wind turbine expenditure around the world fell 55–60 per cent in 2009.[38]

However, we can expect investment to recover sharply, not only as global economies pick up, but also as the green energy revolution gathers pace with new international agreements on targets for emissions. Expect a minimum of $500 billion a year of new green tech spending by 2012.[39]

As we have seen, many green tech projects pay for themselves rapidly, but raising capital for larger projects can be difficult. A major source of new funding is carbon trading.

Carbon offsetting has already created a market that is trading over *$127 billion a year*, growing rapidly.[40] Around 75 per cent of this is the same carbon changing hands more than once, but the process is bringing into the market around 2.2 billion tons a year of CO_2, or 8 per cent of around 27 billion tons of global CO_2 emissions[41] – so long as those funds are properly used.[42] Expect more than 30 per cent of global carbon emissions to be traded in one form or another by 2030, creating a fund for green tech of at least $200–300 billion a year (depending on offset price).

Offsetting allows a company to pay another organization to make carbon cuts. It provides extra financial incentives for the second company to reduce its own carbon emissions. The cost of trading a ton of carbon was as low as $13 at the end of 2009, but needs to be around $30 to drive green tech expansion rapidly.

Seventy-six per cent of Americans believe that global warming is a serious problem and half believe it is a very serious problem.[43]

Some market traders think that the total value of transactions in this new carbon market could exceed $3 trillion a year in the next 10–20 years, which would be double the size of the oil market today.[44] However, almost all of that $3 trillion will be the same carbon credits being switched back and forth around the market by investors.

Offsetting is controversial and open to fraud: the key is strict monitoring and controls to prove that *extra* carbon is saved as a direct result of a grant made. Carbon taxes may be more effective in some situations. 'Green' taxes are harder to avoid and more transparent, but money raised may disappear into paying off government debt and other things. Carbon tax and carbon trades will both be widely used around the world.

Private investors grow again after the global crisis

Private investors are another source of green tech funding, attracted by exciting inventions and big government grants. Venture capital investment increased 16 times since 2001, and rewards have sometimes been spectacular.[45]

In some ways it feels like the dotcom boom of 1996–99: money chasing ideas that are still unproven. Fortunes have already been won and lost in green tech. Share prices were badly hit during the economic crisis, when oil prices collapsed to $35, wiping out margins. Just look at the rollercoaster ride with these three companies:

- Vestas is one of the world's largest wind turbine manufacturers. Its share price soared from Kronas 91 to 692 from 2006–08, but fell to Kronas 369 by the end of 2009.

- Sunways is a leading solar cell power producer. Its share price trebled from €6 to €20 from 2005 to 2006, falling to €4 by the end of 2009.

- Climate Exchange is one of the world's leading environmental exchanges. Its share price leapt from £277 to £2,000 from 2005 to 2008, falling to £780 by the end of 2009.

Great ideas to change the world

The pace of innovation is being assisted by search engines and social networks. Consider for a moment the collective genius, the combined passions, creativity, agility and ideas of 7 billion people.

Just look at the way great, simple ideas now flash around our world at the speed of light. A billion digital natives, in virtual communities, able to focus on practical answers to shared challenges. Or the ease with which someone with a very rare problem can find an exact solution in a couple of seconds.

Scientific knowledge is doubling every 12 months – as we see in the volume of original research into areas like biotech, nanotech, digital technology, nuclear physics and stem cell research.[46] In the past, most of that insight was quickly lost in stacks of printed journals.

The core value of the online world is that knowledge should be available to all. This digital generation expects instant answers, rapid action, transparency and shared knowledge, rather than endless discussions and lawsuits about copyright.

Take the success of Wikipedia, where millions of digital citizens are working together to create the world's premier encyclopaedia for the good of humankind. Then there are software platforms like Linux that can be altered by any programmer, web building programmes like Joomla, and a hundred million blogs, many of which are used by their owners to give away their best ideas.

Emerging nations now produce most of the world's CO_2. With 4 per cent of world population, the United States produces 20 per cent of global greenhouse gases. What happens if every nation achieves the same average lifestyle? Answer: 500 per cent increase.

Open innovation means faster progress

Gone are the days when companies always did research and development in-house. Many of the world's most dynamic and innovative companies now use an 'open innovation' model.

Today's products are so complex that it is almost impossible to find all the skills needed inside a single company.

Car manufacturers are collaborating with smaller and more dynamic companies to develop components for next-generation vehicles. Pharma companies are working with clusters of biotech start-ups.

We are also seeing a new generation of *social entrepreneurs* who use business to solve problems such as carbon-free energy, pollution, poor nutrition and poverty. There are at least 30,000 of them globally, with combined revenues of over $40 billion, working for a more sustainable (and profitable) future.[47]

So, the problem is urgent and the pace of change extraordinary. The following chapters take a closer look at the future of energy, transport, manufacturing, low-carbon cities, forests, water and food. How green tech business will deliver the answers our world needs to survive and thrive for another 5,000 years – at an affordable cost. What the new mega-growth markets will be. How agile and innovative companies will seize market share, and what it all means for your business, personal life and wider world.

First, what about cleaner ways to generate power? If we can find ways to provide unlimited power, at affordable cost, without producing CO_2, we will have gone a very long way towards a more sustainable future. How will this be achieved and how long will it take?

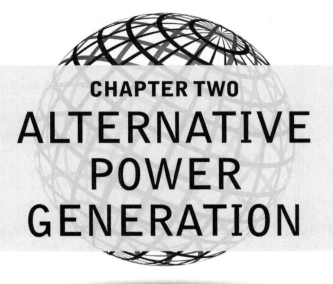

CHAPTER TWO
ALTERNATIVE POWER GENERATION

Solar, wind, tide, waves, geothermal

21 July 2029 at 1.14 pm, +56°C, Fituya Rashed Solar Farm, Southern Libya

After a five-hour journey on bumpy roads and desert sands, the rattling old diesel engine of our battered vehicle ground to a halt, deep in the 5,800 million square kilometres of the Sahara desert.

We could hear the silence, and then as we each climbed out slowly into the searing heat, there was a strange low-level hum. Across the rocky surface of the desert, as far as our eyes could see, were tens of thousands of flat mirrors, each on a short pole, clustered around hundreds of tall towers, the height of huge wind turbines.

Fituya Rashed in Southern Libya is just one of 104 solar farms across the Sahara that together focus 100 billion watts of intense heat onto gas cylinders, to drive thousands of electric turbines. The solar farm already covers 25 square kilometres and can generate up to a gigawatt of power. On the horizon are tall cranes and construction teams who work mainly in the cool of night. They are building a new solar cluster every two days, covering another square kilometre every 12 weeks.

No ordinary human being can survive in such a place as this for more than a few hours, without water and shelter, yet this barren land is the future power-house of Europe. Twenty high-voltage cables run beneath the Mediterranean from Morocco, Libya and Egypt to Spain, Italy, Greece and Turkey and are already delivering more than 22 per cent of the power that Europe uses each year.

Power definitions

MW = megawatt = 1 million watts

GW = gigawatt = 1 billion watts

TW = terawatt = 1 trillion watts

Solar has become the new gold or oil, and desert nations are booming.

We need to build four times the power output of the United States by 2030

Powering the future is one of our most urgent challenges. Our world already uses 5 trillion watts during every second of every day, almost all generated by burning fossil fuels.[1]

Global electricity demand will grow by around 2.5 per cent a year from now to 2030, and 80 per cent of that increase will be in developing nations[2] (1.6 billion in the poorest parts of the world still have no electricity).[3] Even with improvements in energy efficiency, total power consumption will double in parts of Asia by 2020.

We will need 4,800 gigawatts more generating capacity by 2030, four times the entire output of all US power stations today.[4] Globally, only 20 per cent of power is from renewable sources (15–17 per cent from large hydroelectric dams, mainly in the poorest nations).[5]

Half of all US States require utility companies to generate a percentage of their power from renewables.

The good news is that the most efficient wind, geothermal and hydro generators *already* provide electricity for less than 7 cents a kilowatt hour, which is competitive with carbon-based power generation – and their costs are likely to fall below 4 cents by 2020.[6] Solar-thermal generation may fall below 10 cents per kilowatt hour by 2025, including transmission costs and overnight power storage – depending on the size of the project.

We are entering a new electrical age: one where almost all energy comes from electric power, replacing things like gas central heating and diesel in cars. That is why investment in 'green' power generation is now greater each year than in oil, gas or coal power.[7]

Over 200,000 homes in the United States are not on the national grid, growing by 6,000 a year, and 30,000 other homes generate some of their own power (Interstate Renewable Energy Foundation). The UK has around 40,000 off-grid homes.

The average UK household uses 4,500 kilowatt hours of electricity a year for appliances and lights plus 18,000 kilowatt hours of gas for cooking, hot water and heating. US households' power use varies from 4,700 in New York to 16,100 in Dallas – mainly because of air conditioning.[8]

Wind, water and solar could supply 100 per cent of global energy, replacing all fossil fuel use

Our planet is full of energy but most is wasted. For example, there is enough wind in the world to power our planet 5–15 times over (in theory). Our world receives 30 times more solar energy than we would need if direct sunlight were our sole power source.[9] So how could we power the world using only water, wind and solar? How much capacity would we need anyway?

By 2030, on current trends, our world will need 16.9 terawatts of power capacity, at any given moment, assuming no major energy savings.[10] However, if all that power came from renewable sources by 2030, we would need less: maybe only 11.5 terawatts, as a renewable energy economy would be more efficient. That fall would be the same as the output of 13,000 large coal-powered stations.[12]

Water, wind and solar power available in readily accessible locations[11]:

- water: 2 terawatts;
- wind: 40–85 terawatts;
- solar: 580 terawatts.

So how could we generate 11.5 terawatts *only* using water, wind and solar power? There are many other renewable sources of power, but our purpose is just to show the *theoretical* potential of these three, using technology we already have today, based on work by Professor Mark Jacobson at Stanford University and Mark Delucchi from the Institute of Transportation Studies,

University of California.[13] They make many (perhaps unrealistic) assumptions but their study provokes fresh thinking.

1. Water – 9 per cent of supply

- 490,000 turbines – 1 megawatt each.

- 5,350 geothermal plants – 100 megawatts each.

- 900 hydroelectric plants – 1,300 megawatts each (70 per cent exist already).

2. Wind – 51 per cent of supply

- 3,800,000 turbines – 5 megawatts each.

- Would occupy an area smaller than Manhattan – the footprint of turbines themselves, but spread out over 1 per cent world landmass for maximum wind capture, with all space between being available for farming. This is a major advantage over huge solar arrays on land.

- 720,000 wave converters – 0.75 megawatts each.

3. Solar – 40 per cent of supply

- 1.7 billion rooftop solar generators – 0.003 megawatts each (each sized for average house – commercial systems would be larger).

- 89,000 solar power plants – 300 megawatts each.

- Total area that would be needed: 0.3 per cent world surface.

- As with biofuels, large-scale solar could compete with land that is used for agriculture unless confined to places like semi-desert or desert.

We have the manufacturing power globally to achieve such an ambitious energy revolution. Society has made such jumps before. During World War II, car factories were converted in the United States to produce 300,000 aircraft, and other nations made a further 486,000. Our world makes 73 million cars and light trucks every year.

Building renewables on such a vast scale would create supply issues. For example, it would push up prices of cadmium, tellurium, indium, lithium and platinum used in solar cells, batteries and other equipment. Part of this could be overcome with recycling, or by other technologies.

It would also require smart electricity grids to balance loads across very large areas, which vary in wind and sun. High voltage DC lines would need to link these grids so that huge amounts of power can be carried thousands of miles without significant losses (see pages 63–64). And it would require major investment into power storage.

The total cost of such a 100 per cent renewable system has been estimated at around $100 trillion over 20 years, plus new grids, paid for by selling energy. To compare, adding more power generation from today's 12.5 to 16.9 terawatts would cost $10 trillion, using coal power stations.[14] But all traditional power stations use fuel, so we can make a saving here – at least $14 trillion in 20 years, depending on fuel prices[15] – up to $50 trillion.

So then, the renewable technologies we need are available, but how well do they work, at what cost (in every sense) and how quickly will they make a difference? Which are best for business investment, communities and governments? First let us look at solar, then wind, waves, tide and geothermal.

'Alternative power' is widely used to mean renewable, but sun, wind and water will always be with us, so in a way it is more logical to think about fossil fuels as 'alternative'.

Solar power takes off

The sun blasts our world with far more energy every hour than we need to power the whole world for a year.[16] Despite the fact that sunlight hitting the earth is 10,000 times more powerful than the 5 trillion watts of electrical power we use, only 0.1 per cent comes from solar.[17] This is about to change rapidly.

Every square metre of the earth receives an average of 250 watts of sunlight per day[18] – around 1 kilowatt when the sun is overhead.[19] Enough power for the whole of the United States could be generated from 92 square miles of the Nevada desert, an area equal to 9 per cent of the

The poorest nations have more than 40 per cent of renewable power generation, and 70 per cent of the world's solar power.[20]

desert and 1 per cent of the State of Texas.[21] Enough energy to power the whole of Europe could be generated in future from an area 60 miles long by 200 miles wide, out of 3,300 million square miles of Sahara desert. Half the 12,000 square miles would be solar collectors, and the rest would be land taken up with high-voltage cables.[22]

Every roof of every home

Solar-voltaic cells operate differently, capturing up to 20 per cent of the total solar energy at that location, and pushing it down wires to energize electrical appliances. When appliances are used, the energy is released once more as heat. We can convert the roof of every home, office, retailer, school, hospital, government building and factory into an electricity generator – free power every day of the year.

It all depends on solar cell prices, which are falling by 20 per cent every time production doubles. Solar cells will form a major part of power generation by 2050. At present the power from these devices is much more expensive than from solar-thermal. You have to work out the total power the cells will generate over their lifetime, divided by the cost of the whole system including connectors and controls. Right now it works out at around 45 to 70 cents per kilowatt hour, falling by around 10–20 per cent a year.[23] They cannot compete with wind or coal at less than 7 cents per kilowatt hour, so are only viable with subsidies at present, or where there is no cheap access to the national grid – for example lighting road signs in rural areas.

Fedex will soon generate 3 megawatts of solar power:

'Fedex has three solar facilities already running in California, and we have broken ground this past fiscal year on what will be our largest solar plant and our first outside the US, in Cologne, Germany.'

Frederick W Smith, Chairman, President and Chief Executive Officer, Fedex, Annual Report 2008

Huge market for solar cells

Even if solar-voltaic cell costs remain as they are today (not that they will), they will become cheaper relative to coal-fired power stations, if coal-burners are required to capture and store their own CO_2 emissions, or are forced to pay a carbon tax, or to buy carbon credits.

Expect every new roof of new homes in some regions to be at least partially covered by solar cells by 2020. Hundreds of millions of smaller electrical devices and installations will be powered by their own solar cells – whether illuminated road signs, robot lawn mowers or remote mobile phone transmitters.

Sales of solar-voltaic cells are doubling every 24 months.[24] The global market could easily exceed $40 billion a year by 2015 – almost four times the 2009 figure. Production will be dominated by a relatively small number of manufacturers. New technologies will produce solar panels that are much thinner and lighter than today, capturing more energy at lower cost. We will see fierce competition for supply/fit/servicing of solar panels.

Germany and Spain jump into solar technology

In Germany, people installing solar cells are being offered 50 cents a unit for any electricity they wish to sell to the national grid – up to five times higher than the cost of electricity they buy. As a direct result, in 2008 over half the entire global sales of solar cells were in Germany alone, and Germany's own solar cell industry was given a massive boost.

By the end of 2006, the solar generating capacity in Germany had already reached a maximum output of 2,500 megawatts (bright sun shining on all panels at the same time), equivalent to two or three medium-sized coal-fired power stations.

The Spanish government introduced a similar feed-in tariff, and was quickly overwhelmed by the speed at which people started generating their own power. By 2008, Spain accounted for 40 per cent of global solar cell demand. The government planned for 300 megawatts to be built, but 3 gigawatts was the result, and it soon had to reduce the generosity of the scheme. It dropped the feed-in tariff rate to 32 cents from 44 cents, and the market collapsed. Solar cell prices crashed 30–40 per cent and share prices in the industry fell 50–75 per cent. Twenty thousand jobs were lost in the solar industry in Spain alone.[25] Spain and Germany have shown

Exelon is working with SunPower to build a large solar cell plant on an old industrial site in Chicago's South Side. The 10 megawatt plant will have 32,000 solar cells to power up to 1,500 homes.

the rest of the world how easy it is to boost solar cell use across an entire nation. Once sufficient scale is reached, the solar cell revolution will drive itself without any further subsidies. The UK's own sell-back scheme for home generators was launched in 2010 at 41.5 pence feed-in tariff, and other nations are expected to follow.

Free solar cells for your home

Expect to see all kinds of creative finance packages. For example, Solar-City in Silicon Valley leases solar panels to home owners and gives them free electricity, so their 4,000 customers make a net saving. SunRise in San Francisco offers a similar deal, but selling electricity to customers from solar panels that SunRise places on their customers' property. Cities like Berkeley and Boulder are giving people loans for the purchase and instal-lation costs of solar panels, with payback over 20 years as part of property taxes. Ten other States are doing the same. The economics work because of Federal subsidies such as investment tax credits that lower the tax bills of banks financing these projects.[26]

Assuming that solar cell prices continue to fall by 10 per cent a year, then the cost per kilowatt hour will fall to around 6 cents from 60 cents by 2030. But it could happen by 2020–2025 if more nations go down the Spanish, German and British path. Solar cells are made in a similar process to memory chips, and the industry will benefit from scaled-up production.

A two square metre solar-voltaic panel can provide up to 1,500 kilowatt hours a year (1 kilowatt per hour in bright sun).[27] The average home needs 8 square metres, converters and batteries.

Solar-thermal power for entire nations

The cheapest way to get sunlight to produce electricity is to use huge arrays of mirrors to track sunlight during the day and focus the heat. These systems can already produce power for around 20–28 cents per kilowatt hour.[28] New models will do the same for 25 per cent of the cost.

The speed of solar-thermal development is astonishing. From 2010 to 2015 we will see a number of large solar generators, built one module at a time across deserts, using different technologies. Expect copy-cat companies to invade the market. Designs all come down to one thing: computer-controlled mirrors track the sun, heat gas and drive generators.

Solar-thermal power has a long track record in heating water on the rooftops of homes, and industrial-scale power plants in the Mojave Desert have supplied 350 megawatts of power for more than 20 years.

Solar cell companies battle for global dominance

Hundreds of companies are already interested in solar-thermal power as a business, and some of them are actively involved in research, or are building the first large-scale projects. Here are just four.

Andasol

Andasol's first solar-thermal power station became active in Spain during 2008, providing 50 megawatts for 200,000 people. Siemens is expanding Andasol's mirrors by 500,000 square metres by 2012, increasing total power to 500 megawatts. Mirrors lined up in rows north to south, track the sun from east to west, concentrating light onto pipes that contain oil, that is then heated to 400°C. Hot oil is pumped to a heat exchanger to make steam for use in a turbine.

Andasol also stores heat to use for up to 7.5 hours at night, by melting a mix of sodium nitrate (60 per cent) and potassium nitrate (40 per cent). The heat is used during the evening or if there is cloud during the day, enabling turbines to work for twice as long each week. Andasol's power will cost around 27 cents per kilowatt hour (stored heat twice as much). It is only commercially viable because Spain pays a feed-in tariff of 27 cents per kilowatt hour, guaranteed for 25 years. Power is well-matched with demand: sunlight is strongest when people are using the most air conditioning. Spain will be one of the largest markets for solar-thermal, together with the south-west United States, the Middle East and China.

SunCatchers

SunCatchers, made by Stirling Energy Systems (SES), capture over 31 per cent of solar energy. They are self-contained units, which look like large satellite dishes and turn with the sun, heating 'receivers' filled with hydrogen, on poles sticking out into the middle of each dish. Super-hot hydrogen drives a small Stirling engine mounted in each receiver, which generates power.

There is no steam turbine so water use is very low (only to clean mirrors). Each unit generates a peak of 25 megawatts. Huge arrays are being set up across Imperial Valley and Calico, California, to provide 1.75 gigawatts for San Diego Gas and Electric and Southern California Edison. The technology was first developed by Ford Advanced Development Operations, McDonnell-Douglas Aerospace & Defense, and Boeing Aerospace & Defense.

eSolar

eSolar is already able to produce electricity at prices that compete with gas-powered stations. Arrays of hundreds of small mirrors on the ground (heliostats) track the sun to reflect light onto 65-ton thermal receivers, placed on top of high towers, using computer-controlled motors. The mirrors are small and factory-made, and mirror frames fit easily into shipping containers. Software does much of the setup, so non-technical workers can install new modules. Like all solar systems, each unit can be added to, allowing rapid scaling up of successful pilot projects. Existing standard 150-foot tall wind-power towers can be converted to mount the thermal receivers, reducing issues over planning consent.[29]

Sierra Sun Tower generates 5 megawatts for Southern California Edison, on 20 acres of land on which there are two such towers using eSolar technology. Heat from the towers creates steam to drive GE turbines. Google is an investor.

Desertec

Meanwhile, the Desertec project in the Sahara desert is aiming to generate 20 per cent of all the electricity that Europe needs from 2,500 square kilometres of mirrors to supply 100 gigawatts. An additional 3,600 square kilometres will be needed for high voltage cables to transmit the power to Europe.

Desertec power plants will cost €350 billion, with €50 billion more for transmission.[30] Siemens, Munchener Ruck Reinsurance and 10 other corporations are behind Desertec, which also has mirrors that track the sun and focus heat. Desertec thinks desert power will be competitive by 2025. While the total project is huge, it can be built in small stages, as required. The first step is to improve efficiency from 15 to 20 per cent, which will reduce the need for mirrors by a third.[32]

EnviroMission is planning a solar tower in Australia to convert solar to wind power, using a huge 'greenhouse' collector over a square kilometre, built around a tall chimney. Hot air will rise at 15 metres a second up the chimney, by the laws of physics, to drive 32 large turbines. A pilot, almost 200 metres high, was built in 1982 by the German Ministry of Investigation and Technology, south of Madrid.[31]

Solar-thermal power stations need to be built on fairly flat land, with connections over long distances to supply urban centres via national grids. Some systems require water for steam turbines or cooling, which is hard to find in sunniest areas, and large installations may also disturb desert ecology. BrightSource was defeated recently in its plans to build a 5,130 acre solar farm in the Mojave desert.[33]

So, we can see that our world is right on the edge of an extraordinary revolution in solar power, which has the potential to transform electricity production for thousands of years into the future.

Powering earth from space?

EADS Astrium, Europe's largest space company, is planning a pilot space-based power station for launch by 2015, using lasers to send power to earth. Japan has announced a $21 billion plan to power 300,000 homes from space. California has made a deal with Solaren to design power-generating satellites for the state.[34]

Some scientists have proposed that huge satellites be built in geostationary orbit, 35,800 kilometres above the equator, collecting solar power five times more efficiently than solar panels on earth – sunlight is more intense in space.

These satellites would send power to earth in a microwave beam, collected by a huge array of receivers on the earth, over several square kilometres. Power density on the ground would be little more than leaks from a microwave oven. The US Department of Energy concluded back in 1981 that the main issue was cost,[35] but in 2007 the National Security Space Office suggested that the Pentagon might want an energy source like this.[36]

In 2008, the Pentagon was delivering 1.6 million gallons of fuel a day, 70 per cent by weight of all US supplies, just to supply the forces in Iraq, at $5.20 a gallon, including the cost of getting it there. The US military also spends over $1 per kilowatt hour from generators. Power from space microwaves could in theory reduce costs and logistics challenges.[37] The NSSO estimated that the costs of a pilot project would be $8–10 billion, providing power for 50 cents a kilowatt hour, but it is hard to imagine such a system being built, as it would need huge investment in space, careful targeting into a battle zone, and would be very vulnerable to attack in orbit.[38]

ACTION

Consumer action

You can save money, in many parts of the world, by installing your own solar-powered hot water system – with payback time of around six years in hotter nations. For now, it only makes economic sense to install solar-voltaic cells on your roof if your local electricity company is offering a pay-in tariff that is at least three times what you pay to buy power from it. Otherwise there are better ways to spend your money on going green.

By 2025: expect $40 billion a year global sales and 50 million homes with solar panels in the EU alone.

By 2040: expect more than 20 per cent of power in some nations to be from large solar arrays. Solar cell power will be cheaper per kilowatt hour generated than carbon-fuelled power stations. Huge solar thermal power stations in the Sahara desert will supply over 10 per cent of the EU's energy, but planning challenges will continue to block the largest desert projects in the United States.

So, we have looked at the stunning pace of innovation in solar-powered technologies. What about the future of wind power?

Why wind power will dominate our future

Wind power is growing faster than any other type of renewable, excluding large hydropower projects. It only provides around 1 per cent of electricity globally, but could generate 40 per cent[39] to 50 per cent or more.[40] Turbine costs have fallen 75 per cent since the 1980s and capacity has multiplied five times in less than a decade,[41] with $50 billion invested in 2004–2008.[42]

Sweden produces over 30 per cent of its power from renewable energy.

If you add the peak outputs of every turbine in the world, we now have 121 gigawatts of power installed today, 10 times more than a decade ago, and more than twice the peak consumption of the UK.[43] Of course, such peak output from the world's wind turbines is theoretical, requiring strong winds at every site at the same moment. The Global Wind Energy Council expects world wind power to almost double in two years.

Wind power growing fast across Europe

Between 2005 and 2007, Germany's wind power jumped 21 per cent, Spain's 51 per cent, and the United States' 84 per cent. The EU goal of 12–14 per cent wind power by 2020 should be easily reached – it would need 9.5 gigawatts of new wind farms every year, but 8.5 gigawatts was installed in 2008 alone. The European Wind Association predicts that wind will account for 34 per cent of new generating capacity in 2010–2020, and 46 per cent in 2020–2030. By 2020, 180 gigawatts are likely to be wind powered, enough for 107 million EU homes.

Location is very important: windy sites in Denmark produce a kilowatt for 4 cents, the same as natural gas, but up to 80 per cent of Sweden's capacity is unused most of the time. Despite this, studies suggest Sweden could generate up to 8 per cent of power from wind.[44] Sweden generates 30 per cent of energy from renewable sources.

EU wind power (per cent)

Denmark	19
Spain	9
Ireland	6
Germany	6
UK	2
Sweden	1.6

As with solar power, peaks and ebbs in power need to be managed, and transmission losses can be large over long distances between turbines and cities, unless high voltage DC lines are used.[45]

Denmark's own wind generation could rise from 19 to 50 per cent of total average power by 2025 – so long as they are able to balance peaks and troughs using a smart grid linking other nations.[46] On very windy days, Denmark's output already reaches 100 per cent of the nation's needs.[47]

Twenty-five per cent of all EU offshore wind capacity is in Scotland, and UK wind farms could in theory provide more than 30 times all the electricity consumed in the country on the windiest days.[48] Even at 20 per cent of capacity on average days, a network of 2.5 megawatt inshore wind turbines, away from cities, would easily meet all UK demands, again only so long as balanced using an international smart grid. In 2008 there were already 165 wind farms operating 1,944 turbines in the UK with another 34 being built, 118 more had planning consent and 220 were being reviewed for planning – getting approval is the greatest block to large-scale development.[49]

Wind power popular in the United States

Sky WindPower is a California start-up planning to launch giant airborne windmills, tethered to the ground. Italy's KiteGen is planning to do similar things with kites.[50]

General Electric is forecasting that half of all new generating capacity in the United States over the next decade will be wind driven. The 1 per cent generated by wind today could rise to 15 per cent by 2020, and 20 per cent by 2030 (300,000 megawatts).[51] That would reduce CO_2 emissions in the United States by 25 per cent and natural gas use by 11 per cent, save 4 trillion gallons of cooling water, create 500,000 jobs (150,000 directly employed by the wind industry), and contribute $1.5 billion to the economy.[52]

US sales of small turbines are likely to exceed 100,000 a year. General Electric already sells more than $6 billion of wind turbines a year. A single new installation in Texas will soon generate a gigawatt of power – with a capital cost of $2 billion. That will be enough to power the lives of around a million citizens.

The UK government pushed ahead in 2010 with a massive expansion of offshore wind farms, each up to 100 kilometres from the coast and each pro-viding up to 10 gigawatts of power – more than the entire capacity of wind power in the UK in 2009.

Wind power will become more efficient

Huge advances have been made in blade design and operation, so that wind turbines are near their theoretical maximum efficiency of 59 per cent.[53] New blades flex in gusts so that they spill damaging forces without breaking (various methods are being used to vary power and wind pressure at different wind speeds). The most efficient turbines are thus able to adjust their speed to different wind conditions.

A common cause of breakdown is the huge gearboxes, which convert slow revolutions of huge blades into fast revolutions of generators. Enercon has developed a generator that is attached directly to the axle holding the blades, but these generators are much larger and heavier. Reliability has improved dramatically: in 2002 the average turbine was out of action for 15 per cent of the time; that figure is now less than 3 per cent.[54]

Pure profit in five years

Medium-sized wind turbines cost €2 million to build, but the energy they use is free, and they last for at least 20 years. They typically pay for themselves in five years and then make pure profit. Costs fall as turbine size rises. The largest ones produce 6 megawatts – enough to power several shopping centres. Each blade is 65 metres long, similar to the wingspan of a Boeing 747.

 A farmer can earn £50,000 a year from a quarter of an acre with a single installation – compared to just £150 from growing crops for biofuels.

A typical 2 megawatt (2MW) turbine can generate £200,000 of power on wholesale markets – plus another £300,000 of subsidy from taxpayers – over the first five years. The £500,000 total revenues give a great financial return if you have a windy site, planning permission and capital.

Single blades can be more than 250 feet long, which means it is often easier to make them near the place where they will be used. Small turbine production also offers huge opportunities for local medium-sized business, for example with installation and maintenance.

> A single 60-metre-high wind tower can produce 2.3 megawatts using 45 metre blades, in a wind of 11 metres a second. At that wind speed, blade tips travel 230 kilometres per hour, and the gearbox spins 1,500 times a second, making enough electricity to boil 6 litres of water a second. The whole structure weighs 300 tons and sways slightly in the wind.[55]

Problems with wind

However, wind power does present a number of challenges:

- *Wind power needs smart, flexible grids:* to cope with huge peaks at windiest moments. Denmark has to sell wind power to Sweden and Norway at peak times.

- *Many people object to the appearance or noise of wind farms* on hills or coastline.

- *Many wind farms are built in remote places where energy yield can fall significantly.* Long cables to cities mean significant power losses unless DC grids are used (see pages 63–64). Energy may also be needed to build new roads for construction.

- *Unsuitable for city homes:* wind speeds are lower in cities, and air turbulence is created near buildings, so turbines do not 'know' which way to face.

- *Radar confusion for aviation:* images looking like aircraft can suddenly appear if a turbine turns to face a new wind direction. Vestas and Qinetiq are working on stealth blades to reduce the strength of images.

- *Interference with TV, radio or mobile phones:* turbines can interfere with radio signals, either by generating radio waves at the top of the turbine, or by bouncing signals off the blades. Generators can be screened, or blades can be made with less metal.

Sales of $800 billion over 20 years from windy weather

After the 2009 fall in sales linked to the financial crisis, the total global market for wind power will grow again rapidly – and could be more than €7 billion a year in the EU alone by 2020, and €2 billion in the UK. At $1.76 million per megawatt, if 500,000 megawatts were installed globally by 2030, that would mean $880 billion or €650 billion of sales.

The European Investment Bank released €1.4 billion in 2009 to finance loans for smaller onshore wind farms.[56] In 2008, Energias de Portugal (the national utility provider) bought Horizon Wind Energy from Goldman Sachs for $2.15 billion – the highest ever paid for a wind company. The Chinese are about to become global leaders in wind power production, assisted by huge government commitments to domestic wind power generation.

So, we have seen the speed of innovation in solar and wind power, and the impact they will have. Sadly, it is a very different picture with waves and tides.

Waves and tide are hard to use

There is enough wave power breaking on UK shores to supply the entire nation's energy needs three times over. Wave power is more predictable than wind, varies less rapidly, and can harness energy from storms many thousands of miles away. Wave power stations can also be hidden below the surface, causing less visual impact than wind farms.

Wave power is hard to use: steel rusts, while salty water corrodes electrical contacts. Every piece of submerged equipment is quickly covered in barnacles and seaweed, which reduces efficiency, unless painted with toxic coatings on a regular basis, which can only be done by lifting equipment out of the water.

There are a few small pilots, which have struggled to varying degrees. Pelamis Wave Energy Converter looks like a giant red serpent, made of cylinders linked by hinged joints. The cylinders float on the sea. As the joints bend, they pump hydraulic fluid through turbines. The pilot off the Orkneys was successful and the first commercial project is running off the coast of Portugal. They hope to expand at the site to 25 Pelamis machines, saving 60,000 tons of CO_2 a year.

The US Interior Departments' OCS Wave Energy Initiative is a device that works by using waves to push air up and down in a cylinder to produce electric power. Carnegie Corporation in Australia is using a different CETO system for desalination as well as electricity, expecting to power 50,000 homes. Waves pump water through a generator and across a membrane to remove salt and other minerals. There is no offshore equipment, so pumps may last 30 years.

Seawater makes electricity by osmosis

Every cubic metre of river water that flows into the sea could be used to generate 0.7 kilowatts of electricity. Fill a reservoir with sea water and another with river water. Connect the two with a large semi-permeable membrane, which allows water but not salt to pass through. Water moves across to dilute the salty reservoir, and the salty reservoir rises. Now let the salty water flow down to sea level, driving a turbine as it does so. Statkraft has installed pilot plants on the coast at Sunndalsøra in Norway, and in SINTEF's laboratories in Trondheim. It hopes to have membranes that are large and strong enough by 2015.[57]

Tidal machines often break down

Tides are also difficult to harness. Very few tidal power projects exist and funding is hard to find. But tides are regular and varying output is easily managed because it is 100 per cent predictable. The best locations are where strong currents are close to towns – as in Northern Ireland, Norway, France and Canada.

The largest tidal power station is the La Rance barrage in France, which produces up to 240 megawatts. The huge Severn estuary project in the UK has the potential to generate up to 5 per cent of the nation's power, more than 9 gigawatts, if approved. A large barrage project would cost at least £21 billion and would require a £2 billion upgrade to the national grid to cope with a huge surge in power generation every 12 hours. An alternative may be smaller barrages, or even tidal islands, to minimize the impact on wildlife.

So, we have looked at solar, wind, tides and waves – we now need to turn to the most important of all renewable energy sources: one that has dominated power generation in developing nations, is responsible for almost a fifth of all electricity globally, and is one of the most controversial ways to reduce carbon use: hydroelectric power.

> Marine Current Turbines is the world's first tidal energy company to feed power into a national grid commercially, selling to Irish utility ESB. SeaGen turbines use blades that rotate at the speed of a revolving door for 18–20 hours a day. Its first installation is generating enough power for 1,000 homes (1.2 megawatts).

The importance of hydroelectric power

Water power is a vitally important part of electricity generation, mainly in low income nations where labour to build dams is relatively cheap, and the value of the electricity is very high (due to a lack of foreign currency to buy oil or coal). Norway is almost 100 per cent water-powered and worldwide there are around 945 gigawatts of capacity – around 20 per cent of all power generated today. In 2008 alone, 110 gigawatts were added.[58]

Most suitable sites have already been developed in Europe and the United States, but there is huge potential elsewhere. For example, the world's largest hydro project could be the extension of the Grand Inga Dam in the Democratic Republic of Congo, with a possible capacity of 40 gigawatts – enough to power Hong Kong, Israel or New Zealand.[59]

Dams can last 100 years and plants require little maintenance. Unlike other renewable sources, dams can provide power on demand (30 minutes' notice). This feature can be hugely valuable in balancing power loads from wind or solar. Owners of dams can sell electricity for higher prices at peak times.

Hydro projects are popular with funders such as carbon offset schemes because they are large, tangible, long-lasting, and it is clear how a subsidy has made the difference between a project being built or not. Dams also help guarantee water supplies in regions that have varying rainfall, and play a vital part in water management.

But dams are also very unpopular with policy-makers (mainly in developed nations) because they interfere with the natural flow of rivers and may displace large numbers of people living in valleys. For example, the Three Gorges Dam in China affected no less than 1.5 million people, many on very low incomes, who lost land and homes. Their daily lives were destroyed. At the same time, the project brought electricity to 10 million people for the first time – carbon-free apart from energy used in construction. For these reasons, most new hydropower dams are likely to be relatively small scale (10 megawatts or less), easier to fund and lower risk.

However, it is also possible to generate electricity from slow moving water in other waterways. For example, Hydrovolts has developed a way to generate power from slow currents in irrigation ditches. (For discussion of dam building trends and ethics, see pages 130 to 133 on water management.)

So, expect hydropower to be increasingly important, especially in developing nations. There is one other very way important way to generate power without using carbon or nuclear fuel, and that is geothermal.

Power from hot rocks – geothermal

Geothermal power taps heat stored in the molten core of the earth. There is 250,000 times more accessible geothermal power available than is currently being used worldwide. In theory this would be *enough to power the world many thousands of times over*, so long as that power can be distributed from the most suitable geothermal sites to where it is needed.[60] Total global geothermal generation is only around 10 gigawatts, equivalent to 10 medium-sized coal power stations.

Hawaii generates 25 per cent of electricity in this way and California 6 per cent. Huge areas of the United States have hot dry rock relatively close to the surface. In Iceland, five major geothermal power plants produce about 24 per cent of the country's electricity. In addition, geothermal heating provides hot water and room heating for around 87 per cent of the nation's buildings. The cost of geothermal power is usually around 6–7.6 cents per kilowatt hour[61] – in Iceland there is so much of it that some pavements in Reykjavik and Akureyri are heated.

Unlike wind or solar, geothermal is always available and can be turned on and off as needed. The energy source will last for hundreds of millions of years, and its use is expected to grow 80 per cent in 2010–15 across the United States, 9.5 per cent per year. The Federal stimulus packages and Recovery Act funding set aside a total of $750 million for geothermal. Congress allocated a further $45 million for Department of Energy geothermal programmes. There is more geothermal funding available for spending right now than for the entire previous 20 years.

Until recently almost all geothermal power was generated near fault lines in the tectonic plates, where the earth's rocky crust is most vulnerable. The oldest working geopower station is at Larderello in Italy, which provides enough output for 1 million homes and represents 10 per cent of global output.[62]

In theory, geothermal power plants can be built anywhere, so long as you are prepared to drill down deep enough to find hot rock (up to 10 kilometres). In practice, tapping into such depths can release CO_2 and sulphate gases. Tapping geothermal heated water can also cause local land disturbance. Even drilling can cause a mini earthquake – as happened in Basle in Switzerland in December 2006, registering 3.4 on the Richter scale and shaking many government buildings.[63]

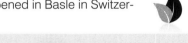

Geothermal heating is not to be confused with heat pumps, which work in a similar way to motors in a fridge-freezer, using pipes laid underground as a radiator for a building. Heat pumps are a very efficient way to heat homes (see pages 101–02 for a whole section on heat pumps).

Heatspring Learning Institute trains building professionals how to design and install geothermal heating and cooling. Over 1,600 people have participated in courses since 2007, from $300 online training to $1,500 three-day programmes. Heatspring had sales of over $1 million in 2008.

Heading towards a carbon-free world

In summary, we have seen that solar, wind, hydro and geothermal power each have the theoretical capacity to provide 9 billion people with far more power than they could possibly want or need, and to do so without emitting a single molecule of CO_2 except in manufacturing, building and decommissioning. When we combine these technologies, the total generating potential is more than sufficient to rid our world forever of carbon-generated electricity. The issues are to do with cost (falling fast) and infrastructure (smart grids) as well as scaling up manufacturing and installations fast enough.

Solar power from deserts will grow at great speed from 2015 to 2025, together with domestic solar water heating, but solar-voltaic cells will only start to have a significant impact on power generation from 2025 when their purchase cost per watt of peak power falls 25 per cent from 2010 levels. More than 20 per cent of UK and United States power will come from wind by 2025, competing on cost without subsidy, rising to over 30 per cent by 2040.

We will also see huge growth in China and other emerging economies. Tidal barrages will prove very successful as large-scale projects.

We can see that in the longer-term, humanity will be able (if we choose) to develop an almost carbon-free and nuclear-energy-free society. Carbon use could then be restricted to making petrochemical products like plastics and for fuels used in planes and ships. But until we get there, which could take us at least 40 years, and probably longer, we have to face the reality that much of our power will be generated from carbon – particularly coal, which is cheap, plentiful and convenient to countries like China.

The question is, how will green tech innovation help us convert an inefficient and polluting fossil-fuel industry to one that is efficient and carbon-neutral, or nearly so?

ACTION

Business action

Every investor should look closely at alternative energy. Expect many start-ups to become major corporations, and many larger corporations to snap up innovative companies in this area.

Every company should consider installing solar-thermal power for water heating, solar-voltaic cells for places where mains electricity is unreliable or far away, and wind power for roofs of factories and tall offices. The payback periods may be excellent and it also sends a positive message to staff, customers and investors about your commitment to climate change action.

Consumer action

Solar-thermal water heating can have a payback period of around seven years, depending on site and country. Solar-voltaic cells are only worth considering if you have a generous tariff for the energy you generate. Only think about wind turbines on your roof or land in rural areas. Water power is an excellent power source if your property is next to a stream or small river – just run a small turbine floating on the water. If your house has easy access to hot rock or hot water coming up direct from the ground, this is a very attractive energy source. Some power companies give an option for you to buy only renewable power – for each unit you use, they have to supply a unit to the national grid. You may want to sign up – it sends a signal to the power company and can help accelerate investment in renewable energy.

CHAPTER THREE
CLEANER COAL, OIL AND GAS

How carbon will be burnt – and what price oil?

Huge plumes of white steam rise thousands of feet into the air from cooling towers so immense that you could fit two Olympic swimming pools inside the base of each one. Soaring above them all is the 259 metre chimney of one of the largest coal-fired power stations in the world.

That chimney gets rid of 15 tons a minute of warm CO_2, around 22 million tons every year. If this single power station were a whole country, it would rank number 76 in the world in carbon emissions.

A continuous stream of long freight trains crank and squeak through the 2 square mile site, into the power station yard, at Drax in the North of England. Each engine is pulling 1,400 tons of coal, which they dump without stopping, truck by truck, as each one reaches the conveyor belts below. Thirty tons every minute is needed to feed the furnaces at full capacity. If all that coal came by road, the flames would burn through a lorry load every 90 seconds.

The coal is carried along to massive crushers, pulverized into fine dust by huge 1.4 ton steel balls at a rate of up to 1,800 tons every hour. The dust burns like gas when blasted with air into the white-hot furnace, producing temperatures of over 560 degrees centigrade.

Burning coal is a very dirty business. If those chimney gases were untreated, over 300,000 tons a year of sulphur dioxide would be released into the air, drifting east with the prevailing winds to form millions of tons of acid rain, which would damage or destroy Scandinavian forests. Most of the toxic gas is washed out using a fine mist of limestone and water.

Huge electrodes and very high voltages remove 1.4 million tons of soot that would otherwise descend onto the countryside or end up turning snow and ice grey over the Arctic. Most of the ash is used in concrete.

Drax is one of the most efficient coal-fired power stations in the world, yet it wastes 60 per cent of all the energy it uses. But it still converts enough to power the lives of over 4 million people – 4 gigawatts of power – more, for example, than three nuclear power stations at Formask in Sweden.[1]

Over 80 per cent of global power comes from burning carbon today, and by 2030 more than half of power will probably still be carbon-generated, despite all the growth in alternatives. Up until the downturn of 2008, China was adding almost *2 gigawatts every week* of new coal-fired power capacity.

Cleaner electricity from coal, oil or gas

The first way to make carbon use cleaner for power generation is to ensure that the power plants are more efficient. It costs around €20–60 million to upgrade a steam turbine system for a medium-sized plant, but this also boosts power output by around 30–40 megawatts, so the work pays for itself in a few years.[2] The most efficient coal-powered stations can achieve around 46 per cent efficiency, operating at around 600°C, with the latest turbines operating at very high steam pressures.[3]

Europe alone has 500 steam turbines that are more than 25 years old and urgently need replacing, including many in former Soviet bloc nations. Ukraine uses energy about three times less efficiently than EU countries on average. Studies demonstrate that if Ukraine's energy efficiency could reach the level of countries like Slovenia and the Czech Republic, Ukraine would come close to being independent of gas imports from Russia.[4] Ukraine may lack the cash to make the upgrades, but that is just the sort of project where carbon trading may help, allowing companies that need to offset their own emissions to invest in saving carbon emissions elsewhere.

Another reason to upgrade is that the main use of carbon-powered stations is changing. In the past they all ran 24 hours a day, but now they are increasingly being used to top up variable supplies from renewables such as wind turbines, particularly in the case of gas-powered turbines. But that means a complete refit, to allow much faster starting times. Upgraded power plants reach optimum efficiency much faster, so that they also waste less energy as they power up.

Zero-carbon coal burning?

Carbon capture is the *only* way to burn fossil fuels without damaging the environment and our future may depend on it, but only so long as we are sure it works safely and reliably. First we have to prove the technology, locate enough suitable sites and lower the cost. Pilots already exist, which are collecting CO_2 from power station waste gases and storing it underground.

The EU has recommended that at least 12 large-scale demonstration projects are launched by 2015 for coal and gas-fired power plants, and that by 2020 all new coal-fired plants should include carbon-capture and storage (CCS) technology. Existing plants are to be 'retrofitted'. These will be paid for by increasing electricity generation prices by 1–2 pence per kilowatt. Meanwhile, the UK will only approve new carbon power stations if fitted with carbon capture and storage.[5]

Opportunities for storage seem to be huge. The UN's International Energy Agency estimates that Canada alone has sites that could store up to 1,300 billion tonnes of CO_2. That would be enough to last Canada over a hundred years, by which time other kinds of energy generation will be used.

In countries like the UK and Germany, where local people have often been unwilling to let CO_2 be stored beneath their land, it looks like most projects will have to pump CO_2 into old oil and gas fields under the North Sea. This means that the location of new carbon-burning power stations may need to be close to where carbon storage is easiest.

Carbon capture is very attractive to large energy companies because it will allow them to continue a carbon-based business in a less polluting way, and because they also have huge skills in piping gases under pressure over very long distances. But some scientists worry that underground stores of carbon may leak, and that the whole idea may be a dangerous waste of effort. They also worry that investment in capture and storage will take money away from much more effective projects.

How to capture and store 100 per cent of carbon

There are several ways of collecting and storing CO_2. Chimney exhaust is a mix of CO_2, nitrogen, nitrogen dioxide, steam and other gases. A simple way to capture 100 per cent of all CO_2 is to use some of the electricity from the power station to separate oxygen from air, to use the oxygen, rather than air, to burn fuel.

When carbon is burnt in pure oxygen, almost all the waste gas is CO_2 and steam. When the gases are cooled, water flows away leaving the CO_2 to be pumped back underground. Vattenfall launched a small pilot carbon capture facility at Schwarze Pumpe near Berlin that is working well, generating 30 megawatts. But local people have protested, and have stopped the CO_2 from being buried underground, so the gas is stored for now in tanks or vented into the atmosphere.[6]

An alternative method is to separate the gases after burning in air, using an absorber plus a solvent, which captures almost 90 per cent of CO_2. The solvent is then heated to 120 degrees centigrade, which releases CO_2 for later storage. The other waste gases are discharged into the atmosphere along with any remaining CO_2. Multinational power-giant Alstom uses solvents such as chilled ammonia to grab CO_2 from power plant smokestacks. Alstom and American Electric Power are running a pilot in West Virginia.

Cooling the planet – is it possible?

Ideas to cool the earth down include geoengineering projects like pumping sulphur into the atmosphere to reflect sunlight back into space, or creating clouds by spraying seawater into the sky from huge ships, or building huge parasols to shade parts of the earth. The huge volcanic eruption of Mount Pinatubo in 1991 injected a vast amount of sulphur and other material into the upper atmosphere and cooled the earth by 0.5°C for some weeks. Of course, geoengineering would do nothing to alter the fundamental drivers of climate change except for a few weeks at a time and would need constant action with unknown side effects.[7]

Another idea proposed in 2007 by a company called Planktos was to dump iron filings into the ocean off the Galapagos Islands to attempt to fertilize the ocean, stimulate the growth of plankton and increase the capture of carbon. The laboratory experiments suggested that every ton of iron filings might remove 30,000–110,000 tons of CO_2, as microorganisms grow, capture the carbon, die and sink to very deep levels of ocean.[8] But this assumes that the organisms are not eaten by others, and many questions remain about possible risks to marine life. A ban has since been agreed by 80 nations on commercial fertilization of the sea.[9]

Other suggestions for geoengineering include space mirrors, artificial trees sucking CO_2 from air, reflective crops, adding carbonate to the ocean (ground limestone) to absorb CO_2, and biochar (buying charcoal). All are controversial, unproven or expensive, or a combination of all three.

The most convenient way to store CO_2 is to pump it back into an oil or gas field, under huge pressure as a liquid. Pressure then rises in the underground store, which assists recovery of remaining oil or gas. A far more controversial storage method is to pump CO_2 into very deep ocean water where (it is hoped) it is absorbed and will stay for a long time. A safer method using water is to pump CO_2 into salty water that forms part of ancient rock formations (saline aquifers). Water easily absorbs CO_2 gas, which turns into carbionic acid (as in soft drinks like Coca-Cola). Saline aquifers hold salty water for millions of years, and carbionic acid will do no damage there.

Another suggestion has been to pump CO_2 into old coal seams that have been mined. Once again there are potential problems of leakage, but intact coal seams have held gas reliably for millions of years.

We need to be certain that the CO_2 will stay underground. We know that natural gas has been safely locked away in the same geological conditions for millions of years, but we cannot be certain that CO_2 will remain as long. Slow leaks would be very hard to detect. There is also a small risk of a 'blowout' at a pumping site, but blowouts are a regular event in oil fields and we have the technology to seal them. A more serious problem is that most power stations in the world are too far away from oil and gas fields to make such storage economic.

Market of $500 billion for carbon capture

So far only three successful projects are running with a combined storage of 3 million tons a year of CO_2 – but the electricity industry in the United States alone produces 1.5 billion tons a year, which would mean finding another 1,500 sites of similar size, or going for much larger installations.

In the United States the FutureGen carbon capture programme has been revived with $1 billion of economic stimulus funding, and is planning a 275 megawatt plant in Illinois, to be working by 2015 – at a cost of $1.5 billion, more expensive per watt than a nuclear plant. China is also exploring carbon capture.

A coal-gasification plant in Beulah, North Dakota, is pumping 1.5 million tons of CO_2 a year over 200 kilometres by pipeline to Weyburn, Sask, where it is re-injected into an old oil field to help recover new deposits. Each of these projects will remove the same amount of carbon over 20 years that would be used in 12 months by 5 million vehicles. BP is doing the same with an oil well in Algeria and is developing a similar project in California. Shell and RWE are also developing such projects.

Green tech consultants will earn up to £20 billion a year globally – 3 per cent of total annual spending of up to $2 trillion.

Norway's national oil company, Statoil, has been removing a million tons a year of CO_2 from North Sea natural gas over the last decade, re-injecting it back into empty wells – another type of carbon capture and storage.

The cost of capturing a ton of CO_2 can vary from $40 to $200 a ton in small-scale pilot projects, and was already close to being competitive at a price of $60 in 2009.[10] The EU cap and trade proposals could provide up to $50 a ton. But if the process is improved and developed on a very large scale, worldwide, the cost could fall to around $15.

Power stations with carbon capture and storage could be twice as costly to build and 30–50 per cent more costly to run, using today's methods, but when you add costs of distribution, marketing, account management and so on, the actual increase to retail prices would be more like 20 per cent. Phased in at a 1 per cent increase a year over two decades, consumers are unlikely to notice much difference compared to much larger fluctuations we have seen in fuel costs. In any case, the added costs will be more than absorbed by energy savings in things like low energy light fittings and so on. But we can also expect innovations to reduce capture costs significantly.

The size of the market for new carbon capture systems over the next 20 years could be greater than $500 billion – a single carbon capture and storage installation at a large plant can cost up to $1 billion to build.

Collecting carbon from the atmosphere

Levels of CO_2 in exhaust gases can be 100 times that in the atmosphere, so efforts to capture carbon other than by growing plants, trees or algae have been limited to power stations. But what if a device could be built that could suck CO_2 out of the air at low cost? Several laboratories around the world have built prototypes that could be scaled up to the size of shipping containers, each able to extract a ton of CO_2 a day.[11]

Some projects spray sodium hydroxide to capture CO_2 as sodium carbonate, which is then recycled to release the CO_2 as gas. Others use calcium oxide to form calcium carbonate, or use ion exchange resins, a polymer impregnated with sodium hydroxide. The CO_2 is later released by blowing warm moist air onto the membrane.

Scrubbers can extract CO_2 from any source, including local heating systems, ships' boilers and so on. They could also be placed directly above the sites where CO_2 will be stored underground – more efficient than pumping CO_2 many hundreds of kilometres from a coal-fired power station.

Most of the cost of carbon capture is the energy required to run the process, including the pumping underground. If at some distant point in the future, the price of energy were to fall to a fraction of what it is today, then it might make sense to put back underground some of the trillions of tons of

CO_2 that are already in the atmosphere, especially if humankind is faced with a far worse climate change crisis than we thought in 2010.

Once again, we see a common theme: technology already exists, which can be widely used if the price is right. Short-term financial incentives can encourage take-up, so we start to see economies of scale, leading to lower prices and the ending of subsidies.

What price for a barrel of oil?

One of the greatest challenges for our world is that oil is so cheap – not to buy, but to get out of the ground in many places. Many oil wells operate profitably at around $17 a barrel – the price in 1999. But oil sold at that price encourages over-use and puts most green tech companies out of business. Fortunately, cheap oil sources cannot keep pace with growing global demand, so the price rises until energy companies are able to bring on-stream enough additional oil flow from more expensive locations.

Since most green tech innovations depend on energy prices being above a certain level to be financially viable, we need to think about what future energy prices could be. First, let us make a big assumption, which is that our world would cope with an average energy price in real terms of around $100 a barrel of oil. That figure is significantly less than the $147 peak of 2008, and only around the same price that oil was in real terms in the peak of the 1970s.

There is a big difference between then and now. Since the 1970s we have enjoyed 30 years of green innovation, increasing fuel efficiency in vehicles by over 50 per cent, boilers by 35 per cent, heat loss in homes by 25 per cent, and in much of manufacturing by 50 per cent. So, most nations are much better protected against the impact of oil price rises than they were a generation ago.

Price of $100 a barrel is a critical point for green tech

At $100 a barrel or above, a hundred million small steps by companies and communities make perfect financial sense, and market forces drive green innovation at every level. Even at $75 a barrel, many green tech businesses start to become highly profitable.

Of course prices could end up far higher than $100, and stay there for a long time; if so, we will see even faster green tech innovation. The risk will then be another deep recession, triggered by high energy costs, leading to a fall in demand for oil, and another price collapse, which then wipes out huge numbers of green tech companies, scaring off future green tech investors for a very long time.

So why should we think that minimum oil prices of $100 barrel are both likely and sustainable? Here are three reasons why such a price is likely to be exceeded:

1 *Demographics:* 1 billion children alive today becoming adults. Population growing from 6.7 to 9 billion over next 40 years.

2 *Wealth generation:* 2 billion young adults in emerging nations are fast becoming more wealthy consumers. Energy use per person in these regions is likely to go on increasing fast.

3 *Oil limits:* oil reserves from old wells are running out. Owners of those wells are keen to slow down the destruction of their assets by price rises. New sources of oil are more costly to extract, and require huge capital investment.

Sixty-six per cent of all oil used in the United States is used for transport (45 per cent is gasoline) – most of the rest is used by the chemical industry. Oil accounts for more than 95 per cent of all energy used in transport in the United States.[12]

It is a fine balance, and no one can be sure where the 'ideal' price for oil is, even if it could be artificially set. Oil prices of $75 are needed as a minimum for the oil industry to carry on drilling and expanding capacity. But oil prices of much more than $100 may take speed out of the global economy, so the situation could easily become unstable. Rapid upturns can quickly outstrip capacity with spikes in oil price, and downturns can lead to price slumps. Both are bad news for energy companies, which need to plan long term.

Peak oil – and when will the wells run dry?

For years, many have warned that the world is near peak output for oil, but it depends on region. Peak oil production was reached some time ago in Europe. What of the future? The International Energy Authority enraged many experts in 2009 by suggesting that peak oil would not be reached for at least 20 years, and that the 85 million barrels a day we used in that year could rise by up to 20 per cent by 2030. Its forecast assumed that oil prices remained high enough to drive high investment in extraction, and that the world fails to take radical steps to control CO_2 emissions, or to invest in green tech. Its 'worst case' forecast would also risk earth temperatures rising by 6°C by the end of the century.[13]

The fact is that that no one knows how much extractable oil the world has left, because it all depends on future market price. The higher the price, the more oil we can afford to extract. On the other hand, as technology improves, old fields become more attractive, even if prices remain the same.

Look how technology and price have affected estimates for the size of the Kern River Oil Field, which was discovered in 1899. In 1942, the owners thought that only 54 million of the 330 million barrels of oil still remained. By 1995, more than 736 million barrels had been extracted – but scientists expected to remove 970 million more barrels. By 2007, Chevron announced that more than 2 billion barrels had now been extracted, and the State of California thought that 627 million more barrels were still available. Total figures had jumped from 330 million to 2.6 billion in 60 years. At every stage, new technology, and higher prices enabled them to get more out.[14]

With today's technology and prices, around 65 per cent of the oil in an average field has to be left in the ground. The US National Petroleum Council estimates that although our world only has *proven* oil reserves of 29 billion barrels, 1,124 billion barrels are still underground, of which 374 billion could be extracted with today's technology, if the price is right. Only a third of the geological formations that may contain oil have so far been explored, so further discoveries are also likely, some of which may turn out to be huge.[15] But there is more to carbon stores than oil.

> ### Higher prices make new oil fields possible to exploit
>
> In September 2009 BP announced that it had managed to drill 9.4 km below the seabed – a world record – and found more oil. The Tiber field is 250 miles south-east of Houston and in a depth of 1,200 metres of ocean, so the find is 10.6 kilometres below sea level. Mount Everest is only 8,848 metres above sea level.

Oil from coal, algae and other sources

While analysts fret about when oil or gas or coal will run out, we need to realize that we already have the technology to convert any carbon source to any other kind of carbon. For example, we can convert coal to gas and gas to solid forms of carbon. Carbon in food can be converted to oil or gas and carbon from oil can also be used to accelerate growth of food (growing in high concentrations of CO_2). So once oil prices rise above a certain point, it becomes economic to start producing oil products from coal – as they were in the early decades of the 20th century.

What this means is that oil prices will tend to find a new level (we can debate how high). There may be spikes and troughs during the adjustment processes, but as prices rise, the point comes where it is viable to turn coal into oil. When that happens, there will be a natural limit to oil prices. There are also other correcting mechanisms: as oil prices rise, green tech also expands more quickly, providing alternative energy sources, and also saving more energy.

The energy in one barrel of oil is the equivalent of 5 labourers working 12 hour days for a whole year. (A barrel of oil contains 6 billion joules of heat if burned.)[16]

One of the largest factors in all of this may be what happens to the vast methane deposits that are being discovered beneath frozen tundra.

Methane to power the future or poison the planet?

It looks like our world has been sitting on huge gas reserves that were previously unknown. Global reserves of natural gas (mainly composed of methane) are around 6,000 trillion cubic feet,[17] double the figure of 20 years ago.[18]

But this is just for gas from traditional sources. Research over the last two decades suggests that energy trapped under permafrost or the sea (mainly methane) could be as great as all the world's oil, natural gas and coal reserves – more than 3 trillion tons. Methane in the region is produced by bacteria that feed on the 950 billion tons of carbon in the top several metres of frozen ground, which covers 20 per cent of the earth's land surface. As ice melts, bacteria are activated and start producing methane gas. One-third to half of all permafrost is now within 1–1.5°C of melting.

Hundreds of billion tons of methane have been trapped in ice crystals over thousands of years as methane clathrate, buried in permafrost in the Arctic.[19] It looks like dirty ice, is quite soft, and bursts into flames when touched with a match. The United States, Canada, Russia, China, Japan, South Korea and Norway are all racing ahead to full-scale production of clathrates, which may begin by 2015.[20]

Clathrates are mainly found within and underneath permafrost, and beneath the seabed on continental shelves, usually at depths of around 200–400 metres.[21] Methane is often present at a concentration of 50 per cent in pores of ice. Layers of clathrate can be hundreds of metres deep, with methane compressed up to 160 times atmospheric pressure.[22]

In 2007 scientists located deposits of clathrates in Alaska that were 80 per cent pure methane (plus ice). There could be up to 0.7–4.4 trillion cubic metres of methane clathrate in Alaska alone, enough to heat 100 million homes for up to 60 years. South Korea has deposits that could meet the nation's gas needs for 30 years[23] while Japanese deposits of clathrates could supply the nation with natural gas for decades – 50 trillion cubic metres.[24]

How methane is mined from ice

One way to release clathrates is to pump CO_2 into deposits. Another is to depressurize clathrate and allow methane to bubble out. In all this there are huge risks: methane is more than 20 times more powerful at warming the earth than CO_2, and once clathrate deposits are disturbed it is possible that leakages could occur in a vast and uncontrollable way. A runaway chain reaction could break up trillions of tiny crystals, triggering landslides or even tsunamis. But pumping in CO_2 allows one gas to replace another, preserving the ice structure more safely, so long as CO_2 becomes permanently embedded in the ice.[25]

If methane were accidentally released on a large scale it would in turn add to global warming, and potentially create another feedback mechanism: warming $\rightarrow$ further release. So methane extraction should be viewed with great caution. In any case, it takes us in the wrong direction, back towards a carbon-dominated world.

We should leave the methane where it is and redirect efforts to wind, solar and other renewables – including renewable sources of carbon such as biofuels made from biowaste and from algae.

Methane is released into the atmosphere as landfill waste rots underground, but the gas can be collected by sealing the surface of old landfill sites, and running pipes to pump the gas out. Water Management's landfill gas and waste-to-energy projects already produce enough electricity to power more than 800,000 homes, saving around 8.2 million barrels of oil a year. Management will invest $500 million in green tech over the next decade and plan to double renewable power generation from methane by 2020.

Biofuels – great promise or great curse?

Biofuels are solid, liquid or gas carbon-based fuels that are made from biological material – mainly plants. Examples include making petrol substitutes from sugar, biodiesel from wheat or recycled cooking oil, or making fuel out of agricultural material such as straw stubble or manure, or from wood chips, sewage or landfill gas. Some kinds of biofuels are a disaster for the poorest in the world and should be banned – anything linked to food, even kitchen waste, which should be fed instead to animals or composted for fertilizer.

Food – to make first generation biofuel

Turning food into fuel has been widely promoted by many national leaders as a great way to beat the fuel crisis, while also reducing reliance on unstable oil and gas suppliers. However, biofuels from food have also been blamed for higher food prices, food shortages in the poorest nations, hunger riots and the fall of governments. As we will see in Chapter 10, biofuels from food are an absurd idea on a large scale. In 2008, 25 per cent of the entire US grain harvest was burned in vehicles, enough to feed 330 million people for a year.[26]

You would have to use twice the entire land area of every farm in the United States just to fill the tanks each year of US truck and car drivers. Even if all grain produced in the entire world was converted to biofuels, it would only produce an amount equivalent to 10–15 per cent of total world energy consumption.

> Novozymes provides a range of products to help society shift from an oil-based to a renewable-based economy. Its technology produces 'second generation biofuels' from agricultural waste, forestry and even municipal rubbish.

This is a really serious issue for global food supplies. Fortunately we can use other biological material to make 'second generation' biofuels, but even then, not without stresses on farms, food and land use.

The US market for biodiesel is already larger than a billion gallons a year and Federal directives require this to rise to at least 36 billion gallons a year by 2022. But almost all of this is being made from food.

Forced by law to burn food in your own car

The European Union required at least 5.75 per cent of all transport fuel to be made from biofuel by 2010, rising to 10 per cent by 2020. Once again, almost all of this is from food. So car owners are being forced by law to burn food every time they drive. Businesses were not only converting food into vehicle fuel, but also stockpiling for tomorrow's biofuel factories that they expect to be built.

Regulators are finally waking up and policies are now starting to change, to try and stop a global stampede to pour food into engines. It is impossible to convert food to fuel on this scale without risking a significant impact on global food prices. A World Bank report published in July 2008 suggested that up to 70 per cent of the massive price jump over the previous two years was due to competition with biofuels.

Safer light from biofuel – and a cooker too

Sixty per cent of rural homes in India have no electricity. The only source of light is a kerosene lamp, or perhaps only the cooker, burning wood or charcoal. Families live in dim light at night, breathing very polluted air. It has been estimated that indoor rural air pollution kills around 2 million people a year. Nimbkar Agricultural Research Institute (NARI), India has pioneered special ethanol lamps, which use low grade 55–60 per cent ethanol-water as fuel made from locally grown organic material, and which can also be used for cooking (called a Lanstove). This fuel is much safer than pure ethanol – fewer accidental fires – and easier to make in a single distillation process. Fumes are less toxic and waste heat can be used to heat a specially designed slow cooker. Ethanol devices usually have to be filled each day by hand, with the risk of burns, and also that the alcohol will be drunk. To prevent these things, cylinders of compressed gas/liquid are provided that are easy to change and cannot be abused. NARI won a Globe Forum Innovation award for the Lanstove in 2009.

Food riots and fall of governments

Food prices really matter. In Asia and Africa we are seeing mass migration of subsistence farmers, drifting into megacities. China alone is seeing 30 million people a year on the move, and Africa will have 750 million in cities by 2025. Most of these people are very poor and now depend on buying food in local markets.

Up to 80 per cent of the daily income of such people is spent buying rice or other grain. When food prices doubled, hundreds of millions of people struggled to eat. Parents had to choose between feeding themselves or their children, selling furniture and even cooking equipment to buy basic food.

And then the riots began. Tens of thousands of hungry people in many different towns and cities in 33 nations protested in 2008, by setting fire to cars and smashing shops. But this is nothing to what we could see in the future, if it is widely perceived that the reason hundreds of millions cannot afford food is because the United States, the EU and other wealthy regions have burnt too much food in their cars, lorries, trains and planes.

First generation biofuels (food into fuel) created a direct link between energy prices and food. The poorest will never be able to compete with industrial giants and vehicle owners, and the end result of using food for fuel is bound to be further food shortages.

Here is a scenario:

1 Oil prices double.

2 Profit margins of biofuel producers rise.

3 Purchases of food for biofuels rise.

4 Global price rise for these crops.

5 Farmers sow more fields with these crops.

6 Less fields available for other crops or for livestock.

7 Other crop prices rise, meat prices also.

8 Price of farmland rises.

9 Price of woodland rises – where trees can be cleared for planting.

10 More trees cleared by farmers.

11 Amount of land under cultivation grows.

12 Amount of biofuel still too small to influence fall in oil price so 3) to 11) continues until the lunacy of such policies is seen by governments and regulations change.

Officials may try to limit the percentage of crops that can be used for biofuel, but how do you enforce such a ban?

Biomass – 'second generation' biofuels can also be damaging

Unfortunately, you end up with a very similar scenario even if there is a complete and fully enforced ban on using any more food in fuel factories, allowing only biowaste or non-edible biomass to be used in future. There is just not enough biowaste available as an agricultural by-product.

Remember that almost all biowaste has been used in the past to return nutrients to the land – ploughing back straw, putting manure on the fields and so on. The more farmers sell off their carbon waste, the more they also lose the attached nitrogen, and the more they lose soil conditioners (humus from rotten vegetation), and that means only one thing: more artificial fertilizers, which are themselves made using huge amounts of energy.

Whether farmers are growing food for fuel or biomass for fuel, scientists are unable to agree what difference biofuels make in terms of carbon saving, when grown on farmland. We need to include energy used in fertilizers, tractors and food transport, and lost in the conversion into fuel. The only biofuel that scientists generally agree gives a clear reduction in CO_2 emissions, and is cheaper than petrol when oil is around $80 a barrel, is sugar-cane ethanol made in Brazil.

Here is the same scenario above – but with a ban on use of food for biofuels, using only biomass. We end up in exactly the same place, with food price rises and increased deforestation:

1 Oil prices double.

2 Profit margins of biofuel producers rise.

3 Purchases of biomass for biofuels rises.

4 Global price rises for biomass.

5 Farmers sow more fields with biomass crops.

6 Less fields available for food crops or for livestock.

7 Grain prices rise, meat prices also.

8 Price of farmland rises.

9 Price of woodland rises – where trees can be cleared for planting.

10 More trees cleared by farmers.

11 Amount of land under cultivation grows.

12 Amount of biofuel still too small to influence fall in oil price, so points 3 to 11 continue until the lunacy of such policies is seen by governments and regulations change.

Short-sighted madness and greed

It was an act of short-sighted madness for US and EU policymakers to insist by laws that every citizen is to burn food in their cars. But as we can clearly see, filling cars with non-edible biomass will also distort farm prices and increase pressures on land use, with disastrous effects in the longer term on forestation as well as food production.

In any case, these things are very hard to control. How do you prove that biofuel on sale in the local store has been made only from straw and not partly from food, for example? We are likely to see hundreds of thousands of farmers around the world secretly converting their food to fuel, to sell on the black market. We know from what happened in 2007–08 that oil prices of only $75 a barrel are more than enough to force this process in a very damaging way. If prices average over $135 a barrel, we are likely to see even faster deforestation.

So, when would such an agricultural disaster grind to a halt? Maybe only when food prices become so high, due to shortages, that biofuel conversion becomes profitable. This whole area will be a huge headache for government regulators, and for all those concerned about food shortages and fighting hunger (see Chapter 10).

Brazil leads in biofuels

Brazil is the world's second largest producer of biofuels, after the United States. Brazil produced 29 per cent of the world's ethanol in 2008, from sugarcane, and is the world's largest ethanol exporter. Brazil began using ethanol for vehicles in the 1970s during the global oil crisis: 85 per cent of all vehicles can use either ethanol or petrol or both, and 25 per cent of all petrol sold is an ethanol mix.[27]

Biomass can be hard to use

Biomass is much harder to convert to fuel than grain. Various methods are used to make fuel from non-food crops, straw and corn stalks, chips, bark and pinecones as well as other biological waste. They include using steam or acids, enzymes or fungi, and catalytic processes. Many pilots exist but few are working on a large scale.[28]

Burn waste gases as fuel

Expansion of landfill methane recovery; burning flared gas at petrochemical installations.

Methane in landfill sites is responsible for 15 per cent of all global methane emissions, natural and man-made. Methane is 21 times more powerful in global warming per ton than CO_2. Since methane causes 4–9 per cent of global warming, landfill emissions may be responsible for 1 per cent of the global warming impact of human activity. Assuming that capture remains only partial, even on well organized sites, and is impractical on smaller ones, the theoretical contribution of such methane capture would be the equivalent of cutting CO_2 emissions by around 0.5 per cent globally.

Of course, the easiest thing to do with biomass is just to burn it in power stations, rather than in vehicles. Global production of biomass electricity is 47 gigawatts – around 1.3 per cent of electricity, and could rise to 2–3 per cent.[29] Unlike other renewable energy sources, it can be turned off and on relatively easily. It can also be burned in disused coal power stations.[30]

Not enough biomass to meet demand

The biggest challenge with biomass is supply: there is no large-scale collection process for growing, harvesting, processing and delivering. Biomass is only likely to be sustainable if grown on low quality land or as a by-product of the food industry. But even low quality land has uses for farming of livestock, so biomass grown as a crop will *always* tend to displace other farming activity or normal forestry. Even if we decide only to use biomass derived from forest waste, such as bark or sawdust/wood chips, we will risk pulling perfectly usable wood into the system. There is not enough local wood waste in most nations to keep all the hungry furnaces going.

In the 2008–2009 global downturn, shipping costs fell so low that biomass in Europe and the United States was soon being sourced from the other side of the world. Drax in the UK now burns peanut husks, straw pellets and olive cake, which is waste from the olive industry. Drax is

Sweden has huge forest resources, and waste from the paper industry could provide enough energy to generate up to 33 per cent of power, which could be used to balance out variations in wind and solar power.

planning to build up to three huge biomass plants, each with a 300 megawatt capacity, the biggest in the world, which will only be viable if a huge new industry is created to feed the monsters.[31] But if supply chains to deliver biomass cannot keep pace, the temptation may be very strong to mix in other agricultural products instead, which could otherwise have been used to feed livestock or people, or to start using decent cuts of wood.

Converting wood-burning homes to electric

Over a billion people cook every day on wood fires. Even a well-designed wood oven can waste 80 per cent of heat from burning, much more than industrial biomass generators using a high-temperature gasification process.

A community could burn the same amount of fuel in a small power station, and cook using electric power. The end result may be better use of fuel as well as cleaner air, especially inside homes. The communities also gain from electric light and so on. These are complex issues and the balance of advantage will alter depending on the local situation.

Seaweed harvesting to burn for energy

So the biofuels debate is moving on – from food to biowaste, to farmed bio-mass and forestry products – and then to seaweed and algae.

Kelp has been harvested in previous centuries in Britain, France, Scotland and Norway, and still is in China. But kelp can also be turned into methane and alcohol in large digesters. What remains is useful fertilizer. The shallow coastline of Scotland is ideal for growing seaweed on floating rafts.

One survey suggests there are around 8,000 square kilometres of suitable water between low tide mark and the edge of the continental shelf in the UK, beyond which the water is too deep to use. The Crown Estate owns most of the seabed up to 12 miles from the coast and commissioned the research. Brown kelp can grow between 16 and 65 kgs of biomass a year per square metre, compared to only 8–18 from sugar cane. Seaweed farms could also encourage other marine life.[32]

Algae fuel for cars and planes

'Third generation' biofuels can be made using algae, which produce up to 30 times more energy per acre per year than food crops or biomass. Growth of algae can be speeded up by cultivation in a higher concentration of CO_2, using processed gases from power stations, for example.

Algae could supply enough fuel, in theory, to meet all of the United States' transport needs, as biodiesel. It would take twice the entire land area of the United States to grow enough soy and palm oil to supply all transport needs, compared to a mere 0.2 per cent of land for algae – 15,000 square miles or 9.6 million acres (the size of Maryland).[33] Algae fuel costs $30 a gallon so far but this could fall if Royal Dutch Shell, BP or ExxonMobil manage to perfect the process.

So how do algae produce so much fuel so efficiently? Algae are very fast growers, doubling their mass every day as they divide, absorbing sunlight and using its power to convert CO_2 from the air into oil inside each cell. Under ideal conditions, algae can produce 24 times more oil per acre each year than palm oil (up to 635 gallons). Some companies claim to be able to produce far more than this, depending on growing conditions.

ExxonMobil has committed $600 million to fund algae development[34] – $300 million to Synthetic Genomics in developing algae as fuels.[35] The company is headed by Craig Venter who was head of Celera Genomics, which ran a privately funded version of the Human Genome Project in the 1990s. He has found a way to genetically engineer algae to make them release the oil they normally accumulate inside their cells, so it floats to the surface.

High-performing algae need to be able to cope with very intense light, high temperatures and high concentrations of CO_2, which they will be fed from nearby power stations. In that sense the process will not be strictly carbon neutral, since they will work more efficiently as organisms if exposed to warm CO_2 waste gas than if they have to extract CO_2 from normal air. They also need nitrogen, which can be provided from treated sewage. And they need to be resistant to viruses, which would be a threat to the giant algae incubators. Venter thinks the process will be 10 times as efficient per acre as growing maize, although capital-intensive and requiring a constant feed of CO_2.[36]

In theory you produce even more fuel per acre – but the limitation is the amount of natural sunlight, nutrients and CO_2. Once you start shining artificial light into brewing tanks, pumping in fertilizers and CO_2, you use up much of the energy (or possibly all) that you get out of the process as you burn the fuel in vehicles, compared for example to using coal to generate power to recharge car batteries.

Another approach is to use genetically modified bacteria or fungi that

Wood waste to drive cars
Choren has built an 18 million litre pilot plant to convert plant and wood waste to ethanol – large enough to fuel 15,000 cars a year. Converting wasted tree branches, pine needles, bark and other wood and paper waste to ethanol or other liquid fuels is a complex process because it means breaking down cellulose and lignin. Choren is backed by Shell, Daimler and Volkswagen.

convert CO_2 into carbon. But all these bio-methods require energy inputs. You cannot split CO_2 into carbon and oxygen without reversing the burning process. Plants, trees and algae do this using sunlight, and if microorganisms do the same then we are just talking about a variation of algae projects.

Expect huge growth of investment in all kinds of biofuels. Be ready also for sudden changes in government regulations as a result of public pressure, and for withdrawal of all tax benefits for biofuels produced from food. Fortunes will be won and lost in biofuels, as companies get caught by the technical and moral challenges.

ACTION

Business action
Think about switching from inefficient to efficient carbon burning, eg oil to gas boilers. Consider biowaste as a heating source – even from your own factory, eg wood chips. Consider biowaste such as cooking oil as a fuel, but take care not to get embroiled in food-for-fuel production or use, which could damage your brand. Look out for new business opportunities such as growing algae for fuel.

Consumer action
You may wish to avoid (if you can) burning food-linked biofuels in your car or home. You may wish to buy power from utility companies that capture some or all of the carbon they use – if you have a choice where you live, and their storage is secure.

So, we have seen how burning of fossil fuels will continue to dominate power generation until beyond 2040, and how huge efforts will be made to make the process more efficient; how carbon capture will be used to create carbon-neutral coal and gas power stations, and how biofuels will continue to create great controversy.

We now need to turn to smart grids, which will make it possible to use power more effectively and to connect huge amounts of renewable power, and also to look at the future of nuclear power stations.

CHAPTER FOUR
SMART POWER AND THE NUCLEAR BOOM

Walking through the damp forest in the rain, we can hear a loud fizzing noise. Above our heads is a tall electricity pylon carrying high voltage power from a nearby nuclear power station to the city. Each centimetre of each line above us is losing power into the air, ionizing particles and radiating electromagnetic energy. We do not know the health effects on people who live close to such pylons, but one thing is sure: huge amounts of power are being wasted every day in every nation of the world, just moving power from one place to another.

Around 7 per cent of power is lost between the place where it is generated and the consumer through switching and power lines, and a further 10 per cent is wasted by consumers who have only a poor understanding of where power is being used in their homes. Meeting peaks in demand is also very inefficient. It is much easier for power companies to run power stations at a steady pace, hour by hour, than to turn huge facilities on and off at short notice. So how can we sort out these problems?

The last-century model was to build huge power stations, transmit current over big distances using high voltage cables, transform voltages down to a usable level, and wire it into homes, factories and offices, and hope consumers use power wisely. The system had no built-in intelligence, apart from monitoring load on a minute-by-minute basis.

A third millennial model is to create an intelligent power network, so that power can flow an infinite number of ways around the community, in either direction, according to local demand, while also allowing the electricity company to reduce demand by some consumers automatically when needed. In this way,

50 million people can become linked together into a 'power community' as both buyers and sellers of electricity, depending on the time of day and on what they are doing.

Managing peak demand means cheaper power

One basic element in smart power management is smart metering: boxes for each property, linked possibly to smart switching-on appliances. If every household, office and factory were using smart metering, it could mean that 5–10 per cent of new power stations may no longer have to be built. Home owners typically cut their power use by 10 per cent in the first six months after getting smart meters, but this settles down to an average saving of 5 per cent once they get used to having the additional information about the power they are using each day.

Good Energy is the first UK electricity company to sell 100 per cent renewable energy – with 25,000 customers by 2009. The power is sourced from 450 independent renewable generators, who all feed electricity into the national grid.[1]

Power companies have huge challenges managing peak demand and the result is wasted energy and extra costs. Take Australia: on the hottest four days a year, energy use can jump by over 50 per cent compared to the average. Ten per cent of the entire generating capacity of the country is used for just four days a year. To recoup such costs, the wholesale price of electricity at peak times soars from an average of AU$50 per megawatt hour to over AU$10,000.[2]

Smart power regulation means that spikes of electricity demand can be managed by automatically turning off certain devices in factories, offices and homes when the grid is under strain. It also means that electricity pricing can be varied from hour to hour depending on demand. For example, it could be that a food company agrees with the electricity supplier that its huge deep freezes can be turned off for up to six hours at a time at peak periods – which is managed by cooling to lower temperatures during off-peak times.

Variable pricing could work based on the following day's weather forecasts. Consumers on variable tariffs would know that if outside temperatures are officially forecast to exceed, say, 40°C, air-conditioning use would rise and as a result they will be charged 20 per cent more than normal that day for electricity. To compensate, on low demand days they could be given a discount so that overall their bills would be the same if they took no action to vary consumption. In the example above, the frozen food company would only lower freezer temperatures at night, when the forecast is a heat wave for the following day. The alterations in temperature could be controlled automatically by price warnings sent online from the power company.

Intelligent power management would mean installing a special power monitoring device into every home, office, factory, school and government building. Additional controls would need to be installed in every device to be remotely turned off at peak times.

Smart metering is ideally suited to owners of electric vehicles, who can set chargers to operate only when hourly prices are at their lowest. Smart metering can also help us manage the big variations in energy production on windy or calm days, in regions with high wind-generating capacity. On windy days, prices will fall.

Smart grids will be up to 1,000 times larger than the internet

Every conventional electricity meter in the EU will be replaced by 2020, by law.[3] Venture capitalists in the United States have recently invested more than $1 billion in smart grid start-ups – two of them, GridPoint and Silver Sprint Networks, raised $220 million and $170 million. Siemens hopes to win orders for $8.5 billion in the next five years. Cisco believes that the communications network inside these smart grids will be 100–1,000 times larger than the internet.[4]

Brattle Group estimates that a smart grid could benefit the US economy by $227 billion over the next 40 years.[5] Part of this will be helping prevent power cuts, which cost the US economy around $150 billion a year. But just as the original electricity grids facilitated huge economic growth in the last century, smart grids will be the backbone of green tech economies in this century. Without smart grids, many green technologies just do not work.

Boom-time for smart metering and smart grids

President Obama's stimulus package contained $3.9 billion for smart grid development. Germany has made smart meters compulsory in all new buildings. German utility companies are spending €15–25 billion on smart grid technology – part of a total grid investment of €40–50 billion.[6]

Excel Energy has set up a smart grid in Colorado, so households get paid for energy they generate and share their power with neighbours. Smart meters in homes can be read remotely at frequent intervals, helping to plan loads on the system more easily.

The UK is aiming for universal use of smart metering by 2020, and China is also transforming its grid. Around 73 million smart meters will be installed worldwide in 2009 alone – the United States is aiming for 41 million installations by 2015. A nationwide smart grid across the United States will cost around $165 billion.[7] Morgan Stanley estimates that the total market for smart grid technologies will increase from $22 billion to $115 billion from 2010 to 2030 – an average growth of 8.8 per cent, making smart grid technologies one of the most exciting growth markets for the future.[9]

> A trial of smart meters by the Carbon Trust in the UK shows that they cut energy bills by 5 per cent and emissions by 12 per cent, by making it easier for people to watch their power use.[8]

More than 40 start-ups are developing home area networks attached to smart meters that will allow households to watch their power consumption closely, turning off devices around the home with a single switch, and controlling every electrical device. Google and Microsoft have also developed products like PowerMeter and Hohm to do similar things.[10]

At the heart of every smart grid is Advanced Metering Infrastructure or AMI – devices made by General Electric, Itron and Landis+Gyr. More than 76 million have already been installed; expect 155 million to be in use by 2013. These meters often form wireless networks of their own, where each meter can pass on information to the next one in the street, using technology developed by companies like Silver Spring Networks and Trilliant Networks.[11]

How to build 30 virtual power stations

These are companies that sell electricity to power companies without generating a single watt. EnerNOC is one such virtual power station. It has agreements with many different companies, which it pays for permission to be able to shut down non-essential equipment at peak times. Over 2,400 firms have signed up, representing control over 3,150 megawatts, which is the equivalent of around 30 peak-power plants.[12] EnerNOC provides businesses with its free PowerTrak to keep tabs on their energy usage via the internet.

Pacific Power and Gas has a similar power crisis on hot days in California. It has to double output during the summer months in California – up to 20,000 megawatts. The company is installing 10,000 smart meters every day and is aiming to include 5 million homes by the end of 2011. It expects this will trim peak demand by 10 per cent.

Smart metering systems pay for themselves because they can be read remotely, either by using wireless internet or mobile phone technology, or by short-range readers outside the property as vans drive around.

DC grids send power further

But we need more than meters in homes. Many companies are looking at ways to help build a more efficient 'supergrid' across the whole of Europe and far beyond, which works on direct current (DC) rather than alternating current (AC). With DC you can send power down a line 1,000 kilometres long with a loss of only around 1.7 per cent, compared to 15 per cent for AC, and DC cables are also easier to install underground.[13]

Europe already has a small DC grid linking Scandinavia, Germany and the Netherlands.[14] High voltage DC lines become financially viable at around 1,000 megawatts and over distances of more than 600 kilometres. For example, the 1,400 line between the Chinese provinces of Yunnan and Guandong will transmit at 800,000 volts. Compared to a traditional AC line, it will save around 35 per cent in costs over 30 years. Undersea power losses are so great with AC cables that DC works out better for distances as short as 60 kilometres.[15]

So why is AC so popular with national power companies, and why is DC so unusual for moving electricity across a nation? DC is like the current you get from a torch battery: electrons move only in one direction. With AC, the current moves back and forth 50 times every second, and every time the direction changes, a little energy is lost as radio waves, as the magnetic field alters. This effect does waste power but is very useful for electricity companies: when they push huge amounts of energy through coils of wire, it creates strong magnetic fields, which induce current to flow in any other coil of wires nearby even if they are not connected. That is how transformers work.

Let us imagine a generating company has a 10,000 volt cable. All it has to do to bring the voltage down to 100 volts for use in homes is to connect its 10,000 volt supply cable to insulated wire that is coiled round a piece of steel 10,000 times, and place another coil of wire nearby that has only 100 turns around a piece of steel, which supplies your home. This example is obviously very simplified, but illustrates the point. Such transformers are cheap, easy to make and need little or no maintenance.

In other words, AC cables constantly leak power, from every metre, every minute of every day. DC cables leak almost nothing. But using DC is difficult: you have to find a way to push the voltage up or down, and that means complicated equipment. But the same equipment can be helpful in isolating parts of a national grid from collapse, when one fault triggers another in a cascade that shuts down power across a whole region. DC lines act as firewalls.

Next generation grid

- Transmit power thousands of miles on DC high voltage power lines.

- Manage fluctuations in supply and demand with smart switching, smart metering to balance suppliers like nuclear (always turned on) and wind (variable).

- Power storage – paired up reservoirs, compressed air or hydrogen, heat, batteries (including tens of thousands of vehicle batteries).

Big batteries – new ways to store national power

Life would be easier for power companies if they had ways to store huge amounts of power to balance variations in supply and demand. Indeed, without advances in this area it is hard to see how alternative energy production can really take off.

One way to store power from hydro-electric installations is to link two reservoirs together at different levels. When there is low demand, electricity is used to pump water to the higher dam, which can be released at times of peak demand. In 2000 the United States had 19.5 gigawatts of pumped storage generating capacity, accounting for 2.5 per cent of generating capacity. More energy is consumed in pumping than is generated, and losses also occur due to water evaporation, electric turbine/pump efficiency, and friction. In 2007 the EU had 38.3 gigawatts net capacity of pumped storage out of a total of 140 gigawatts of hydropower, representing 5 per cent of total net electrical capacity in the EU.[16]

Another way to help manage peaks and troughs is to build vast batteries. VRB Power Systems supplies 'flow' batteries with hundreds of gallons of electrolytes. Pumped in one direction, it absorbs power, and in reverse the power is released. It costs $500–600 to store a kilowatt hour and the system is only 70 per cent efficient.[17]

Compressed air has also been used as a storage method by the Alabama Energy Cooperative since 1991. Coal-fired power plants are used to pump air during the night into underground salt caverns to a pressure of 1,000 pounds per square inch. The air is fed during the day into a turbine burning natural gas – which usually has to compress its own air to feed the process. This increases the overall energy output by 33 per cent.[18]

An alternative to compressed air is compressed hydrogen. Surplus energy is used to split hydrogen and oxygen by electrolysis. The hydrogen is stored at high pressure in underground salt caverns, which typically will leak around 0.01 per cent a year, according to Siemens Energy Sector. This is because rock-salt walls behave like a liquid, sealing leaks automatically. Any cavern already used for short-term storage of natural gas would be suitable.

Around 60 salt caverns are being built in Germany. If only 30 were used, they could provide a short-term store of around 4,200 gigawatt hours of electrical energy. Whenever extra power is needed, the hydrogen can be fed almost instantly into a nearby gas turbine. Each cavern is capable of providing a baseload of 500 megawatts of power continuously for up to a week, which is the equivalent of 140 gigawatt hours of power, compared to only 40 gigawatt hours of total power storage across the entire nation in 2009. The costs of long-term storage will be less than 10 cents per kilowatt hour, half the cost of compressed air. Siemens expects to have large-scale pilots up and running by 2013–15. The hydrogen could also be used to mix with gas from biomass to make additional liquid biofuel;[19] the oxygen released from splitting water can also be sold for use in furnaces.

A third way to store power on an industrial scale is to build vast batteries – or to create 'virtual battery farms' by using the battery power of hundreds of thousands of electric cars that are all plugged into the grid (see page 77–79).

Expect new opportunities for consulting services offered to clients in partnership with electricity providers, providing energy audits, discussions about new tariffs, managing peak demand and so on.

Next-generation nuclear boom

Whatever you may think about nuclear power, whether you love it because it is reliable and carbon-free, or hate it because of contamination risks, the fact is we are entering a new nuclear age, barring another major nuclear accident. The Three Mile Island accident in 1979 and Chernobyl in 1986 have both become distant memories.

In 1986, the Chernobyl plant developed a fault and reached 150 times its normal power level before its water turned to high pressure steam and blew the plant apart, stopping the nuclear reaction. Thirty-one people died in the immediate event and an area of 20 square miles centred on the plant became too dangerous to live in. A wide area to the west across Europe was contaminated to a slight degree – as far as Wales in the UK.

Around 4,000 people will die or have died already from cancer, among the 600,000 people who were exposed, according to the Chernobyl Forum, a regular meeting of IAEA, other United Nations organizations and the governments of Belarus, Russia, and Ukraine. In its death toll, Chernobyl was equal to the Bhopal chemical plant explosion in India, or to the number of people dying in road accidents every five to six weeks across the EU.[20] It was very significant, and a catastrophe for those nearby or onsite at the time and shortly afterwards. It also caused huge fear and anxiety, but it was not a regional disaster on the scale of a Tsunami or a major earthquake, for example.

It did stop investment though, and for the last 20 years innovation in nuclear-related technologies has been minimal. That is now changing rapidly, and we can expect to see more progress in improving nuclear power generation in the next 10 years than we have seen in the previous 30.

Centrica has invested £5.2 billion in nuclear and wind energy and will spend £15 billion more by 2020, including £2.2 billion on nuclear and £3 billion on wind farms.[21]

The rush to build nuclear

There are 436 nuclear generators already producing electricity and a similar number are being planned, of which 125 will be in China and only four in the United States.[22] Most power stations in use today are getting old, because most nations stopped building them two decades ago. Old steam turbines in these power plants may date back to the 1970s or 1980s and are often wasteful. For example Siemens is upgrading the generators for the St Lucie nuclear plant in Florida, which will increase the power output from each reactor by 100 megawatts, with a short payback period.

New nuclear plants cost at least $5 billion to build, which means government help is usually needed. They will probably take around a decade to go online from start of construction. Both Italy and the UK are building reactors for the first time in 20 years, with other EU nations set to follow. The UK announced 10 new nuclear reactors in 2009, built on existing nuclear sites, the first ones to be up and running by 2018. Each will supply a city the size of Manchester for 60 years, at an estimated cost of £5 billion. As a result, the government expects that nuclear will supply up to 25 per cent of UK power by 2025, compared with 13 per cent today.

Japan has produced 30 per cent of its power from nuclear for decades. The government slashed through legal hurdles and imposed a decision that had been held up by arguments for years.[23] Some scientists warned that the new reactors would take too long to build to deal with the gap in power generation that was likely to arise when old nuclear and coal power plants would have to be decommissioned. Others pointed out the risks of nuclear power, the likelihood of running over budget on construction, and unsolved problems of waste storage.[24]

Meanwhile, Sweden is planning to overturn a 30-year ban on new nuclear plants, proposing new reactors on existing sites. The country was at the forefront of anti-nuclear campaigns following the Three Mile Island accident in the United States in 1979 and voted in a referendum a year later to phase out nuclear power. Sweden's 10 nuclear reactors at three plants – Oskarshamn, Ringhals and Forsmark – supply roughly half of the country's electricity, while two other reactors at the Barseback site have been closed over the past decade.[25]

The United States backed away from nuclear power a decade ago, as did many industrialized nations. In 2009 it was building only a single new reactor, but running 104 old ones – almost twice as many as France. But things are changing. NRG Energy hopes to start building new plants in Texas with partner Toshiba using the Japanese company's proven design. Entergy and other nuclear utility companies formed NuStart Energy Development in 2004 with the goal of constructing new generations of reactors.

China is erecting 16 reactors with 90 more proposed, data from the Nuclear Association shows. The US Nuclear Regulatory Commission has also received 18 applications.[26] Japan already makes 30 per cent of its electricity from nuclear, and has said it may want more, while India's Prime Minister, Manmohan Singh, has said that his nation may seek a 100-fold increase in atomic capacity over the next 40 years.[27]

Companies with nuclear expertise will grow fast, with recent contracts awarded for $115 billion to General Electric, Toshiba, Westinghouse Unit and Paris-based Areva.[28] France has a more advanced nuclear economy than any other nation (see Figure 4.1): it decided to go nuclear in 1974 and around 80 per cent of its power comes from 59 nuclear plants, so anyone driving an electric car in France is driving on nuclear energy. But the country stopped building new plants in the 1980s and a government report in 2002 called the programme 'a monster without a future'.[29]

But in this new nuclear age, France is also thinking more positively about new nuclear investment. France has a huge competitive advantage in providing nuclear skills to other nations, because of its experience not only in building and running nuclear plants, but also in a novel reprocessing technique that means less radioactive waste.

Nuclear non-proliferation treaties mean that non-nuclear nations can only build reactors if they do not thereby gain the ability to make nuclear bombs. That means they need other nations to help them with enriching uranium to make fuel rods, and with disposal of fuel waste.

FIGURE 4.1 *Nuclear Share in Electricity Generation in 2007*

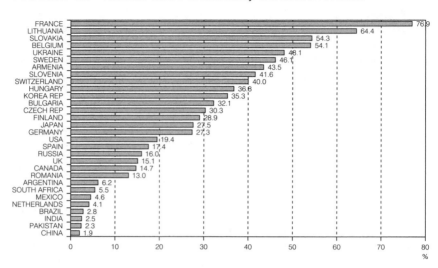

Source: The International Atomic Energy Agency.

The true cost of nuclear power

The true cost of nuclear power is very hard to calculate, partly because the costs of long-term decommissioning and storage are unclear, and partly because most of the first 400 nuclear power plants built were paid for partly or entirely by governments, which have not always given figures for their total financial outlay.

EDF's existing nuclear power plants in France are making electricity for around €30 per megawatt hour, and sell that power for around €39 per megawatt hour, according to Citigroup. EDF will need to invest €400 million to extend its life for each plant from 40 to 60 years, which will mean most of them can still operate beyond 2030–40. EDF plans to build four new nuclear plants in the UK, four in the United States, two in China and one in France. Citigroup estimates that the cost of power from these could be in the region of €55–60 per megawatt hour or up to €70 if projects run over budget.[30]

These new power plants can be expected to be active by 2020 and still producing power in 2060–70, so their owners are taking a bet on what price they will get for their electricity, on average, over that period, which will depend on energy prices generally. They will earn more than fossil fuel generators by being (almost) carbon-free. Carbon taxes on coal, gas and oil power stations, carbon emission permits or requirements for carbon capture will all make nuclear energy prices more competitive.

Nuclear energy could supply all the world's electricity

In theory, nuclear power alone could eventually solve the world's entire electricity problems without burning carbon, except in construction and decommissioning, and in mining or reprocessing fuel. Depending on the methods used, up to 4.8 per cent of all output energy is needed to prepare fuel – 1.7 per cent if newer centrifuge technology is used.[31]

The following eight countries account for 93 per cent of global uranium production: Canada (23 per cent), Australia (21 per cent), Kazakhstan (16 per cent), Russia, Niger, Namibia, Uzbekistan and the United States.[32] In each case the mines are of high-quality ore. However, uranium is as common as zinc or tin. It is present at very low concentrations in granite, sedimentary rock and sea water (0.003 parts per million).[33] Coal ash in places like Yunnan province in China can contain up to 315 parts per million of uranium – higher than low grade ore in countries like Namibia.[34] There is more energy in the uranium impurities in coal than in coal itself.[35]

> A single atom of uranium-235 produces 10 million times as much heat as is produced by burning an atom of carbon in coal. Running a reactor for four years produces enough plutonium to run it for one more year provided the plutonium is extracted and put into new fuel rods.[36]

Uranium reserves depend on price

There is more than enough uranium in today's mines or from other accessible sources to supply demand for many decades. As soon as there are shortages, the price will rise, and as we have seen with oil, as soon as that happens the amount of commercially available reserves of uranium will increase. Very little uranium exploration took place from 1983 to 2005, but in 24 months of intense searching, the world's known reserves increased by 17 per cent.[37]

As with oil, total reserves of uranium depend on price. At around $130 per kilogram, there are around 5.57 million tons of known reserves,[38] which would last around 100 years at current rates of use.[39] But fast neutron reactors are being developed that will be up to 50 times more efficient in using uranium than models in use today, which would mean the same reserves would last our world at least 2,500 years.[40]

These newer types of reactor are started up on plutonium, which is a waste material from conventional reactors. The plutonium is surrounded by a blanket of natural or depleted uranium, which is then enriched. One ton of ore can yield 60 times more energy than a conventional reactor.[41]

How much uranium do we need?

Our world is using around 65,000 tons of nuclear-grade uranium every year to produce around 370 gigawatts of power, but only 40,000 tons a year are being extracted from mines. The rest comes from civilian and military sources, as well as from reprocessed fuel and re-enriched uranium.[42]

Old nuclear weapons are a great source. Since 1987, the United States and former Soviet-bloc nations have agreed to reduce their arsenals by 80 per cent. These weapons contain uranium enriched to 25 times that needed for power plants. Since 2000, around 30 tons of high-grade military uranium have been used each year, equivalent to 10,600 tons of uranium ore, supplying 13 per cent of the world's nuclear power needs.[43]

Another source is 1.5 million tons of depleted uranium, which dates from civil and military enrichment activity since the 1940s, increasing by 35,000 tons a year. Most of this is available to mix with recycled uranium or as a future fuel for fast reactors.[44] (Thorium can also be used as an alternative to uranium in CANDU reactors or others designed for the purpose. Thorium is three times as abundant as uranium.)[45]

'Unlimited' uranium from seawater at affordable cost

> Seawater contains enough uranium to power our world for over 5 million years.

Uranium costs are only 1–2 per cent of the total bill for nuclear power, so even if uranium prices were 10 times of those today it would not make a dramatic difference to viability, especially if uranium were used more efficiently. Once a certain price is reached, it will be possible to start extracting almost unlimited amounts of uranium from sea water.

Seawater contains around 4.6 billion tons of uranium, with 32,000 tons flowing into the sea in river water every year. Over two decades ago, Japanese scientists developed a very small-scale method of extracting uranium from seawater using amidoxime, in a passive process powered only by waves and sea currents. Uranium atoms are trapped when they come into contact with a cloth impregnated with amidoxime.[46]

The Japanese Atomic Energy Research Institute (JAERI Takazaki Research Establishment) has calculated that the cost of recovering uranium from seawater using this method would be around 5–10 times higher than mining uranium. More than 80 per cent of the cost is in creating huge metal cages to carry the absorbent materials, and also creating supplies of amidoxime.[47] But recent improvements in the process may reduce the price of uranium from seawater to around $300, equal to the peak price of uranium in 2007 – and well within sight of what nuclear power operators can afford to pay without pricing nuclear electricity out of the market.[48]

So, even if the *entire* world's power came from nuclear energy, the uranium in the sea could last humankind over 5 million years, using today's relatively inefficient reactors, and 5 billion years with more efficient technology.[49] In that sense, uranium power generation must be considered a far more sustainable solution than burning up scarce fossil fuels, setting aside concerns about contamination, accidents, nuclear weapons proliferation and so on.

What will happen to nuclear waste?

Old fuel rods contain highly radioactive material, which continues to give off large amounts of heat. They are placed in huge tanks of water until they cool down. Fuel rods are then chemically reprocessed to remove leftover uranium and the plutonium that has formed.

Each power station produces an average of 1.5 tons of radioactive material each year, which is often then fused into glass to make a total weight to be stored of around 15 tons.[50] Total nuclear waste from old fuel is growing by around 12,000 tons a year.[51] Engineers are uncertain where the best place to store such waste long term is. In the meantime, companies like GNS make canisters costing €1.5 million each that are designed to store nuclear waste for 40 years. Holtec International and Ensa build containers to last about 100 years.[52]

Nuclear fusion – unlimited power with lower risks

There is a better way. Heating water for electricity turbines using rods of uranium is a clumsy, costly and last-century process. We will see big progress on next-generation nuclear energy, using a totally different process. Instead of splitting large atoms (fission), power plants will merge small ones (fusion). They use fuel sources that are abundant, produce little pollution and have almost zero risk of being abused by terrorists or rogue governments.

Fusion research in the United States and the USSR was linked originally to nuclear weapons programmes and took place in secret until the 1958 Atoms for Peace conference in Geneva. Soviet scientists made a breakthrough in design of a doughnut-shaped structure called a 'tokamak' to contain fusion reactions, and fusion research became more established. However, the cost and complexity of the devices involved increased to the point where international cooperation was the only way forward.

Small fusion reactors have already been built in Culham, UK, the Cadarache research centre in France, and in Japan. In all three, nuclear fusion released enough energy to keep the process going.[53] In 1997, JET in Culham, UK produced a peak of 16.1 megawatts of fusion power (65 per cent of input power), with fusion power of over 10 megawatts sustained for over half a second.[54]

In 2018 a huge new fusion reactor on the Cote d'Azur will go live, fusing two heavy isotopes of hydrogen (deuterium and tritium) to release huge amounts of energy and generate 500 megawatts of fusion power. Assuming all goes well, a demonstration plant called DEMO will then be built, which will produce steam and drive turbines to make 1 gigawatt of net electrical power (after supplying power to itself to keep the process going), enough to supply half a million homes.[55]

The physics is similar to what takes place in the sun; on earth, without the huge mass of the sun, it requires temperatures of around 150 million °C. That is 10 times as hot as the sun itself. The walls of the reactor are made from water-cooled steel slabs half a metre thick, coated with tiles made from beryllium. The terrific heat will be absorbed by 3 million cubic metres of water a year.[56]

The reactor will cost $10 billion to build and is called the International Thermonuclear Experimental Reactor (ITER).[57] It is a joint project of China, the EU, India, Japan, South Korea, Russia and the United States. The ITER is just the latest in a long series of projects based on a tokamak, which keeps very high temperature fuel away from the furnace walls using strong magnetic fields. Without this, the furnace would melt rapidly. Tokamaks have been built by Joint European Torus (operating since 1983 in the UK), JT-60 (1985, Japan), T-15 (1988, Russia), ADITYA (1989, India), NSTX (1999, United States), EAST (2006, China) and KSTAR (2008, South Korea).[58]

Deuterium can be extracted from the sea in virtually unlimited quantities, but tritium is very rare – only about 20 kilograms exist in the whole world. Future fusion reactors will have to make their own tritium, from lithium when bombarded by neutrons from the nuclear reaction. Fortunately lithium is as common as lead.[59] Fusion does not produce any long-term waste. Low-level waste will result from activation of some parts of the machine. All waste can be easily treated and stored onsite.[60]

There are many challenges to overcome with fusion technology. The central issue is not whether the science works – it does in the sun and on a very small scale on earth – but rather when fusion will be a commercially viable energy source.

ACTION

Business action

Smart metering gives you huge opportunities to reduce fuel bills by 20 per cent or more. First, appoint someone in your team to attack energy consumption at every level – start by monitoring power use by department, floor, business unit or whatever. Set yourself a tough target and explain the reasons to everyone. Secondly, look at areas where your power consumption could be timed more flexibly and, if this is significant, talk to your utility company about an off-peak rate, or giving them the ability to turn off some of your equipment at peak times in return for a large discount.

Consumer action

If you are not already being offered a smart meter by your utility company, go and buy a small device to clip onto your meter, which will give you an instant readout from somewhere convenient in your home, so you can monitor your consumption hour by hour. It will help save money and carbon. Make a monthly record of last year's power use and aim to save at least 10 per cent. Hunt down hidden power users such as a forgotten battery charger or an old fax machine.

In summary, we are entering a new nuclear boom that will continue to accelerate so long as there are no more major accidents on the scale of Chernobyl. Nuclear energy is a proven technology in which there has been little innovation for over 20 years. We can expect many improvements in efficiency and in handling nuclear waste, as well as in safety. We can also expect innovations in uranium mining, extraction, refining and reprocessing. More nations will want to 'go nuclear', which will pose dilemmas for countries wishing to prevent nuclear capabilities from being used to create more nuclear weapons. On the other hand, growth in demand for uranium will give an added incentive for countries with nuclear weapons to cannibalize them and turn warheads into electricity.

CHAPTER FIVE

BETTER CARS, TRUCKS, TRAINS, PLANES AND SHIPS

*How new technology will transform travel
of people and goods*

The enormous Airbus 380-F lifts into the air with a small shudder, with its 330 tons of fuel for 525 passengers, which it will carry 8,200 miles. Just one of the 240,000 aircraft leaving the runway of Heathrow Airport this year, carrying 70 million passengers. Each person will cause more CO_2 emissions during the flight than in their entire lives on the ground over the last year.

But what of the future? There are already 475,000 aircraft in the world if you include 60,000 helicopters[1] – but less than a quarter are large commercial passenger planes.

People love flying. It is part of our genetically programmed desire to explore. Flying is just one part of the huge transport revolution, now responsible for 30 per cent of global emissions (3.5 per cent of global emissions are aviation, 10 per cent are cars). Over the next 40 years, the number of cars on roads worldwide could reach 3 billion. China could have as many cars by 2050 as are in the world today.

If we save an average 40 per cent of energy per mile (and we can), it will reduce today's global emissions by 12 per cent – but the number of miles travelled per year is expected to soar. We need far more radical answers, for example using renewable energy for most car and train journeys.

Revolution on the roads

Expect to see rapid improvements in fuel efficiency using petrol and diesel, and many new ultra-efficient hybrid vehicles (cars that run on petrol or diesel and also generate their own electric power). Even if we only see a 30 per cent energy saving in 30 per cent of vehicle miles driven in developed nations over the next decade, we will save at least 9 per cent in motoring energy use (at today's rate of miles driven a year). That will be the same as cutting today's global emissions by more than 1 per cent. But such a figure is very conservative, particularly regarding freight.

Greening of the world car fleet is happening rapidly. JD Power Consultancy estimates that a third of emission cuts by 2020 will come from improving petrol and diesel engines, and 14 per cent from miles driven in electric vehicles.[2] Consumer fuel costs and government regulations are forcing the pace of improvement. That is why Honda and Toyota have worked so hard to develop some of the world's most fuel-efficient vehicles, including hybrids. GM and Ford continue to be held back by fuel-hungry models, including inefficient SUVs and pickup trucks.[3] If all vehicles in the United States were hybrids and half were plug-in hybrids (with larger batteries so they can also charge up from the mains electricity supply), US imports of oil would fall by 8 million barrels a day or by 80 per cent of daily consumption.[4] So conversion to electric vehicles is also a way for the Federal government to reduce energy dependence on other nations.

Electric cars

Electric vehicles are one of the most important ways to reduce motoring costs, reduce carbon use in transport, improve air quality and reduce global warming. Carlos Ghosn, CEO of Renault and Nissan, expects battery-powered vehicles to be 10 per cent of the market by 2020. Models like Nissan's Leaf and Chevrolet's Volt have led the way. But for electric cars to really take off, governments need to encourage the first few thousand sales, to get prices down, and also to encourage recharging points across cities.[5]

Governments are pouring hundreds of millions into subsidies and incentives for electric cars, with ambitious targets to transform travel in cities. Many government economic stimulus packages for the auto industry have been linked to green tech, of which a huge proportion is things like battery technology.[6]

Sixteen million new cars a year are sold in the EU alone (2.4 million in the UK). If we assume that up to 25 per cent of the smallest car market could be electric cars within 10 years, that would mean over 1 million sold each year, at an average cost of €11,000. Electric car sales would then be worth at least €11 billion a year in the EU.

Electric cars more efficient

Vehicle batteries are charged from a power socket at home/garage or at work. Energy is saved when braking to recharge batteries. Motors in wheel hubs provide power and can also work as generators to recover energy when breaking, the mechanics are much simpler than with petrol or diesel, and there are hardly any maintenance costs. The current distance of around 100 miles between charges will soon double and 80 per cent of battery recharging will happen in 30 minutes.

Electric cars can produce much lower emissions than burning fuel in mobile engines, but it all depends on how the electricity is generated. Burning petrol or diesel in a vehicle can be inefficient compared to the most efficient coal-fired power generators. When petrol is used to power a vehicle, only 15–20 per cent of the energy is usually captured to drive it forward,[7] compared to 40 per cent in making electricity in an efficient coal power station – half as efficient. Some electric cars have a motor in each wheel, others use one for each axle, or just a single motor – and these things can also affect efficiency.

It is true that a small amount of power is lost between power station and battery, and 20 per cent of electricity put into the car is lost in heat (batteries and other components). But even when we include these things, we can see that 'coal-powered' electric cars are likely to be better users of fossil fuels than diesel or petrol vehicles.

Where wind, solar, wave, tide or nuclear power is used to charge batteries, electric cars have zero emissions when in use. Either way, air quality improves dramatically in cities as the use of electric vehicles increases. Owners can also save a huge amount of vehicle tax on petrol or diesel since taxation is far lower on electricity. It typically costs only 1 or 2 cents a mile in battery charging.

One thing is certain: if half a million people are driving electric cars across a nation, oil consumption will fall dramatically, while coal or gas power consumption will rise in the short term. However, the existing US grid could probably cope with powering 70 per cent of all car journeys if all vehicles were electric, without any new power stations, assuming each car is driven for no more than 42 kilometres a day.[8] Every new owner of an electric car is sending a powerful message to electricity companies to go green. Electric vehicles will create huge pressures on power companies to scale up carbon-free electricity prduction. Buy now, and make the power companies follow on.

Green Tomato Cars is a taxi firm running Toyota Prius hybrids, also offsetting all emissions. Through clever branding the company has taken off with more than 100 vehicles and a turnover of £3.5 million. It launched a franchise in Sydney and is looking for other cities.

Battery problems will be overcome

The performance of electric cars is improving dramatically with astonishing acceleration in the most expensive models.

Tesla electric sports car

The acceleration of this sports car is awesome, jaw-dropping – 0 to 60 miles per hour in 3.5 seconds, and a very responsive braking system recharges the batteries. The Tesla can travel up to 200 miles without a recharge, depending on how hard you drive. However, the batteries weigh 400 kilograms, only last five years and are very expensive to replace.

Auto makers need a car battery that is light, will last 15 years and allow 5,000 charge cycles, but today's lithium-ion batteries can need replacing in just two to three years of heavy use, while old-style acid batteries are bulky, too heavy and can be damaged by irregular, light use. Even though the car may only cost 2 cents a mile or less in electricity, the battery could add as much as 40–50 cents a mile in depreciation/ replacement charges, depending on the pattern of driving.

The goal is a price of $300 per kilowatt hour of current (enough to drive a car for 40 miles, assuming 3 miles per kilowatt hour).[9] Battery performance will double in the next three to four years and costs will fall.

High-power lithium can pack four times as much power into a car battery, using nanotechnology. Batteries charge faster, allowing up to 350 miles of driving. They could be mass produced by 2015 at affordable cost.

Batteries are going to be one of the biggest green tech businesses – powering not only phones and other small devices, but also cars, trucks, buses and just about any large piece of equipment that does not have a permanent electricity connection. Expect sales of hundreds of billions of dollars. President Obama's economic stimulus provided $2.4 billion to fund battery innovation and electric car projects:

- $45.1 million to UQM Technologies;

- $34.3 million to Exide Technologies;

- $118.5 million to Ener1;

- $229.2 million to Johnson Controls;

- $249.1 million to A123 Systems.

Car batteries will have another purpose: linked together when charging at people's homes, to create virtual storage by power companies, to assist their power management at off-peak times. This will make it easier for them to plug in huge numbers of wind and solar generators. Smart grids will allow power to flow in both directions, so that each battery can become a power source to other people in the neighbourhood for short periods of time. If 200,000 electric cars were plugged into the German national grid, it could make 8 megawatts of power available almost instantly, giving more flexibility than the nation currently needs. (For more on this and smart grids, see pages 61 to 63.)

Massive boost to electric cars in Israel and Denmark

Expect many governments to give huge incentives to people who want to buy electric cars. Israel and Denmark are leading the way.

Better Place is a major new joint venture with Renault-Nissan, based in Israel. Better Place will supply batteries for electric cars and 500,000 charging points, which look like parking meters, as well as a battery-swop service at service stations. The aim is to subsidize car sales out of revenues from keeping them going – similar to mobile phone companies. They are aiming for 10–20,000 cars in Israel alone, launching in 2011.

The Danish Oil and Natural Gas Company has a similar scheme in Denmark. Both Israeli and Danish governments are providing major support, while Renault-Nissan has committed to supply the two nations with 100,000 electric cars by 2016.[10] In Australia, the Macquarie Capital Group is also part-nering with Better Place, hoping to raise $1 billion for a similar service in Brisbane, Sydney and Melbourne. Better Place has become one of the world's fastest growing start-ups.

China will soon have a large electric car industry. Take BYD for example, which makes mobile phone batteries for Motorola and Nokia, and started making vehicles in 2003. BYD has combined both divisions to sell e6 electric cars, with a 10 per cent stake by MidAmerican Energy – part-owned by Warren Buffet's Berkshire Hathaway, making it a profit of $1 billion in a year. The founder of BYD, Wang Chuanfu, is the richest man in China, with a fortune estimated at $5.1 billion.[11]

Over 300 million old tyres are thrown away in the United States every year. Enviro has developed a way to recycle huge numbers of old tyres into pure steel, liquid oil, and granules of carbon black, which can be re-used to make more tyres. Every gram of material is recovered. The oil is clean enough to power generators, can be sold for heating and also keeps their factory running. The secret is heating 4 tons of tyres at a time to very high temperatures, in the absence of oxygen, so the tyres melt and decompose without burning.

Hydrogen and fuel cells – the answer to battery problems?

Many people talk about the 'hydrogen economy' or water-powered cars. They envisage millions of cars burning hydrogen gas in their engines, or using hydrogen to power their fuel cells to drive electric cars, emitting nothing but water vapour. However, making hydrogen requires electricity to split water into hydrogen and oxygen, and in an area where most power comes from coal, these hydrogen cars are running on coal power.

Hydrogen is also difficult to store and transport. It is a very 'thin' gas, which seeps through microscopic cracks, so gas can be lost when piped under pressure over long distances. Total energy per cubic litre (liquid hydrogen) is less than carbon-based liquid fuels, so tanks also have to be larger. Filling a normal sized fuel tank of 75 litres (20 US gallons) with hydrogen at room temperature and pressure will only take a car 1 kilometre.[12] We will find new ways to pack more hydrogen into smaller tanks, using nanotechnology and other innovations, but power output will remain a challenge.

Hydrogen could be used in fuel cells, which make electricity at the same time as making water from hydrogen and oxygen. Less heat is lost than burning hydrogen, but they cost thousands of dollars per kilowatt hour to build.[13]

For all these reasons, it seems unlikely that tomorrow's global auto industry is going to switch to hydrogen anytime soon. Meanwhile, fuel cell development is being rapidly overtaken by huge gains in battery power and efficiency.

MIT researcher Daniel Nocera is developing a way to split water into hydrogen and oxygen using sunlight, so people can make and store hydrogen to use in their own fuel cells at home.

Lithium – shortages in future?

Lithium will be highly prized as the stampede grows for car batteries. The metal is also needed for pharmaceuticals, aircraft, glass, heat-resistant cooking ware, air conditioners, synthetic rubber and so on. Lithium batteries are in 90 per cent of laptops and over 60 per cent of mobile phones.

Better trucks for freight delivery

Electric cars are only part of the answer to more energy-efficient driving. Seventy per cent of all EU freight is moved by road, and trucks use 12 per cent of all oil consumed in the United States, but the energy efficiency of most

Car sharing – anywhere

Zipcar is a car sharing scheme for major cities, with an annual fee of $50 and hourly rental. Members hire vehicles scattered across the city. Every reservation includes 180 miles of driving, and a card to pay for fuel. Drivers book a nearby car online and tap its windscreen with a chip-enabled Zip Card (or use their iPhones) to unlock and drive the vehicle away. They have central controls with vehicle tracking and automatic lock down if stolen. Drivers also get instant diagnosis and personal advice if something goes wrong. Zipcars are now in 50 cities including London, Boston, Washington DC and New York, following a merger with Flexcar, with 6,000 vehicles for 675,000 users.

trucks is as low as it was 40 years ago, while cars have doubled their fuel economy. We will see a giant leap in efficiency of new trucks – at least 40 per cent in the next decade.

Colani has already built a prototype that uses 41 per cent less fuel than usual, while Mercedes-Benz claimed a world record for its Actros truck, cutting fuel use by 50 per cent, partly by using 'superwide' tyres to replace each pair, together with aerodynamic reshaping.[14] Up to 40 per cent of truck energy is wasted by pairs of tyres as they roll along the road at speed. Single very wide tyres reduce rolling resistance by 4 per cent.[15]

Here are some of the many approaches being taken by truck manu-facturers and green tech start-ups, and some possible savings. Figures are of overall truck efficiency unless otherwise stated. You cannot add all the savings together, as some reduce the impact of others:

- Low energy tyres – save 11 per cent of the rolling resistance to reduce fuel use by 4.3 per cent.[16]

- Better streamlining (skirts, fairings and filling gap from trailer to cab) – save 12 per cent (long-haul trucks use up 35 per cent of their energy in wind resistance.)[17]

- Air jets at the back of the container/truck (another way to reduce wind resistance) – save 5 per cent of fuel.

- Longer length by 1.5 metres – save 5 per cent of energy per cubic metre of load.

- Better diesel engine design or lubricants – save 15 per cent.[18]

- Hybrid electric-diesel engine – save 30 per cent.[19] Each hybrid truck could save more energy than nine hybrid cars.[20]

- Use waste heat to boost power or drive air conditioning, etc – save 5 per cent or more.[21]

- Better gearbox/transmission – save 1 per cent.[22]

- Shock absorbers that generate power (Genshock) – save 3–5 per cent, generating up to 1 kilowatt of continuous power.[23]

- Slow down: 65mph down to 55mph – save 20 per cent.[24]

- Driver training – 5–10 per cent depending on the driver.[25]

We can expect very rapid innovation in this field. For example, the US Department of Energy has launched a $45.5 million programme to get 378 mid-sized hybrid trucks on the road by 2011, with Eaton power systems on a Ford chassis. Bright Automotive aims to replace 50,000 trucks with plug-in hybrids by 2014. Each will save 16 tons of CO_2 a year.[26]

Clean Power Technologies uses waste heat from truck engines to generate steam. This is stored and used when needed to help drive the engine or to power other equipment such as refrigeration units. The company claims 40 per cent energy savings and is starting tests with two Canadian freight companies.[27]

Other manufacturers are experimenting with truck engines as electric turbines to power motors, similar to many diesel trains. E-traction has developed electric motors for truck wheels that replace heavy engines and gearboxes. The electricity comes from a diesel generator. The trucks run 40 per cent further than usual for every litre of diesel. Ten trucks will be delivered in 2010 and 36 ton versions will be on sale in 2012.[28]

One problem with redesigning trailers is that they often belong to a different firm from the cab owner, and there is no incentive to make the loads more efficient. One way to solve the problem is regulation, requiring all trailers to meet new efficiency ratings.

Wind resistance is similar for long and short trucks, so longer trucks use less fuel per metre. Combination vehicles with four trailers are allowed in Australia, but in many US states even a second trailer is forbidden due to safety fears. Japanese researchers are working on ways to create caravans of trucks, with only a metre gap, using multiple sensors, saving up to 20 per cent of fuel at a cost of €1,800 per truck.[29]

Another reason for allowing longer trucks is to make it easier to move containers from ships, trucks and railways. Ships and trains can use 45 foot and 48 foot containers, but EU rules limit trucks to 40 feet (12.1 metres). Ships and trains charge almost the same for small or large, so small containers waste money. They are also hard to pack with EU standard-size pallets. A foot and a half (half metre) of extra length would save energy, time and cost – and reduce the number of lorry journeys – but could be a social nuisance unless weights were restricted (remember many trucks carry mainly air and packaging).

Buses and coaches – instant extra transport capacity

One of the fastest and cheapest ways for government to expand public transport in urban areas is to increase the number of buses and routes, as well as providing high speed bus lanes through congested streets.

New bus routes can be set up almost overnight, and the buses themselves can be bought and run at a fraction of the cost of building a new metro system. If well-used, the carbon per mile per passenger can be lower than any other form of transport. But it all depends on occupancy. According to the US Department of Energy, a bus with average occupancy (nine people) is more polluting than six cars with average occupancy (1.57 people).[30]

Stagecoach, based in the UK, is one of the world's largest public transport corporations. In Scotland, some of its buses run on used cooking oil. Passengers get free tickets in return for bottles of used oil. Travellers have spread the message across the community. Stagecoach benefits from reduced fuel costs, free publicity and a stronger, energy-conscious image.

Many cities are developing bus networks that operate like a metro on rails. Concrete dividers keep the buses and other traffic apart. Riders pay before travel and wait in enclosed stations with raised platforms so they are at the right level to enter or alight from the bus. For example, Columbia's Rapid Transit lines handle 1.6 million trips a day, and have removed 7,000 private buses, reducing bus fuel and pollution by 59 per cent.[31]

Bicycles can transport a million people a day

The most sustainable transport is usually walking or cycling, especially for short distances over congested routes. While many efforts are being made to improve cycle routes in cities, it still means you need to own a bike that works and is always in the right place at the right time.

Velib is a successful bike hire scheme across Paris that was launched in 2007 and has grown to 20,000 bikes at 1,450 stations. It costs one euro an hour plus one euro a day to become part of the scheme. There were more than

30 million rentals in the first couple of years. The entire funding came from JC Decaux, the world's second largest outdoor advertising company, in return for Paris signing over the income from a large number of billboard ads.

Paris receives all revenues plus a fee of around €3.5 million a year. In return, the company has total control of 1,628 city-owned billboards – the city is allowed to use half the space for public-interest messages. The company takes 12 per cent of all subscriptions from around 200,000 people. Other cities like London and Bristol in the UK are planning similar schemes, despite worries that the entire Paris fleet of 20,000 bikes was stolen or vandalized within the first two years, costing €8.5 million.[32]

Faster rail passengers and slow freight

Next generation trains – faster, lower cost, competing with more air routes

Rail is a very energy-efficient alternative to road travel, but only if trains are reasonably full of passengers or loaded with freight. Switching containers from lorries to rail can save huge amounts of fuel. Every ton of freight that goes by rail, rather than road, reduces energy use by 33 per cent or more if the distance is over 100 miles, on an average freight train. A single freight train can remove 50 heavy trucks from roads, and a train can move a ton of freight more than 430 miles on a single gallon of fuel – albeit at slow speed.

Eurostar claims that flying from London to Barcelona causes 277 kilograms of carbon emissions compared to only 40 kilograms by rail – but it does depend on how full those trains and carriages are and other factors. However, an EasyJet booking of a direct flight online could cost as little as £47 compared to rail tickets to Paris, and on to Madrid at the lowest price of £290.[33]

Across the United States, rail carries:[34]

- 40 per cent of all tons of freight;
- 70 per cent of vehicles (made in the United States);
- 30 per cent of grain;
- 65 per cent of coal;
- more miles than trucks, boats, barges or planes.

Electric trains use up to 30 per cent less carbon per mile than diesel (emissions from coal-fired power stations that supply the track, compared to emissions from a diesel train), so electrification is one of the most important ways to save rail energy.[35]

Even so, an electric train cannot compete with an average car containing four passengers, in energy per passenger mile, if that train is only half full. And the calculations are even worse if you include *all* the energy used by electric railways (buildings, laying and maintaining tracks, providing power to railway stations), which can more than double emissions per mile, depending on the line, compared to energy building and maintaining roads.[36] Of course, if a train is running from one city to another with some empty seats, and you want to travel in that direction, the additional energy used in carrying you as an extra passenger is almost zero. On that basis, taking a train over driving saves a huge amount of energy.

Compare the average energy used for each passenger per mile on Amtrak trains in the United States with cars:

Amtrak: 2,700 BTUs (British Thermal Units)[37]
Car: 3,400 BTUs for petrol cars (1,700 BTUs for Toyota Prius hybrid)

One reason for the relatively small difference is low seat occupancy on Amtrak trains. While auto and airline fuel efficiencies are improving by 2–3 per cent every year, Amtrak's fuel efficiency has increased by just 0.1 per cent in the last decade.[38] Fuel efficiency varies with design. For example, Virgin's long-distance electric Pendolino trains in the UK carry passengers for around 28 grams of carbon per kilometre if half full. But Virgin's smaller diesel electric Voyagers emit 74g, even though they are similar in age.

That 74g per kilometre is 50 per cent more than a car uses per person with four people in the vehicle. If you are travelling more than 200 miles on a Voyager that is 75 per cent empty, your emissions per mile will be the same as it would have been if you were flying the same distance in an 80 per cent full plane.[39]

Regenerative braking saves around 20 per cent of energy on slower trains with many stops, and is being used more widely, but most innovations on trains have focused on safety, speed and comfort – all of which have resulted in extra weight, now a major issue with high-speed trains.

There is hardly a rail route in the world that can compete with road from a cost point of view, without huge subsidies for rail or huge fuel taxes for vehicles (or both), unless the route is longer than 500–1,000 miles. The big question is, what would happen if those same taxes and subsidies were spent on more efficient road vehicles – for example encouraging the use of electric cars in cities?

Desiro City trains tell passengers where to sit, count the number of passengers per carriage to work out how to adjust the air temperature and turn air conditioning off in empty carriages.[40]

High speed rail boom – 5,000 more miles in Europe

High speed track costs at least $35 million per mile, before buying trains, and therefore usually requires government assistance.[41] The attraction is taking people out of planes for intercity travel. The high speed TGV line from Paris to Lyon virtually closed down air travel between the two, and the line from Madrid to Barcelona halved air travel within the first six months of opening.

There are 3,480 miles of high speed railway lines in mainland Europe with a further 2,160 miles under construction and 5,280 miles planned for the future. France already has 1,100 miles of high speed track and more than 400 trains. Spain has made huge steps to expand high speed rail since 1989, and will have the longest system in Europe by 2012. By 2020 it is likely that more than 90 per cent of the population will be within 31 miles of a high speed rail station.

High Speed 2 track in the UK is being planned to be able to cope with speeds of up to 280 miles per hour, running from London to Birmingham and eventually on to Glasgow.[42] Over 60 years, the line could save 30 million tonnes (29.5 million tons) of CO_2, worth maybe £3.2 billion if traded on the carbon market, by diverting passengers from air travel to rail. High speed rail works best where there is at least 100 miles between stations, as it takes time and energy to accelerate to maximum speed.

US trains running slow

The United States lags behind Europe in passenger rail, but is way ahead on freight, where very long trains can run at slow speed for several thousand miles at low cost using relatively little energy. The US Department of Transport has identified 9,000 miles of high speed rail corridors. Such a mega-project could create 4.5 million permanent jobs, (1.6 million in construction), save 125 million barrels of oil a year, and create $23 billion in economic benefits in the Midwest alone.[43]

President Obama announced $8 billion of Federal funds for the United States' first high speed passenger rail routes, barely enough to link two cities over a short distance. California's planned high speed links alone could cost $40 billion.

China is the country to watch – rail expansion

Russia is spending $1.5 billion to upgrade 401 miles of track from Moscow to St Petersburg, with new trains from Siemens operating at 217 mph. But China will soon have the world's largest high speed railway, with 3,700 miles of track and trains built by Bombardier Sifang – a joint venture between Chinese business and Bombardier.

China already has the world's first Maglev train track, which uses magnetism to suspend trains above rails, running at up to 501 km/h (311 mph).

The track was built by Siemens, but these kinds of technologies will be within China's own manufacturing capabilities in future.

Making better use of what we have

Countries like the UK have seen a boom in rail passengers, as more people choose rail to commute, partly forced by the rising costs of city living, and encouraged by faster journeys. The easiest way to get more out of rail is to use existing tracks more heavily:

- Increase train frequency – reduce minimum 'safe' distance between trains, or slow down some trains. Use smart train signalling and better emergency controls. Run more trains at off-peak times. Let faster trains overtake local services. Use automatic train operation – robots cause fewer delays than drivers.

- Remove seats – pack 50 per cent more passengers into short-haul trains. Most seats are empty at quiet times, and a nuisance at crowded peak times. Many rail operators in the UK and other EU nations have removed seats to gain peak capacity, but in doing this they may also put off some passengers who hate standing.

- Increase train length – add extra carriages, and only open some carriage doors at shorter stations. Long trains save wind resistance.

- Do more essential maintenance at night.

- Increase the number of slower freight trains at night – and clear lines for passengers by day. Separate slower freight trains from intercity services.

- Increase train height – two-level trains usually mean new tunnels and bridges, and rewiring overhead cables, which can cost many tens of millions of dollars.

- Lighten trains – reduce power consumption and track damage.

The future of trams and other urban rapid transport systems

We will also continue to see rapid growth in urban, electric light railways, with high frequency and capacity, running below or above streets. More than 160 cities already have rapid transit systems, with over 8,000 kilometres (5,000 miles) of track and 7,000 stations. Twenty-five cities have systems under construction.

They can be expensive to build, but can be woven into a busy city without taking up much land area, integrated into other transport systems. Most new light railways in the last decade have been built in Asia, many with driverless trains, on elevated tracks.

So, we have seen how road transport will be decarbonized, and become more efficient, and how rail use will grow, but what about air travel?

The future of air travel

Aviation is the fastest growing cause of emissions

Flying causes 3.5 per cent of global CO_2 emissions, and this will jump to more than 15 per cent by 2050 unless action is taken, especially as other uses of carbon are likely to fall.[44] Emissions from flying doubled from 1990 to 2004, and are now the fastest growing cause of global warming.

The number of UK air passengers jumped from 4 to 228 million a year from 1954 to 2005. Around 5 per cent of EU emissions are from planes, increasing by an average of 1–2 per cent every 12 months.

If you fly to Australia from Europe, you will release 9 tons of CO_2 – almost twice the amount the average UK home produces in a whole year.[45]

But planes affect the earth in other ways: satellites show that clouds from a single jet can reduce sunshine over an area of 20,000 square miles at a time. Soot and water vapour triggers more cloud formation, and on busy flight paths, sunlight can be cut by 10 per cent – globally around 1 per cent.[46] Clouds reflect light back into space but also insulate the earth and the net effect is warming – equal perhaps to an additional 1.5 per cent of global CO_2 emissions.

Flying can use less energy than driving if the plane is at least 80 per cent full, journeys are longer than 400 miles, and the average number of people in the car is 1.4 or fewer. It depends on the plane design, car engine and other factors. We also need to add an amount for energy in building and maintaining runways and passenger terminals, compared to motorways and urban roads. The fact is that building airports is a fast and convenient way to create new high-speed transport infrastructure, which is one reason why governments do it so often.

Increasing fuel efficiency

The aviation industry is under intense pressure to reduce carbon use, mainly because up to 40 per cent of their costs is buying fuel (2008 oil prices; 15 per cent in 2000), even though aviation fuel is untaxed. Flying has a huge (unfair) tax advantage over road travel in countries like the UK where more than 80 per cent of petrol prices can be tax. We can expect aviation charges of some kind in any new global agreements on carbon use – whether they are require-ments to offset emissions or taxes of various kinds.

BA expects efficiency to improve every year by 1.5 per cent across the industry until 2020, and carbon-neutral growth after that.[47] New planes are already 70 per cent more efficient than 40 years ago and 20 per cent better than 10 years ago. We can expect a further 25 per cent energy saving by 2025 for new planes – less than 3 litres of fuel per passenger per 100km flown, which is less than a small car in 2010, with a single person travelling.

One challenge in improving the efficiency of planes is the very long service life of aircraft. Many flying today are already 30 years old, and most new planes sold in 2010 will still be flying in 2040. Airbus expects to deliver 25,000 new aircraft worth $3.1 trillion over the next 20 years, but this will still only be a small fraction of the global total. Planes sold in 2010–20 may only contribute 1 per cent of aircraft miles flown by 2020.

Replacing old planes is certainly an effective strategy for an individual air-line. For example, Alaska Airlines will save 18 per cent of fuel by replacing MD-80 planes with 737–800s. But what happens to the old ones? History shows they usually land up being sold to less wealthy airlines in emerging nations, so continuing their inefficient working lives. What can be done about these older planes? Fuel use can easily be reduced by adding pointed wing tips to improve air flow, saving from 7 per cent in Learjets to 3.5 per cent in Jumbos (Boeing 747s). Some can also be fitted with better engines.

Expect fuel economy to also be improved by:

- Fuller plane occupancy – almost all weight in a large plane is the plane itself plus fuel, so the cost of extra passengers is marginal. An empty 747–400 weighs around 340,000 pounds, or 800,000 when fully loaded on take-off – but only 250,000 of those extra pounds is actual passengers or cargo. Almost all of the rest is fuel.

- Better air traffic control, including more direct air routes, which can reduce emissions by up to 18 per cent on short-haul flights, especially into congested airports like Heathrow, reducing the time spent flying in circles waiting to land. UK air traffic control is aiming for a 10 per cent cut in CO_2 per flight by 2020 with better routing. Europe and the United States are upgrading their entire air traffic systems to save energy.

- Flying more slowly – best with larger, narrow wings. Every aircraft design is a compromise, with wings optimized for the speed that the aircraft is expected to fly at, most of the time.

- Steeper landing paths – the more time the plane spends at higher altitudes, where air is thinner, the less air resistance and less fuel used.

- Increased use of turboprop aircraft for shorter distances (better fuel use, partly as planes are optimized to spend more time at slower speed).

- Reduction in plane vapour trails – detection, dynamic avoidance (altitude corrections), lower altitude long- and short-haul flights. That means new in-flight technologies and new traffic control systems, but lower altitude can also increase fuel use, so fine adjustments are best.

Flying on biofuels – added pressure on food prices?

A 50 per cent blend of biofuel and kerosene is likely to be approved in the US soon. Converting jet engines to use pure biofuel will be costly unless they are a perfect match for kerosene. And there will be pressure to make sure that planes are not burning food, forcing up food prices (for more on biofuels, see pages 49–58). If planes start using a limited supply of biofuels, it will mean less is available to burn in cars and trucks, so there will be no 'green' advantage.

Aircraft are the *only* form of transport apart from ships that will have to go on using carbon-based fuels for the next 30 to 40 years. Batteries are too heavy, solar cells too feeble, and fuels like hydrogen are too bulky and provide too little energy to be useful in planes. Planes are like ships in one respect: they cannot refuel during their journeys, which are often many thousands of miles. Therefore they are very dependent on being able to store the maximum amount of energy in a small space.

Ships can use (even) less fuel

Ninety per cent of all products made each year are carried in over 47,000 merchant ships.[48] It's the equivalent of shipping 1,000 tons of products over 30 billion miles a year and results in 5 per cent of all carbon emissions each year.[49]

Container ships use very low amounts of energy per mile, per ton, compared with any other form of transport. It can cost more to drive a full container on a truck for 120 miles than to ship it from London to China. This is a highly specialized and consolidated industry: 10 per cent of all container ships work on behalf of DHL, for example.[50]

Ships can save 25 per cent just by slowing down by 10 per cent, reducing global emissions by 1.25 per cent.[51] We can save at least 40 per cent more, or 2.5 per cent of global emissions, with better hull shapes, propellers, rudders and engines. Fuel can be more than 15 per cent of the cost of shipping containers around the world. Less fuel also means less soot and sulphur dioxide. Some have suggested that the use of bunker fuel in ships' engines is killing 60,000 people living near coastlines every year, through air pollution.[52]

Hyundai Heavy Industries and Daewoo Shipbuilding and Marine Engineering have created new energy-efficient 'thrust fins' that are mounted to the ship's rudder. They reduce water turbulence from the propellers and convert it into extra thrust, reducing fuel use by up to 6 per cent. We can also expect new marine diesels to improve in efficiency by at least 2 per cent over the next decade. Expect other fuels to be used, such as liquid petroleum gas, already powering a Norwegian ferry built by Wärtsilä, with 20 per cent CO_2 savings compared to bunker oil, and zero sulphur emissions.[53]

Another way to reduce fuel use is to harness wind power – on diesel ships. In 2009 a 133-metre cargo ship sailed from Germany to Venezuela, towed by a 160 square metre giant kite, which soared 100–300 metres above the deck, where winds are stronger and more reliable. The kite pulls with the equivalent of 6,800 horsepower, is computer controlled, does not require extra crew and operates in moderate winds, supplementing engines. SkySails developed the kite and believes it can reduce fuel costs on each ship by 10–35 per cent, saving more than 146 million tons of CO_2 a year, equivalent to 15 per cent of Germany's emissions. Large fishing boats can also be fitted with the kite.[54] KiteShip is working on a similar product.

Savings can also be made by more efficient loading and unloading of containers, better container interchanges (huge ports that work like postal sorting offices), and by using more smaller ports along coastlines to reduce the distance that containers have to travel by road or rail to or from ships.

Keeping freight moving – logistics

Ships may be very efficient, and freight trains too, but goods still have to be moved to and from ports or rail yards, and that is often where freight costs jump, and most energy is wasted. Every switch from one kind of transport to another also causes delays.

Managing freight is a major issue for every manufacturer, wholesaler and retailer. Companies can die within weeks if their supplies of vital goods are interrupted, and as international trade grows, so does the complexity of managing a large factory.

Managing global supply chains

For example, Audi manufactures several hundred A6 vehicles every day, each built to individual owner requirements. On every door there are 85 components, creating 50,000 product combinations. Supplying the factory 'just in time' with just the right number of each component is a vital task.[55]

The European logistics industry is worth around €1 trillion a year. Rail freight, air freight, lorries, warehouses, distributors, shipping terminals, river barges, depots, couriers and post offices – all are part of an intricate system to deliver goods. Infrastructure built today will influence economic growth for over 200 years. In Roman times, new roads brought trade and wealth to local communities. Every crossroads or bridge became a meeting place, a market, a management centre. Those Roman roads still influence the pattern of life in countries like England today. Canals did the same in the 1700s and railways in the 1800s and 1900s: an impact that has endured even if the canals have fallen into disuse and railway lines have closed.

The EU plans to extend the number of functioning rivers and canals, to take 500,000 trucks off the roads by 2020.

Speed is central to the future. Many people expect delivery by 10 am following an online order the night before. Pharmacies and garages already require 3 pm delivery for orders taken that morning. That can mean just 30 minutes to pack and send. It also means great accuracy in selecting items: if only one in 20 mail order deliveries have to be restocked back into a warehouse, it can wipe out all the profit of the business.

The Leipzig hub for DHL is an astonishing site. Every night, planes fly in from across the world. By 2 am the last flight has landed and by 5 am they are almost all airborne again. An automated system sorts up to 100,000 packets and boxes an hour, off one plane for reloading onto another. Packages shoot down conveyor belts at over 30 miles per hour, every one monitored at least 50 times during the entire process. The new hub is much more energy efficient than the old site in Brussels airport, and is well linked to road and rail.

The DHL hub for duty free shops at Heathrow receives 700 inbound deliveries a week and repackages these into 300 outbound deliveries to 323 stores belonging to 146 retailers based in five terminals at the airport. In 2008, the combined delivery system saved 217,369 kms of driving and 157 tons of CO_2 emissions.[57]

Fedex uses more than 1 billion gallons of fuel a year, delivering 7.5 million packages daily by air and ground. It has invested in alternative fuels, fuel-efficient aircraft, hybrid-electric delivery vans and all-electric prototypes – aiming to save 20 per cent of emissions by 2020.[56]

The whole of the logistics industry is learning from the energy and cost savings achieved by retail giants such as Wal-Mart, Carrefour and Tesco. Just-in-time, forward planning, use of RFID (radio frequency identification device) technology to track every package, efficient distribution and rapidly responsive systems, which give total knowledge about what is where – we are talking about total integration. However, this speed and complexity can mean more emissions. From the energy-saving point of view, keep more stocks in the warehouse and on factory floors, send more by ship and plan ahead. But that also ties up capital, and may mean more stock is wasted if fashions or technical requirements keep changing.

So logistics is a fine balance between many different conflicting business pressures, and the balance will change for each company and for each product. Where items need to evolve fast and get to market without delay, we are seeing a return to local manufacturing.

A key issue is better hubs. Logistics companies cannot make best use of rail for, example, when rail yards are far from motorways, maybe in congested city centres, far from ports, which may also be blocked by heavy traffic during the day. Expect big investment in hubs and high speed corridors, such as motorway extensions that take trucks right to the dockside, and to marshalling yards of ultra-efficient rail-loading companies.

We have already seen huge advances in loading and unloading ships. Even a decade ago, a single crane operator, guided by computer, was able to completely empty and refill a large container ship in a port like Dubai where most containers are unloaded only to go onto a different vessel. But we have not seen such advances in managing rail freight or lorries. One reason is the scandal of *cabotage*, or empty containers (see below).

Wal-Mart has reduced fuel use by 25 per cent, cutting down on packaging, and using smart routing software to reduce truck journeys, aiming for a further 25 per cent cut by 2015.[58]

'Reducing greenhouse gases quickly will save money for our customers, make us a more efficient business and help position us to compete in a carbon-constrained world.'[59]

   Lee Scott, Wal-Mart CEO

EU rail freight is chaotic

The EU rail freight system is in chaos, with many different rail authorities, regulations and ownership structures. The EU has tried to force nations to make railway companies work better together, but many countries have failed to comply.

They lack:

- independent infrastructure managers to oversee railway operators;
- independent bodies to solve competition problems;
- laws to allow track access charging.

The Czech Republic, Germany, Spain, France, Italy, Slovenia, Romania, Estonia and Greece all have railways that are operating on last-century models, in direct violation of EU law.

Twenty-five million miles a year driving empty trucks

And then there are the empty trucks. A single major retailer in the United States wastes 25 million miles a year driving empty delivery vehicles back and forth across different cities and states and between states. It is a major issue in Europe too.

The European petrochemical industry is responsible for 8 per cent of all EU freight, transporting 1,500 million tons a year at a cost of €60 billion.[60] The average freight cost per ton is €12 more than in the United States for a number of reasons, including road congestion, but one important reason is too many trucks filled with almost nothing but air.

Take for example a factory that makes plastic drinks bottles. Lorries arrive heavily packed with raw plastic at the factory, and others take new bottles away, but each is filled with air and the lorry load is very light. Those empty bottles may be transported hundreds of miles to where they will be filled and capped. A waste of time, energy and money. That is why companies like Coca-Cola have built 'hole in the wall' factories, partnering with drinks packaging companies like Rexam. Two factories share a wall on the same site, through which bottles pass from Rexam to Coca-Cola. But such partnerships require 20-year vision and planning, with a near unbreakable commitment.

Thirty per cent of all EU trucks carry nothing at all

Just look at all those empty trucks due to cabotage:[61]

Cyprus + Ireland – 40 per cent of international trips, and 50 per cent of national trips;

UK – 30 per cent of international trips, and 34 per cent national trips.

Here is a shocking thing. EU governments are forcing tens of thousands of trucks to run around empty on their roads – to strangle competition from truckers in nearby countries. The EU Road Haulage Package allows only three further deliveries in seven days in member states once a truck driver has arrived with a full load. If a truck driver tries to make sure he or she goes home with a full load, and has already reached the limit, he or she will go to prison. It is as outrageous as that.

It is true that diesel tax is lower in France than the UK, so British truckers may fear that European trucking firms will be able to undercut delivery prices, by driving across the UK on French fuel. Two million trucks a year enter the UK, mainly having just refuelled in France. There are similar tensions in many other nations. But cabotage also applies in some situations to *shipping* cargos.

Product exchanges save wasted journeys

Then there is the madness of identical products passing each other every day on highways. Imagine two online retailers selling the same DVD player in Berlin and London. The Berlin retailer wins an order from a customer near London. On the same day, the retailer in London receives an order for an identical product from a customer near Berlin. There are two ways to deliver: each could courier their package across Europe, or they could agree to local delivery – maybe even within a few hours. That is assuming they both know about the other order, and have an agreement to cooperate. Product exchanges save time, cost and energy, and are easy to create online. Suppliers place stock on their website, buyers source it, and an integrated transport network delivers it.

Save 100 million kilometres of truck driving across EU

Every day many thousands of trucks drive long distances across Europe carrying identical chemicals in opposite directions from different sets of suppliers to factories. If both companies were part of a product exchange, they could swop their stock online. Polish polyethylene, for example, would go direct to a Polish factory, and the same for French. Over 100 million kilometres of trucking could be saved if chemical suppliers worked more efficiently. That's equivalent to 10 million litres less diesel burnt, saving at least €20 million in costs. Setting up and running such a product exchange would cost less than €250,000 a year.

Chemical manufacturers often make their products slightly different so that product swaps are more difficult. However, product substitution could still happen quite easily in many cases. Companies can be resistant to product exchanges, because they fear customer relationships will weaken, especially if they realize how much easier it is to get the product delivered from a competitor

There are 4,000 road haulage companies in the EU, and the largest only has 2 per cent of the market, so organizing efficient freight is difficult on a large scale.

nearby. Expect product exchanges to develop in many parts of the world for petrochemicals and other commodities.

ACTION

Business action
There are hundreds of ways you can save energy and emissions on travel and logistics. First review travel expenses and other perks to make sure staff are incentivized to use greener travel, but be sure you also consider efficiency – for example you cannot easily build teams with virtual meetings. Don't automatically assume that rail is better than road or air: it depends on distance and how many others are travelling in the same car, carriage or plane. Give your staff a communication budget instead of a travel budget so they can choose to spend travel money on technology to save travel, eg better videoconferencing systems. Consider replacing some of your fleet with electric or hybrid vehicles. Review all your logistics and give teams tough energy-saving targets. Make every effort to use empty lorries by selling space to other organizations.

Consumer action
You can buy electric cars today (or hybrids). Be sure to include the cost of replacing expensive batteries in your calculations, even though new battery prices will fall. A typical lithium ion battery for the smallest car today can cost over €5,000 and may not last more than three years. Just one long-haul flight can produce more carbon emissions than everything else you do for a year, so think about how much you fly. You may want to fly less or offset (buy a carbon credit – see pages 165–71). The best way to save energy travelling is to walk and cycle wherever possible.

So, logistics is often very wasteful. It is not enough to improve the efficiency of individual trains, ships and lorries. We need central planning and large-scale infrastructure development. That means bigger 'hubs and spokes' operations, more shared journeys, more transparent pricing and less red tape moving goods across borders.

In many parts of the world, freight takes longer to clear customs than to be shipped from one port to another. An absurd amount of time and effort can be wasted on getting official approval for import, export and so on. Much of this can be streamlined using electronic tagging and e-registration. All of this will also save emissions.

We have looked at ways to create unlimited green power, and to make big reductions in travel emissions. But what about cities, in which most people on earth now live, and which are responsible for more emissions than anything else?

CHAPTER SIX
FUTURE CITIES: LOWER CARBON TO CARBON-FREE

The air is filled by honking horns and puttering engines of a hundred motorized rickshaws. Overcrowded buses belch and shudder as they lurch their way to the next stop, people hanging onto doors, packed inside, bags hanging out of windows. The air is hot, humid and irritates the lungs.

Today is a good day. Yesterday, the airport in Mumbai was closed when pilots complained they could not see more than a metre in front of their faces. Welcome to the life of megacities and the problems of smog, created by a chemical reaction of sunlight and pollution.

Smog is nothing new. In the 1950s, London was hit by smogs so thick that they were called 'pea-soupers'. Thousands died on the worst days, impossible to see more than a metre ahead. The Clean Air Act was soon passed, banning coal or wood burning and things improved. Delhi recently passed a similar Act forcing buses and taxis to convert to liquid petroleum gas and the improvement has been huge.

Cities are responsible for 75 per cent of global energy consumption and 80 per cent of all greenhouse gas emission[1] – if you include the energy used in construction and demolition, cooking, heat, lighting inside buildings and cooling, people commuting, freight deliveries, water supplies, street lights and so on. Most people in the world today live in cities, and most large cities have major problems with pollution – air, water, noise, dumping of rubbish and sewage.

By 2020, 300 million will move from rural areas to cities in China alone, plus a further 400 million people across Africa. We will soon have 100 megacities, each with more than 15 million inhabitants.

Most people in megacities live in slum dwellings: shacks that start off made from bits of wood, cardboard and plastic sheeting. Soon you see one, two or three storey buildings begin to rise up, squashed against each other, fighting for space and light. Electricity soon arrives – maybe a twist of wire from a streetlight.

When mains water arrives, new troubles begin. With no drains, it may only be days before slum areas are sliced by networks of shallow, narrow ditches filled with dirty water from washing, cleaning, leaking pipes and sewage – plus rotting rubbish.

From low carbon to zero-emission cities

Cities need formal planning and that requires visionary leadership. Take Wuhan for example, as a typical, rapidly growing megacity of 10 million people, the largest in Central China. The local government has a 20-year plan for expansion, is building new high-density suburbs for 7 million more people on industrial wastelands surrounding the city, as well as new railway stations and other infra-structure. In 2005 only 50 per cent of waste water was treated, now it is 80 per cent.

> Lights left on in a typical small office use enough energy in a year to heat a three-bedroom house for five months. The average office wastes £6,000 a year leaving equipment on when not in use.

What about carbon-neutral cities? The government of Abu Dhabi is creating an eco-city called Mazdar, over an area of 6.5 square kilometres, for 40,000 inhabitants and 70,000 workers. It is being built in desert and will cost Abu Dhabi $22 billion, but they hope Mazdar will boost the economy by 2 per cent. Buildings will be covered in solar panels, and people will travel in electric robot-driven vehicles. Two-thirds of the energy used will be from solar, and all water will be recycled.

We saw in the last chapter how new cars, buses, trucks and trains will transform city life, but most city energy is burnt up in buildings and things like lighting the streets. Here are some easy ways to save huge emissions at low or zero cost. Just a few simple steps can reduce energy consumption in many cities by at least 30 per cent, using technologies or methods that are already proven, and which will mostly pay for themselves: low energy street lights, making buildings last longer, use of polymer concrete, better insulation, heat pumps, better boilers, combined heat and power, better heating controls, roof gardens and better city design.

1. Low energy street lights

Street lighting improvements are a great way for governments and municipal authorities to meet their new carbon reduction targets without spending any money.

Street lighting uses up to 5 per cent of all electricity in some nations – around 40 per cent of the total we use in lighting. This can be cut easily to less than 2 per cent with new lamps. That's a huge amount of energy – without any real cost since the whole operation is paid for rapidly out of energy savings.

New technology street lights can pay for themselves in four years, and go on saving up to 60 per cent of usual annual electricity bills thereafter. These lamps burn five times as long (10 years) and use less than half the energy (50–60 watts each). However, energy is used in manufacture and in installation, including fittings.

The cost of replacing all EU street lights will be £300 billion, but at 2008 prices that will save more than $70 billion in energy costs every year. Converting millions of lights is a huge operation but only needs to be done once.

New business worth €15 billion a year

In the EU alone, 120 million street lights need replacing, plus another 500 million outside lights, at a unit cost of €300 each and €300 labour. If we assume that 75 per cent of public lights will be replaced within 20 years, then the market in the EU will be worth €2.7 billion a year. Economies of scale will be important in awarding government contracts, as well as a track record in delivering large low-cost programmes. Expect many opportunities for regional and national operators.

But we can go further than street lights. Replacing just 700 sets of traffic lights with Light Emitting Diodes (LEDs) can save a city €1.2 million every year. Across a country the size of Germany that would work out at €140 million, reducing power use from 1.3 billion kilowatt hours to just 175 million. City councils typically recover all their costs in two to four years. Siemens is a world leader not only in the technology, but also in creative financing, with repayments funded out of savings, and almost zero financial risk.[2]

2. Make great buildings – to last longer

Most of the energy in a city is used to heat and light, build or pull down buildings, but the good news is that over half this can easily be saved with a combination of approaches. Things like:

- polymer cement;
- better insulation;

- prefabrication/pod building (for example in blocks of flats or hotels);
- more use of local materials;
- recycling building materials;
- green roofs (insulation and better water use);
- making buildings last longer.

It all starts with the design of buildings in the first place, for longer use. Forty per cent of all the energy used during the lifetime of a typical commercial building is spent putting it up (30 per cent) and taking it down (10 per cent). So it is a complete waste of effort to build properties that we know will only have a limited life.

It is a great scandal that so many buildings are designed to start falling down in less than 40 years. Most office blocks are designed with a life expectancy of only three decades – whether it is walls, concrete structure, window fixings and so on. Maintenance costs soon start to soar, health and safety risks grow, until the owner prefers to pull the whole thing down.

Such poor quality would never be tolerated in the housing market. Imagine a new home being built that the contractor knows will crack up after 30 years,

and be almost beyond repair 40 years from now. Such a company would be prosecuted in many countries. How could you get a long-term house loan? Most homes in wealthy nations are designed for a life of at least 100 years. Most houses made of brick or stone in Europe that are already 80 years old will probably still be standing in 2150.

Green Coast Enterprises builds storm-resistant buildings. It has 24 units completed for $7 million in New Orleans, most of which replaced homes lost in Hurricane Katrina.

We need to encourage architects, engineers, contractors and buyers of commercial real estate to be more responsible. Plan buildings as bold architectural and long-lasting statements, which will be loved by generations to come. Future-proof buildings by creating flexibility in how they are structured, use higher quality materials, and design for flexible use. We cannot afford to clutter our cities with yet more near-identical blocks of glass and steel, which add zero long-term value to society. We can expect far greater efforts to upgrade existing buildings.

3. Polymer cement – save up to 3 per cent of global emissions

Construction is responsible for a large amount of the world's energy use, much of it in cities, and a huge amount is in using cement.

Up to 7 per cent of all carbon emissions globally come from the use of 2.5 billion tons a year of cement.[3] Half the emissions are from energy in making it, and the rest is released when water is added. A ton of CO_2 is released into the atmosphere for every ton of cement used.

Polymer cement alone could save more than 2 per cent of global CO_2 emissions, reducing the total energy used to construct new buildings by up to 10 per cent. It is made by adding different materials to ordinary cement, and uses up to 40 per cent less energy per ton than ordinary cement. In many cases these new concrete polymers are also lighter (less transport costs) and offer better insulation. A common ingredient is ash from coal-fired power stations.

We need more research into the long-term strength of polymer cement. We need to be certain that it is safe to use in safety-critical situations – for example in high-rise office blocks or to build huge bridges.

Market of €5 billion for polymer cement in Euroland alone

Expect sales of more than €5 billion a year across the EU alone – the total sold as premixed concrete. Growth of the market could accelerate dramatically if building regulations change in some nations, requiring polymer concrete to be used wherever possible. The construction industry is under increasing pressure to reduce energy consumption, and polymer cement is an easy way to do this.

It is hard to develop strong patents for polymer concrete processes, so competition is likely to be strong from every existing concrete manufacturer. They will adapt rapidly to this new market.

Novacem is going a stage further to develop cement that naturally absorbs CO_2 when mixed with water containing magnesium oxide. California-based Calera is planning to use seawater to capture carbon dioxide emissions in cement from a nearby power station. It bubbles power plant flue gases through seawater, using the CO_2 in the gases to precipitate carbonate minerals for use as cement or aggregates in concrete.[4]

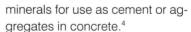

In the United States, PSEG utility company is knocking on the doors of its 2.1 million electric and 1.7 million gas customers offering improvements such as insulation and low energy lighting. Duke Energy is rolling out its own 'save a watt' campaign across several States.

4. Better insulation

What about existing buildings? The fastest way to reduce energy use in homes, offices, factories, schools and hospitals is to insulate them better – saving up to 40 per cent at low cost. A thick blanket of fibreglass wool in the roof can save 15 per cent of the heat lost in a home or small office, and also keep the place cool in summer. Property owners can recover the entire cost in reduced heating bills in less than three years if energy prices are high, eg oil more than $80 a barrel.

Cavity wall insulation is also fast to install and instant in impact. A large house can be completed in a day, by injecting foam, saving a further 10 per cent or more of heating bills, again with a short payback period. Thick carpets help reduce the 10 per cent or more of heat lost through floors, reducing air contact with cold floor coverings and also preventing draughts. A sheet of reflective insulating material behind radiators on outside walls will save up to 25 per cent of heat lost through that area of wall.

Many governments and utility companies are providing interest-free loans or grants, and this is one of the most cost-effective things they can possibly do to alter the carbon footprint of an entire city, if done on a large scale.

5. Pump heat to save 50 per cent energy

According to the International Energy Agency, over 40 per cent of primary energy use worldwide and 24 per cent of global emissions are from heating and cooling buildings. Up to 50 per cent of this can easily be saved in many locations by installing heat pumps – Sweden is the world leader in this.

You can pump heat or cold from 1–2 metres underground more cheaply than burning gas, coal or oil or using traditional air conditioners. Fuel bills can be halved in many cases. This is quite different from

> Heat pumps could reduce global energy use by 2 per cent by 2030 if installed in 1 per cent of homes and offices a year, in developed nations.

geothermal energy, where heat is being tapped from deep into the earth's crust (see pages 36–37).

Up to 70 per cent of new homes in some parts of Sweden, 45 per cent in New Zealand and 30 per cent in Switzerland are already heated by heat pumps. The UK government is hoping for around 500,000 systems to be installed in five years.

Heat pumps work by using the same process as in a fridge or freezer. A compressor pumps gas from one side of the system to the other. Where the gas pressure is low, temperature falls, and where the gas pressure is high, temperature is high. In a freezer, you can feel the heat of the compressed gas by touching the warm radiator at the back.

Heat pumps in homes do the same thing on a larger scale. In winter, the compressed gas is used to heat radiators, while the cooled gas is under-ground in pipes that are being gradually re-warmed by the surrounding earth or rock. In summer, the pump can be reversed, so that the pipes underground get hot, and are cooled down by the earth and rock around them, while the pipes inside the house get very cold. Heat pumps save the greatest costs when they are being used to replace oil-fired central heating boilers, but also save money compared to gas.

Eighty per cent reduction in home heating bills

Rehact has found a way to reduce heating bills for home owners by over 80 per cent – so the system pays for itself in just two years. The secret is combining heat pumps with other energy-saving steps that can easily be installed in new homes.

Heat pumps do have some disadvantages, as they take a while to get going and work best at lower temperatures – under-floor heating for example. However, heat pumps cost their owners little or nothing in the longer term, because they add to the capital value of the house and pay back their installation costs in around 15 years. One of the largest cost elements is digging trenches or deep holes for the pipes outside the house. If this is done when the house is being built, the costs are far lower than trying to install it afterwards.

Expect many governments in developed countries to require heat pumps to be used on most new building projects. And as sales rise, unit costs will fall. Global heat pump sales per year could be at least €15–25 billion.

6. Better boilers save more heat

One of the easiest ways to save energy in buildings that have boilers is to make sure that all oil, gas, coal and wood is burnt more efficiently. Old-style boilers typically waste 60 per cent of all the heat generated. Condensing boilers waste only around 10 per cent. They do this by using heat in chimney gases to pre-heat water that comes into the boiler.

Condensing boilers can be 50 per cent more efficient

If everyone in the UK with gas or oil central heating installed a high efficiency condensing boiler with up-to-date heating controls, it would save enough energy to heat nearly 1.9 million homes for a whole year, and around 6.7 million tons of CO_2.[5] These boilers can pay for themselves in as little as two to three years, depending on fuel prices.

New condensing boilers can utilize up to 98 per cent of the heat released as fuel is burnt (thermal efficiency) compared to new non-condensing ones that are around 78 per cent efficient, and older boilers that are only 55–65 per cent efficient.[6] But in practice, 98 per cent thermal efficiency is rarely seen in homes, and 90 per cent is more realistic. This is because condensing boilers work best when the water returning to the boiler from radiators is less than 50°C, to allow condensation in the heat exchanger of water from the waste gases, but domestic systems are not usually optimized in this way.[7]

Condensing boilers are more complex and can break down more easily. They need fans to expel cool waste gases, and a drain to capture water from waste gases, which is acidic and corrosive. Condensing boilers are up to 50 per cent more expensive to buy.

With today's new domestic boilers already achieving up to 98 per cent efficiency in well-designed systems, it is clear that most innovation in combination boilers over the next decade will be to reduce manufacturing costs, to make installation easier, and to run the control systems in more intelligent ways.

The potential market for condensing boilers is huge in almost every nation, including refitting controls, installation and advice. The UK spends £1.3 billion a year on new domestic heating systems – refurbishment (77 per cent), first time installations (14 per cent) and new build (9 per cent).[8] The most popular boilers are 'combination, condensing'

> Efficient heating systems use clean water. Heating systems produce corrosion and the result is dirty water and deposits, which restrict flow, make boilers less efficient and increase costs. Reducing the amount of dissolved material in water can increase the efficiency of heat transfer, using filters and materials that do not corrode.

(70 per cent of sales), which means they heat hot water directly for washing, without using a hot water tank.

Across the EU as a whole we can expect sales of new, more efficient domestic heating equipment of more than €7 billion a year, or €140 billion by 2030.

7. Combined heat and power generation (CHP)

A great way to save energy is to combine heat and power in the same unit. Large, centralized power stations are very inefficient, wasting up to 66 per cent of the fuel they burn. If power stations are sited close to cities, towns, villages or industrial sites, this heat can be used to heat homes and businesses or used in manufacturing. Heat capture technology has been used for decades in the former Soviet Union, and is also well established in Denmark and the Netherlands where around half the nation's energy is produced in this way.

Combined heat and power plants can be up to 95 per cent efficient. It does mean, however, that power stations end up closer to where people live –

running against a trend over the last 20 years that has been to build new ones far away from cities to reduce local air pollution. But location is mainly an issue for coal-fired power stations, and even there, as we have seen, new technology can reduce soot and noxious gas emissions dramatically.

We can combine heat and power the other way round: instead of converting power stations to local heating boilers, we can convert heating boilers to mini power generators. The capacity of CHP plants can be huge. For example, the Immingham CHP plant in Humberside, UK, supplies two refineries with heat, steam and power. It is being expanded and will soon have the same electricity generating capacity as one of the nation's largest nuclear power stations, Sizewell B.[9] In the UK alone, CHP units could generate as much power as 10 new nuclear power stations at a fraction of the price, and be built much more quickly.[10]

Cogeneration could be expanded rapidly on larger industrial sites, making use of heat energy that would otherwise be thrown away by industry. Many corporations are already using cogeneration to reduce fuel bills, reduce product prices and gain extra sales. They also benefit by telling a great 'green' story, which helps the image of their brand, and reduces the carbon footprint that they hand on to other larger manufacturers that are using their products to build their own.

Take car manufacturers for example. In their annual reports they give figures for the total carbon they use overall, and many are now calculating the carbon footprint of each vehicle they make. Only a small proportion of that carbon is their own, in energy used by their assembly lines. Most is emissions from companies that supply dashboards, foam seat covers, electrical wiring, batteries, engine parts and so on. Every time one of their suppliers does anything to reduce their own carbon emissions, it feeds through into a greener vehicle overall.

CHP can be used in other settings, on a smaller scale. For example, both Southampton and Woking Councils have hidden CHP generators in their car parks, generating both power and heat for public buildings.[11]

Cogeneration has grown rapidly since 1978 in the United States. Con Edison distributes 30 billion pounds of 180°C steam each year through its seven cogeneration plants to 100,000 buildings in Manhattan, which is the largest steam district in the world. The maximum power output is around 2.5 gigawatts.[12] The distribution system is

Woking Council in England has installed power units that produce electricity and heat, and linked them to form a private mini-grid. Streetlights are solar or wind powered, urinals in public toilets use no water, and solar cells on railway stations generate power. The council's carbon emissions have fallen 77 per cent and it saves up to £1 million a year in fuel.

why New York manholes often emit steam. Other major cogeneration companies in the United States include Recycled Energy Development, and leading advocates include Tom Casten and Amory Lovins.

We can also expect further development in micro CHP (up to 5 kilowatts maximum power) and mini CHP (5 to 500 kilowatts), once prices come down. Micro CHP is suitable for individual homes and today provides power for around the same cost as solar-voltaic cells.

However, if the boiler in a home is already capturing up to 98 per cent of the heat it burns, it is hard to see why it would be worth paying a lot more in capital costs to try to make electricity using the same equipment, unless the electricity company was charging a lot more per unit than the owner can make electricity for themselves, or unless the electricity company is buying surplus power at an attractive price.

8. Better technology to control temperature

Older office buildings, schools, hospitals, hotels and government buildings often waste around 40 per cent of their energy in heating or cooling, because of poor systems and controls.

Huge amounts of energy can be wasted when some parts of the building are too hot and others too cold. For example, in one corner of a glass tower block, temperatures may soar when the sun is shining through the windows. Thermostats get turned down. Other people then feel cold and bring in extra heaters.

Take a typical conference hall or hotel ballroom. As people arrive the room feels too cold so the thermostat is turned up. The system takes two hours to respond, but by then the audience is also generating heat. By lunchtime it is far too hot, and the system is turned down. By mid-afternoon, delegates are again too cold. The answer is a more intelligent and responsive system. For example, some systems track occupancy of each room by the electronic tag (RFID) in each ID badge, adjusting temperature and heat/cooling requirements automatically. Building controls can be managed remotely.

Many companies are cashing in on this huge new market to upgrade older buildings. Johnson Controls is a world leader in heating and cooling buildings as well as systems management. It often saves 40 per cent of energy bills by offering a free service to the owners of buildings, carrying out a power audit, looking at all the heating and cooling equipment, ducting, boilers, heat exchangers, controls and so on. It then recommends a package of new technologies, and may install them for free, paid later on out of the energy savings that the building owner enjoys over the following three to four years.

Innovation in this area is not just limited to large companies like Johnson Controls. Ice Energy is a small company based in California that uses cheap energy at night to create huge blocks of ice that are used to cool buildings during the day. This also takes advantage of the fact that air temperatures outside the building are lower at night, so less power is needed to refreeze water.[13]

> Szencorp upgraded its HQ in Melbourne, built in 1987. In 12 months its power bills fell by 61 per cent, and water use fell to 90 per cent of the industry average. The following year, both water and power use fell by a further 30–35 per cent.[14]

9. Roof gardens to cool cities

Green roofs or roof gardens can also save energy and improve the environment, keep flat roofs cool in summer and also help insulate in winter. They can require little maintenance and reduce energy bills significantly.

Twelve per cent of roofs are 'green' in Germany already – 12.5 million square feet of green roofs were installed in Germany in 2001 alone. The Tokyo government estimates that if half their roofs were green it would save a million dollars every day in air conditioning energy use, which is why the city requires at least 20 per cent of all new roofs to be 'green'.

Green roofs are of three types: ornamental roof gardens requiring high maintenance, roofs with shallower soil and narrower range of planting, while the third type is made up of sedums, mosses and whatever else establishes itself naturally.

How roof gardens work to keep buildings cool

A layer of soil is placed over a waterproof roofing material, with raised sides to prevent soil washing into drains when it rains. The soil is planted with vegetation that can withstand extremes of heat, cold, dampness and drying out. Cooling happens not just because of shading the roof surface, but also because up to 60 per cent of all rain is retained on the roof in the soil and, as it evaporates, it acts as an air conditioner, cooling the entire surface. Plants also lose water by transpiration, cooling their leaves down. Water loss is higher than at ground level because wind speeds are greater.

The impact can be huge. For example, studies on Chicago City Hall showed that roof temperatures fell by up to 30°C on hot summer days and surrounding areas were cooler by 9°C, after green roofs were planted. We know that with every degree less difference between internal and external temperature, the fuel bill can fall by up to 10 per cent.

Chicago-based Green Tech has also adopted green roofing. One third of its roof is covered by sedum plants that absorb rain. Green Tech stores up to 48,000 gallons underground, to use later for landscape irrigation. Other downpipes empty onto land rather than into drains, and the parking lot drains into ditches containing water-loving plants.

The US National Association of Homebuilders estimates that green buildings will account for 5–10 per cent of all new housing starts in 2010 – up from 2 per cent in 2005.[15]

Benefits in addition to improved insulation are: reduced storm water runoff, preventing water pollution by keeping contaminants in the soil, longer roof life, reducing the heat of an entire neighbourhood, encouraging plant and animal biodiversity, improved sound insulation and leisure opportunities for users of the building. Roof gardens also increase the capital value of buildings and their marketability.

The saving of energy per square metre is very complex to calculate, and varies with construction methods. In a typical Central European location, savings have been estimated to be up to €50 for each square metre a year in reduced fuel bills.[16]

Build flat roofs for extra weight

However, roof weight can increase by as much as 30–95 kg per square metre for roof gardens depending on depth of soil, when saturated by heavy rain, so most roofs need strengthening. Maintenance can also be costly if a garden is intended. If green roofs completely dry out, they can become hotter than gravel roofs in the height of summer.

The UK could be the largest potential market for green roofs in Europe with an estimated 50 acres of roofs across the City of London that could be suitable for conversion, at £50 to £120 a square metre for ornamental roof gardens to less than £10 a square metre for moss and natural vegetation cover. Hundreds of companies will service this demand, ranging from specialist roofing companies to design, planting and maintenance.

10. Better city design

Another way to reduce energy consumption is to design cities so people have to travel less.

During the period from 1960 to 1990, fuel was cheap and car ownership soared. Across countries like the United States the plan for most cities was to develop suburbs, with low density housing spread out over a large area. Vast tracts of forest land in the United States have been infiltrated by roads and housing, often so widely spaced that most residents can only see a few neighbouring properties through the trees. And scattered at intervals are retail parks. The result is a way of life that depends on driving large distances to shops, to college, to restaurants and so on.

Many city authorities are rethinking such models in favour of creating more local and energy-efficient communities. For example, Miami has set a target to reduce emissions to 25 per cent below 2006 levels by 2020. City leaders are redesigning the city with new mixed-use developments, so people can walk to shops and use public transport. They are also planning an eight to 10 mile streetcar project to connect residential areas with business districts.[17]

ACTION

Business action

If your business is in a large building that is more than a decade old, assume you are wasting around 40 per cent of energy in heating and cooling unless someone can prove otherwise. Set immediate targets for energy reduction, and contact any one of many specialist organizations to give you an energy audit and show you what to do. Include energy conservation in your capital spending and insist on a five-year maximum payback period. If you are responsible for commissioning new buildings, insist on a minimum 40-year expected lifetime when talking to architects. Use all your buildings to make statements about your corporate attitude to sustainability, and appoint someone to 'green' every part of your real estate. Make sure your boiler is efficient, and consider a combined heat and power unit if you have a factory or large complex.

Consumer action

Your home is the first place to think about energy savings. Look at all your fuel bills and assume unless someone can prove otherwise that you can save at least 25 per cent with a few simple measures. Turn down the thermostat by a single degree and you will save around 10 per cent instantly. Increase your roof insulation to at least the thickness required for new buildings by law. Deal with draughts in windows and doors with low cost foam strips. Place reflective foil insulation behind radiators on outside walls. Replace your old boiler with a condensing boiler and install radiator thermostats (and remember to adjust them). Consider a wood burning stove (smokeless models for cities) if you have access to a lot of wood waste from forestry, manufacturers or building companies. If you are redeveloping a property or buying new, look at installing a heat pump, and add the cost to the mortgage.

Summary

Most of global carbon emissions are related to life in cities, in the buildings we construct, use and break down, and in our daily living. Every business and every home owner has huge opportunities to save money. City planners and regulators can also play a powerful role in shifting cities to low-carbon, sustainable communities. Just 10 simple initiatives can save energy use in many cities by at least 30 per cent at low cost, when payback periods are calculated in the equation.

CHAPTER SEVEN
GREEN PRODUCT DEVELOPMENT AND IT

New manufacturing methods and more energy efficient, environmentally friendly products

In a Stockholm food factory, 400 million grains of rice an hour are flowing vertically like a great waterfall in front of a row of cameras, built into a sorting machine the size of a small desk.

Each grain is separately photographed to check against an image of a perfect grain. Every time a damaged grain is seen, or a husk or a piece of grit, a tiny puff of air from a pin-head opening pushes the falling grain into a hopper of rejects, for animal feed.

Welcome to the technology of Buhler: its machines sort 70 per cent of all rice sold on world markets today, and sliced frozen carrots, peas or broccoli. Your kitchen is probably full of food that has been checked by Buhler's robots.

Breathtaking engineering, precise design, and almost zero tolerance for error – you will find genius wherever you look in industry today. Buhler has found hundreds of ways to make its machines more efficient and cut carbon use in manufacturing.

Wherever you look in product design and manufacturing you will find green tech innovation. Here are just a few examples of the depth and speed of change.

Procter and Gamble has cut water use by 52 per cent, energy by 48 per cent and waste by 53 per cent since 2002. It has used profits to deliver almost 1 billion litres of clean water to the poorest nations. As a result of these things, the company was added to the Global 100 most sustainable corporations in 2009, and is in the FTSE4Good and Dow Jones Best Corporate Citizens List, which encourages people to buy their shares.[1]

Tomatoes from CO_2

British Sugar grows millions of tomatoes using CO_2 from its gas turbine generators. It captures every molecule of waste gas and pipes it 1 kilometre to a 26 hectare greenhouse where it grows 75 million tomatoes a year – 37 million more than it would have done without the extra CO_2, which acts as a bio-boost.

Cadbury has reduced packaging across many product lines – for example it saved 202 tons of plastic, equivalent to 24 million plastic bags, by making thinner plastic cases for Easter eggs. It is planning to cut seasonal packaging by another 25 per cent.[2] Marks & Spencer, Tesco, Asda and Sainsbury all continued or increased sustainability innovation through the 2008–09 downturn, with efforts ranging from better refrigeration to reducing packaging waste and ending free plastic bags.[3]

Smurfit Kappa is Europe's leading supplier of corrugated packaging and has worked with Spirax Sarco to reduce energy use by 20 per cent at its factory in Weston-super-Mare, England, by recycling condensate and flash steam back to the boiler. It also halved water treatment chemicals used and its water bill fell by £300–400 a month.

Pernod Ricard produces wines and spirits in 70 nations. It has improved boiler efficiency, upgraded evaporators and driers in distilleries, and reduced steam by 35 per cent since 2002. Adnams makes real ale using a Huppman condensing boiler that saves 30 per cent of its fuel, and the company uses waste heat for brewing. It built a giant turf roof and solar panels for 80 per cent of its hot water and collects rain water for vehicle washing and toilet flushing.

Patagonia is an outdoor clothing company. Since 1993 it has diverted 130 million drink bottles from landfill, by only using recycled plastic for the polyester it uses in fleece jackets. Its mission is to give 'maximum attention to product quality' while 'striving to do no harm' to the environment. It believes that its actions have strengthened the brand and contributed to its profitable growth.

Xeros is developing a washing machine that uses only 2 per cent of the normal amounts of water and energy, and a tiny amount of detergent, using 20 kg of re-usable plastic chips that absorb moisture and dirt with no rinse or spin cycle needed.

Stop fires without polluting the earth

Carpets, curtains, clothes and furniture are often treated to prevent them catching fire. But these chemicals are based on bromides and are very toxic to human health as well as to the wider environment. Deflamo has developed new fire retardants that are just as effective, are based on food-grade materials, are totally harmless, and cost the same.

Nanotechnology is saving energy in many industries and transforming many processes. It is a form of engineering that uses structures only a few atoms in size. NanoLub is a nanotechnology-based lubricant, made by ApNano Materials, which reduces fuel consumption by 5 per cent, and gear box wear by five to six times, as well as lowering engine temperature and noise, without harming the engine. It contains nanosized particles of tungsten disulfide, which form a slippery adherent film on all moving surfaces. NanoLub is added to oil or grease, and forms a durable coating so that moving parts are protected for longer, even if there is a serious oil leak.

PiezoMotor is a Swedish company that makes very tiny electric motors for mass-market applications like handheld devices, household electrical devices, car manufacturing and medical equipment. These can move levers or rods one nanometre at a time and weigh less than a few grams. They cut usual power consumption almost to zero when doing complex tasks, compared to ordinary motors, and are the equivalent to the jump in power efficiency from old light bulbs to light emitting diodes.

Spectris has developed ceramic-tipped blades for the paper and pulp industry that last five to eight times longer than steel and have less run-in time. It has introduced many other innovations to save energy across a wide range of industries.

Clorox collaborated with the Sierra Club; a 116-year-old US environmental organization, to develop effective cleaners. Today, Green Works products are found in most grocery stores. Bottles carry Clorox labels below their own logo and are endorsed with Sierra Club's emblem.

We could list thousands of other manufacturers who are making huge cuts in the resources they use, at the same time as increasing output. What we are seeing is this: whatever you make, distribute or sell, green tech innovation can save you money, enhance your products, help your image, open new markets and increase your market share.

Making steel and iron more efficiently

The steel industry is vital to the rest of manufacturing and is receiving special attention. Iron and steel mills consume 20 per cent of all energy used by industry and cause 30 per cent of industrial CO_2 emissions. Energy is 33 per cent of a steel mill's running costs. To make steel, coal is first turned to coke by heating to 1,000°C without air, and cooled, usually by water, creating huge clouds of steam and dust as well as polluted water and wasted heat.[4]

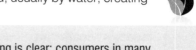

Siemens has developed dry cooling for red-hot coke, using heat for electricity generation, producing a peak of 17 megawatts of generating capacity per ton of coke, enough to power 30,000 homes. Such systems are working in places like Poland's ArcelorMittal plant with many more being installed in countries like India.[6]

One thing is clear: consumers in many countries are thinking more about ethics when they make decisions. Spending on things like fair trade coffee or eco-friendly products tripled in the UK over the last decade to £36 billion a year, but consumers are often held back by the fact that such products often cost more.[5]

Energy savings of 45 per cent can be made by milling steel in a continuous process, from pouring molten metal to rolling and coiling. Some parts of the process are now 10 times more efficient.[7]

Recycling saves raw materials and energy

Sustainability in manufacturing demands much more than saving energy, however. Even if we manage to halt climate change, we are still facing shortages of materials such as precious metals, damage to ecosystems and loss of biodiversity, all part of our total footprint on the earth.

Recycling is vitally important to sustainable manufacturing, and itself saves huge amounts of energy. For example, recycled aluminium saves 95 per cent of the energy it takes to make new aluminium. A single recycled aluminium can saves enough electricity to power a plasma screen for two hours. Recycling a ton of aluminium cans saves 9 tons of CO_2; a ton of glass saves 0.3 tons of CO_2. Germany recycles 64 per cent of municipal waste compared to only 34 per cent in the UK. In 2003, UK recycling saved 30 million tons of CO_2 – the same as taking a third of all cars off the road for a year.[8]

Recycling has become a huge industry in emerging nations. Take for example the Dharavi slum in Mumbai, the largest in Asia. Over 80 per cent of all Mumbai's plastic waste is recycled there, together with metal cans, paper, cotton and other materials – thousands of tons every day. Microloans have been used to set up some of the 400 recycling units. The industry now produces $1.3 billion of recycled output a year.

The paper and cardboard industries have led the way on recycling for decades – see the special feature on the industry on pages 144–47.

Recycled packaging takes a lot of space so trucks have to visit busy recycling points several times a day. BigBelly is a combined bin and compactor. Each has a normal capacity of 32 gallons but can compress 200 gallons of waste. They are solar powered and send radio alerts when full, so no trips are wasted. Philadelphia's BigBelly bins are saving the city $875,000 every year. Boston has installed 42, and New York, Vancouver and Vienna are following on.

Dangerous waste into clean energy

Cortus has found a way to convert dangerous industrial waste, sludges and biomass into clean gas for power generation or heating. The small amount of toxic material that remains is then used to make concrete. The process is highly energy-efficient and profitable.

The EU Recycling Directive requiring 100 per cent recycling of old cars has created a new market for massive recycling machines made by ARN, which sort each old car into different types of material. Engine oil and remaining fuel are removed, and then the vehicle is shredded into small bits of waste material, using an enormous cutting and grinding machine. Hundreds of millions of tiny pellets are sorted automatically into 16 different hoppers, ranging from copper, to steel, glass, PVC, rubber and several kinds of plastics.

An alternative to traditional recycling is to turn waste directly into parts for new products. Terracycle has over 50 items selling through Wal-Mart, Target, Home Depot, OfficeMax, Petco and Whole Foods Market, and is one of the fastest growing eco-friendly manufacturers in the world. It pays schools for old drink pouches, energy bar wrappers, yogurt cups, chip bags and other waste, which it transforms into products such as handbags, shower curtains and kites.

'Cradle to cradle' is taking off as a concept of zero waste: from production to throwing away and re-use of all materials, whether in manufacturing or real estate. Walter R Stahel first coined the term in the 1970s, and a formal 'C2C Certification' has been created by McDonough Braungart Design Chemistry (MBDC) consultants.

'Restore' refilling stations are kiosks in retail stores that allow consumers to refill empty product bottles. A machine reads a bar code, mixes the product, refills the bottle, and prints out a discount coupon. The kiosk reduces costs for manufacturers, retailers and consumers, keeps plastic out of landfill and reduces water consumption. There are machines in 22 stores in eight states in the United States, with revenues of around $1 million.

Sometimes the most sustainable thing to do is stop making a product altogether. One of the biggest wastes of packaging and transport energy is the 200 billion litres of bottled water that are sold every year, generating 1.5 million tons of plastic waste. Producing and transporting them accounts for 170 million tons of oil. Triflow is a tap that delivers hot, cold and refined water from a single spout, using three separate outlets. Purified water is made using a canister under the sink.[9]

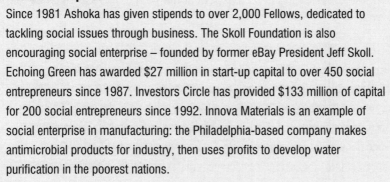

Social enterprise

Since 1981 Ashoka has given stipends to over 2,000 Fellows, dedicated to tackling social issues through business. The Skoll Foundation is also encouraging social enterprise – founded by former eBay President Jeff Skoll. Echoing Green has awarded $27 million in start-up capital to over 450 social entrepreneurs since 1987. Investors Circle has provided $133 million of capital for 200 social entrepreneurs since 1992. Innova Materials is an example of social enterprise in manufacturing: the Philadelphia-based company makes antimicrobial products for industry, then uses profits to develop water purification in the poorest nations.

Reforming the digital world – green IT

We now need to turn to one of the most serious issues in our carbon-burning world: energy use by computers and other IT equipment, which is already consuming 10 per cent of all electricity in the United States, and 5 per cent globally.

At the rate things are going, over 10 per cent of the entire world's power bill could be spent on running computers, the web and other digital devices, by 2030. This is a massive and urgent issue. Most people think that computers save energy by making our world more efficient, but the opposite is often the case.

New chip design, lower energy screens and better use of data storage could reduce energy use in some businesses by as much as 30 per cent. Web servers consume 1 per cent of global electricity, growing 14–20 per cent a year. One 50,000 square feet data centre can use around 5 megawatts on a continuous basis – equal to the needs of 5,000 homes. US data centres use the equivalent of a full year's output from seven 1,000 megawatt power plants – more power than used by the State of Mississippi. Cooling uses almost as much energy as the servers themselves.

Energy can be saved easily – new power supplies for example (Google's are 90 per cent efficient). Or power management software, more efficient chips, new cooling systems, use of fibre-optics, turning servers on and off depending on load (200,000 servers can power up in less than 5 minutes) or heat exchangers to cool server farms and heat nearby homes. Every one of these cost savings is a new business opportunity, and most pay for themselves rapidly.

Adjusting cooling to the numbers of active servers; separate sections of IT rooms to run at different ambient temperatures according to equipment need; placing air conditioning units closer to equipment to reduce distance air has to travel – all these actions can help.

Google servers use millions of dollars worth of power every month. The company is aiming to be carbon-neutral – and to generate 50 megawatt hours of renewable energy by 2012. Google already has one of the world's biggest solar power arrays (9,200 solar panels that cover its corporate headquarters). Together with its philanthropic arm, Google.org, it set aside $10 million for a programme to speed the development of plug-in electric cars, invested $20 million in wind and solar companies, and pledged tens of millions more for an ambitious initiative to find ways to make renewable energy cheaper than coal.

Virtual servers use spare capacity in large IT departments

Most large companies use only a fraction of the server capacity they have, yet these machines burn up energy every hour of the year. Virtual servers save energy by allowing many different users to share the same equipment. Energy savings can be huge – almost $300 a year per virtual server and 300 kilowatt hours of power each year. IBM has rolled out virtual servers and storage in-house and many other companies are following.

Many smaller companies are already sharing space in huge data archive centres, which store vital data each night, and millions of individuals are sharing servers by using companies like Norton/Symantec for their own backup.

A further challenge is equipment left on standby, which wastes 5 million tons of CO_2 every year in the United States alone. Yet a single chip can reduce standby energy use to almost zero.

Hazards from 500 million old computers

Green IT also means careful attention to disposal and recycling – reducing the amount of toxins in manufacture; reducing lead, cadmium and other pollutants in circuit boards, connectors, batteries and components; and enabling 100 per cent capture after disposal.

Silicon Valley Toxics Coalition estimates there are over 500 million obsolete computers in the United States, with 130 million mobile phones being thrown away each year. Over 70 million of these computers are already in landfill.

E-waste is now 2 per cent of solid municipal waste in the United States, and contains many hazards that can end up polluting water or endangering wildlife. Computer screens and old TVs are responsible for 40 per cent of all lead pollution in landfill – mostly lead in the glass itself, but also in printed circuit boards and components.

Plasma screens use four times as much energy as old TVs. In the UK alone a new plasma screen was sold every 15 seconds in 2008.

Some plasma screens cause a ton of CO_2 emissions a year in the power they use. If all UK plasma screens were on at once, it would drain all the power from two new nuclear power stations (2.5 gigawatts). This is just one reason why the 18 terawatt hours of UK power used in 2009 will jump to over 30 terawatt hours in only three years.

More than 1,000 chemicals used in IT factories have been linked to cancer, reproductive problems and other illnesses. Apple has banned a long list of toxic substances from its products, including asbestos, cadmium, mercury and lead.

Intel has already reduced the use of substances that contribute to global warming and is working to replace isopropyl alcohol, a solvent known to cause smog, which is used to clean silicon wafers.

One hundred per cent recycling and recovery

Hewlett-Packard recovers over 250 million pounds of hardware and print cartridges a year, aiming to reuse 2 billion pounds of products by the end of 2010. As prices of precious metals have rocketed, it has become profitable to dip old circuit boards in acids and solvents to collect gold, cadmium, lithium and so on.

Only 10 per cent of 1.5 million phones thrown away in the United States are recycled. Batteries contain important metals that are toxic in landfill. The Rechargeable Battery Recycling Corporation (RBRC) recycles 200,000 cell phone batteries a year into other things such as foundation material for roads. Ninety-nine per cent of each battery can be used. Many organizations are now trying to encourage people to hand in their old phones, including eBay and Verizon Wireless.

Energy savings from IT – more elusive than thought

So what about the huge promises of energy savings from IT? The paperless office has yet to materialize in most places. Paper printing has actually gone up, although we will eventually see a firm downward trend. Green IT means encouraging people to print out less material, printing onto lower quality paper, and ensuring 100 per cent paper recycling (see pages 144–47 on the future of the paper industry).

Virtual teams and virtual working – impact on travel

Virtual teams and virtual working have often been cited as powerful ways to help the environment. One could say that every phone call is a way to prevent travel, and (partial) home working is reducing travel to work.

However, video calls have been slow to take off, and most people prefer to be physically present at important meetings. The paradox is that executives are using video more – watching YouTube or uploading their own material.

Vodafone estimates that videoconferencing has recently saved it over 3,000 business trips.

Many senior executives in rapidly growing multinationals are already spending six weeks a year cruising at 35,000 feet. They are doubling the amount they travel every two to three years. So what happens in the *next* two to three years? Answer: we have to find radically better ways to work across huge distances. Companies that increase the proportion of virtual team meetings may gain significant competitive advantage – but only if those virtual meetings become (almost) as effective as meeting face-to-face.

There are many different tools to aid team collaboration, but most people leave the video turned off. The reasons are emotional. Video provides a huge amount of data – not just about the person's facial expression, but whether they look tired or happy, energized or frustrated. Video tells us whether they ironed their shirt, or still have wet hair after a shower. When working from home, video shows us the pet running around the room and the children's clothes hanging over a chair. Huge amounts of data leak across, and that is why people feel vulnerable. Video also feels unnatural when located only in the board room.

> 'Through the use of our own TelePresence (video conferencing) technology alone, we saved thousands of hours of employee and customer travel, resulting in a dramatically reduced carbon footprint.'[10]
>
> John T Chambers, Chairman and CEO, Cisco Systems

It is the same with video cameras in phones: use is almost zero for live calls. Yet 100 million people a day upload clips they have just made. People love creating video about themselves – carefully edited to reflect their image – but fear that live video will damage that image.

We can make video links feel more natural – for example washing an entire wall with the always-on image of a 'sister' office at another location. The cost of a major video link upgrade can be paid for out of saving long haul flights to a single meeting.

So, we have looked at manufacturing and green IT, and seen that one of the most important advances in manufacturing has been to make huge reductions in the use of water. Water is one of our most valuable resources, and is vital to our future. How else can we make sure there is enough in the future to sustain a good quality of life for all?

We will look next not only at water, but also at forests and food.

IBM reduced its total carbon emissions by 40 per cent from 1990 to 2005. In 2005, it launched 'A Better Planet' to encourage innovation, and invested $20 million into 'Big Green Innovations': advanced water management, including scenario forecasting for projects like hydroelectric dams; alternative energy, for example smart grids to manage national energy supply and demand, including electricity from domestic power units (solar/wind); and carbon management, eg a dashboard showing day-to-day emissions, hot spots and areas for savings.

ACTION

Business action

There are hundreds of actions to consider if you make products. Appoint a leader whose total responsibility is to calculate and then reduce your carbon footprint, and tell everyone where you are aiming for. Be ruthless in cutting waste at every level. You will improve morale and image as well as profitability. Reward every new idea for improving manufacturing efficiency and publicly honour people. Assume that however efficient you think you are, there are probably 10 per cent more savings that could be made each year – simply because technologies improve, the cost of innovations fall, knowledge increases, and lessons learnt in one part of the business roll out across others. Increase recycling of waste and also use of recycled materials in manufacturing. Set a minimum target for the proportion of raw material you want from recycled sources and work with your suppliers to achieve this.

Consumers may be keen to help slow climate change (so long as the cost is modest), but they are often confused about what the greenest choices are. That is why clear product information is vital.

Allow people to cash in their budget for work-related air travel and install state of the art equipment in their own offices or homes. What is the point of wonderful video systems at work when so many calls take place across time zones very early in the morning or last thing at night because of time zone differences?

Consumer action

Choose products that have low energy ratings and which have been made by manufacturers that you think are careful of the environment. Aim to increase your current level of recycling by 25 per cent over the next 12 months and talk to others in your household about why and how. Avoid food products that are in your view over-packaged. Make products last longer and get them repaired if possible when they fail.

CHAPTER EIGHT
SOLVING THE WATER CRISIS

Land turning to desert – near Bulawayo

As far as the eye can see, the entire African landscape is brown, dusty and thirsty. The air is shimmering in the heat. Many trees have lost their leaves in the drought and every blade of grass has shrivelled up. Starving cattle and goats wander aimlessly without energy, searching for food and water, supervised by tired children and old men.

Women, with babies on their backs, weave their way past them, up the hillside, carrying heavy containers of water on their heads. They are preparing breakfast for children at the village school, 2.5 kilometres away from the local river, which is their only remaining water supply.

Each time they return to the river valley, they find a hot bed of sand. The only water is hidden beneath, which they reach by digging big holes by hand, every few days a little deeper. And every animal around them is waiting to drink as soon as they have gone.

This is Zimbabwe – the area around Bulawayo after many months with no rain – but it could easily be a number of other regions in Africa.

Lack of water is the greatest challenge facing humankind in many parts of the world, and the problem is increasing. Water is the difference between rainforest and desert, the basis of all life on earth, and without it, every plant, animal and human is soon dead. More than a billion people lack access to safe drinking water, 2.3 billion people already live in areas where there is not enough rain to farm without difficulty, vulnerable to drought, and 3.5 billion will probably do so by 2025.

By 2050, 4.5 billion will live where water is scarce. Populations are growing, people are getting wealthier and are using more, and weather patterns are changing in ways that are hard to predict.

Across the world's most arid regions, deep wells are drying up and water tables are falling. At the same time, water supplies are being damaged by pollution from waste water, industrial contamination, fertilizer runoff and by saltwater as groundwater levels fall near coastlines.

Aquifers under Beijing, Delhi, Bangkok and many other major cities are almost empty. The flow of water is reduced much of the year down huge rivers like the Ganges, Jordan, Nile and Yangtze. Between Kazakstan and Uzbekistan, the 68,000 square kilometre lake known as the Aral Sea has shrunk to 25 per cent of its normal size, leaving a salt-encrusted wasteland.

Water crisis in China

China is just one nation where water is becoming scarce, threatening the nation's ability to grow food, manufacture goods, or provide basic needs for those living in cities.

China's greatest rivers have their source in the Tibetan plateau, which contains the world's third largest ice store, with 36,000 glaciers, most of which are shrinking. Levels of black carbon in the ice have soared since the 1990s from coal burning and industrial pollution, contributing to melting.

In 20 years, 18,000 miles of ice have shrunk by 4.5 per cent. As a result, 3,000 of the region's 4,000 lakes have dried up. Permafrost is melting. The snowline has risen from 4,600 to 5,300 metres and grasslands have turned to desert. More than 30,000 herders have been forced to find new ways to live.

As glaciers shrink, water flow into the Yellow and Yangtze rivers is falling. The Yellow river supplies 20 per cent of the Chinese people, with 50 large cities along its journey of 3,395 miles. During a recent dry spell recently it almost dried up for 226 days.[1]

'Many conflicts are caused or inflamed by water scarcity. The conflicts from Chad to Darfur, Sudan, to the Ogaden Desert in Ethiopia, to Somalia and its pirates, and across to Yemen, Iraq, Pakistan and Afghanistan, lie in a great arc of arid lands where water scarcity is leading to failed crops, dying livestock, extreme poverty and desperation. Extremist groups like the Taliban find ample recruitment possibilities in such impoverished communities.'

Professor Jeffrey D Sachs, Director of The Earth Institute

Conflicts over water

River basin management brings together all those whose lives are affected by a river. Take the Danube for example, which is 2,850 kilometres long, passing through or bordering Germany, Austria, Slovakia, Hungary, Croatia, Serbia, Romania, Bulgaria, Moldova and Ukraine. A key issue is pollution upstream, which robs nations further downriver of useful water and creates health risks or kills fish. The EU has set up groups to try to manage such rivers better.

There are 360 quintillion gallons of water in the world, 97 per cent of which is in oceans, while 50 per cent of the world's freshwater is found in six nations.

Water wars could be a reality in future. For example, Uganda cut Nile water flow by 33 per cent to let Lake Victoria fill up in 2006. Egypt claims 82 per cent of Nile water under a 1929 treaty, which was updated in 1959 to give Sudan most of the rest. Low rainfall, greater use of irrigation around the lake and over-use of hydropower generation by Uganda (it had added flow into the Nile in previous years) were all blamed for lower lake levels, which recovered by 2009.

How much water does our world need?

An average person uses 1,000 cubic metres a year for growing food, hygiene and drinking – equivalent to 40 per cent of an Olympic swimming pool.[2] If the poorest nations gain a standard of living equivalent to wealthy nations today, then water demand will be three times the figure of 3,350 cubic kilometres seen in 2000.[3]

The average EU citizen uses 150 litres a day: 33 per cent personal hygiene, 33 per cent flushing toilets, 13 per cent for washing clothes, and 8 per cent for washing dishes. Some is easy to save: running a tap while brushing your teeth wastes 5 litres a minute. The UK could save 180 million litres a year if people stopped doing this – enough to supply 500,000 homes. More can be saved by using less water flushing toilets. That will mean less need to replace leaking pipes, less need to build new reservoirs, less need for desalination to supply London, less energy used to pump, process or treat water.

But the figure of 150 litres a day jumps to 4,645 litres if we count water to make the food we eat and the products we buy:

Tomato	**13 litres**
Slice of bread	50 litres
Orange	58 litres
Egg	146 litres
Pint of beer	170 litres

Burger	2,400 litres
Cotton ball	4.5 litres
Sheet of paper	13.6 litres
Cotton T-shirt	4,000 litres
Leather shoes	9,600 litres
Pair of jeans	**11,000 litres**

Much of this 'virtual water' in your shopping bag is from other nations, because the products were made there, or grown there. Countries like Sweden do not need the additional virtual water, but may be adding to pressures on water supplies elsewhere by importing food or cotton, for example, from a very dry nation.

Houses using only their own rainwater

The average person in the UK uses around 150 litres of water a day. If you want to live using only rainwater, then that will probably mean reducing personal use to around 80 litres a day, depending on your roof area and location.

Water saving only really benefits local communities. It is not as if Sweden can start exporting water to northern Africa, and water savings in Stockholm cannot even be traded effectively as virtual water (see page 129), unless the extra water in Sweden can be used to create more food or more products in the country. So in water-rich nations, the main reason to save water is to save energy in treatment and pumping, and use of chemicals such as chlorine.

Spending on water improvements

Booz Allen Hamilton estimates that to provide enough water for all uses by 2030 the world will need to invest $1 trillion on water conservation, maintaining and replacing infrastructure and building sewage works. In low income countries, the best investments are usually to capture more rainwater in reservoirs, ponds, lakes and dams as well as in pumping stations, boreholes, roof collection and so on.

Water investment also stimulates the economy, which is why $11.8 billion was included in US Federal stimulus packages to upgrade water systems. A further $9.4 billion is being planned by the State of California alone.

Water is too cheap in most nations

The cost of water is far too low in many nations for it to encourage saving or serious investment. Water companies often lack a strong financial incentive to save billions of gallons lost each year through leaking pipes, because it may cost less to find more water in other ways. In most nations, water has no real price for domestic consumers, because they enjoy unlimited use for a fixed cost, if they do not have metered water. And as every economist knows, whatever is free in any society tends to be wasted until it has to be rationed, which is exactly what is happening with water.

Many farmers in places like California have fixed water allowances each year and have no motivation to use less than their quota. This is madness in a State that has such low rainfall. In parts of Australia a market has developed, allowing such unused quotas to be bought and sold, so efficient farmers can make extra income out of conserving water.

Cyber-Rain XCI System checks the weather forecast online and then controls sprinklers. Each unit costs $399, with a payback period of around a year in California for people who have water meters. The $4 million, six-employee company sells primarily to landscape contractors, but also sells direct through Amazon. The company saved 9 million gallons of water in just the first few months.

Innovations to save water

Huge savings can be made in most nations without great difficulty. Americans already use 20 per cent less water per person than a decade ago. A ton of steel made today requires only 2 per cent of the water it did in the 1940s.

Smart metering for water is one way to reduce demand, with pricing that varies according to the local situation. Companies like Elster and Sensus are investing in this, while IBM is installing a smart water grid to monitor use in every household in Malta.

Sustainable water use

- Collection – roofs, roads, rivers and streams, contoured farmland, ditches and ponds.
- Long term storage – underground aquifers, new dams and lakes.
- Distribution – repair leaky pipes.
- Metering in homes, offices and factories.
- Farming – drought resistant crops, drip irrigation.

▶

- Industry –innovations in manufacturing.

- Domestic water-saving devices – washing machines, washing up machines, taps and showerheads that aerate water.

- Clothes – which can be cleaned with minimal or no water – nanotech coatings.

- Recycling 'grey water' rather than dumping into sewers – output from sewage treatment plants goes direct to water treatment plants or used for irrigation or flushing toilets.

- Grey water systems in homes and offices re-use water to flush toilets or for irrigation/watering garden.

- Male urinals – no water to flush. Nanotech coating prevents adherence of toxic waste, sprayed every couple of hours.

- Desalination – lower energy methods.

Reduce water use on farms

Since farming is the world's biggest user of water, even small increases in irrigation efficiency will help national water supply. One way is to build dams to catch rain in non-growing seasons, but much of this evaporates away. Underground storage reduces this to almost zero. Alternatives are drip irrigation systems and new crop varieties.

PureSense has developed a smart irrigation system that monitors soil moisture and controls water use.

Australia is the most arid continent after Antarctica, and rain has declined by 25 per cent in recent years. Water levels in the great 1,500 mile Murray River recently fell to their lowest in 116 years, while local reservoirs were only 20 per cent full. In a dry year, harvests of 1.2 millions of tons fall to only 15,000. Meanwhile, coastal cities are investing in desalination.

A third of water used in farming is lost in leaks and evaporation. Coleambally Irrigation is working with 320 farmers to control water use, with smart irrigation channels and monitoring. It monitors flow, temperature and salinity at remote-controlled gates over thousands of acres. Its central system can spot new leaks quickly. Water use has fallen, and some farmers are now starting to trade the water that they save: 1,000 cubic metres sells for $360.

Large numbers of new companies are developing systems for smarter use of water in farming – like Hydropoint Data Systems and M2M Communications, as well as multinationals like IBM. Hydropoint WeatherTrack watches weather and soil moisture, and smart irrigation is sensitive to the needs of each crop on an hour by hour basis. If widely used, it could save 17 per cent of water use in a dry state like California by:

- switching from flood to sprinkler and drip systems;
- reducing watering during drought-resistant stages of growth;
- monitoring water content in soil and air temperature/wind.

Intel and Chandler City – managing water better

As we have seen in the previous chapter, industry can be a major drain on local water supplies and corporations need to work with local communities to use water responsibly. Take for example Intel, which is the largest consumer of water in Chandler, a small city that is now part of the continuous urban area extending out of Phoenix, Arizona. Intel produces computer chips in an area the size of 17 football fields, employs 10,000 people and has invested $9 billion. The factory uses 2 million gallons a day of drinking water, which is purified further to remove small amounts of dissolved compounds, leaving salty sludge that goes to an evaporation pond.

The ultra-pure water is first used to wash chips, and then used again by air scrubbers that clean up the plant's emissions, or used in huge air conditioning towers, while more waste water is used to irrigate plants in the parking lot.

Intel pumps 1.5 million gallons a day into a $19 million desalination plant that it built for the city. The water is made clean enough to drink, and pumped 600 feet down into a sandstone aquifer beneath the city. Intel has replenished 3 billion gallons so far, recycling 75 per cent of water that the factory uses. Intel has gained in image popularity and government approval, which has made it easier to get permission to expand.

Water use is a vital part of the total eco-footprint of any large manufacturer, since carbon use can be reduced by increasing water use, and the other way round. Carbon footprint, greenhouse gas impact and water consumption need to be looked at together.

As in many industrial processes, it is hard to measure Intel's total eco-footprint. You need to do more than look at water use, or power consumption, and include indirect use of water as well as the impact of the lives of all employees on the local environment.

For example, the Intel site uses as much power as 54,000 average homes. Much of this comes from the Palo Verde Nuclear plant outside Phoenix, which itself uses huge amounts of water for cooling turbines, turning 20 billion gallons a year into steam from cooling towers. And then there are 10,000 additional employees who now live in Chandler, meaning new homes in the desert, their own energy and water use, parking lots that create their own heat islands, requiring more air conditioning power to be used, and so on.

London – leaking 180 million gallons every day

London's 7 million inhabitants have a growing water crisis – despite 28 inches of rain a year. A third of the city's 20,000 miles of water pipes are over 150 years old, leaking a third of supplies. It would cost $3.6 billion to replace all the pipes. Thames Water is gradually replacing them on a planned schedule, installing water meters to encourage water savings (an average of 10 per cent) and working hard to detect the largest leaks with a smart water grid using iStaq monitoring devices under manhole covers, to measure flow, pressure and water level. Each sensor can send e-mail or text alerts within seconds of a pipe bursting. They are made by the start-up Qonnectis.

Thames Water's most controversial project is a new desalination plant in the Thames Estuary, designed to deliver 35 million gallons a day during drought. Since this is only 20 per cent of that lost from leaking pipes, many have suggested that it would be more logical (even if more expensive) to spend more on new water mains or new reservoirs.

International Development Enterprises India (IDEI)

IDEI has developed a simple treadle pump that has lifted more than 750,000 farmers out of poverty. It has diversified into drip irrigation systems and is selling its products worldwide. The organization uses Bollywood films and stars to get its message across.

Cleaning water with iron filings

In many parts of the world there are bore holes full of water that cannot be drunk because of industrial pollution or natural contamination. For example, 40 per cent of 50,000 wells tested in Bangladesh are contaminated with dangerous levels of naturally occurring arsenic.[4] We can expect to see many innovations in this area.

One new approach is to use iron filings, as used in the Taopu Industrial District of Shanghai. The project treats 60,000 cubic metres (13 million gallons) a day of industrially contaminated water – as much as you might expect from a small town. Iron powder has been used to treat groundwater for more than a decade. It removes dangerous substances such as arsenic and trichloroethylene (used in paint stripper).

Non-biodegradable industrial chemicals are attracted to the iron filings which react with them, oxidizing into rust in the process. The treatment facility uses 100 tons of iron filings, all purchased locally, and which last around two years. Compared to other methods they were using, nitrogen removal has soared from 13 to 85 per cent, phosphorus from 44 to 65 per cent and dyes from 52 to 80 per cent. The project was developed by Lehig University in Pennsylvania and Tongji University in Shanghai.[5]

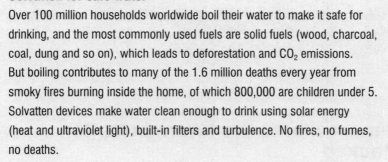

Solvatten for safe water

Over 100 million households worldwide boil their water to make it safe for drinking, and the most commonly used fuels are solid fuels (wood, charcoal, coal, dung and so on), which leads to deforestation and CO_2 emissions. But boiling contributes to many of the 1.6 million deaths every year from smoky fires burning inside the home, of which 800,000 are children under 5. Solvatten devices make water clean enough to drink using solar energy (heat and ultraviolet light), built-in filters and turbulence. No fires, no fumes, no deaths.

Making virtual water – a trillion cubic metres a year

Because most water we use is for growing food, the easiest way to increase the amount of water available in cities for washing, cooking, drinking or making things is to grow less food and import more. The savings can be astonishing. Your nation may be buying wheat, but is also buying another country's water – which we could call 'virtual water', since it is never imported.

It takes 1,000 litres to grow 1kg of wheat – a cubic metre. So a single 40kg bag of wheat uses up the same amount of water as a large 40 ton water tanker. *Importing a single 40 ton lorry of wheat is the same as importing 2,500 lorries' worth of water (100,000 tons), enough to fill four medium-sized container ships.*[6]

The amount of water traded around the world in food sales is probably more than 800 billion cubic metres a year – the equivalent of 10 Nile rivers. If all tariff restrictions on food imports were removed, virtual water would probably double to more than 1.7 trillion cubic metres.[7]

Nestlé encourages better water use

Nestlé has increased production by 68 per cent in 10 years, but reduced water use by 30 per cent, aiming for a further 2–3 per cent over the next five years. Its bottled water business has reduced the additional amount of water to make a litre of bottled product to 1.76 litres – a fall of 26 per cent since 1999. Nestlé has encouraged farmers in Parma, Italy to use smart irrigation (digital monitoring and control of drip irrigation) for vine-ripened tomatoes. A new coffee processing plant in Kochere Woreda, Ethiopia, uses only 4 per cent of the usual amount of water to process green coffee beans, saving 26 million litres per crop. All waste is turned into organic fertilizer, reducing water pollution by 99 per cent. Nestlé has also trained Vietnamese coffee farmers to use drip irrigation in Dak Lak, reducing water use by 60 per cent.

Dams – vital to the future but often attacked

We saw in Chapter 2 how water power from dams provides around 17 per cent of all the world's power, mostly situated in the poorest nations. At the same time, these dams are vital to water management. There are 48,000 dams of significant size worldwide, with a surface area of around 400,000 square kilometres,[8] and many more are planned. Yet many are being decommissioned and organizations like the World Bank have been discouraged from lending for large dam projects. Campaigners have criticized governments that are planning to build dams, and businesses that carry out their construction.

Dams can destroy ecosystems, clog up rivers, prevent fish from breeding, destroy wetlands, and deprive millions of low income farmers of land. The Three Gorges dam on the Yangtze River, central Hubei province, displaced more than a million people when completed in 2006. It is 185 metres high and 2,309 metres long, and is the largest concrete structure in the world. The World Commission on Dams estimates that 40–80 million people have been displaced by large dams (defined as being higher than 15 metres) – mostly in India and China, between 1950 and 1990.[9]

Dams can also create new health risks. Between 1947 and the early 1980s, large-scale water projects were a factor in the 75 per cent increase in cases of schistosomiasis, flukes, nematode worms and bilharzia. Around

60 per cent of the world's largest 227 rivers have been fragmented by dams.[10] The natural flow of the Yangtze River will be disrupted by 46 large dams planned or under construction, while the Danube and Amazon are also vulnerable.[11]

Much of the water from dams can also be wasted on inefficient irrigation – perhaps up to 1,500 trillion litres a year, or 10 times the entire water consumption of Africa. Large amounts of sediment can be trapped behind dams. In an extreme case, the turbines of Sanmenxia Dam were shut down in 1964, after only four years operation, because the reservoir filled with silt.[12] Decomposing plant life in the sediment can cause significant emissions of methane and CO_2 – in some cases the same as a coal-fired power station with equivalent capacity to the output of the water turbines.[13]

PlayPumps get more water from the ground

In many parts of Africa, women and children walk over 3 kms to fetch water, which they carry on their heads. Diesel or electric water pumps are often broken. PlayPumps are attached to children's merry-go-round equipment. As the children play, they pump water to large storage tanks connected to a pipe and tap. Each pump costs $14, and is made by Roundabout Outdoor.

Restricting water flows can also damage economies further down the river. The diversion by India of the Ganges, before it reaches Bangladesh, has caused an estimated $25 million in losses for an agricultural project in north-west Bangladesh, and increased the salinity of water in fishing areas in the Bay of Bengal.[14] Dams can increase erosion of river banks and beds. Silt that usually washes down a river can help replenish erosion of river beds and banks, and in some cases, silt-free water from dams can mean that the river cuts wider and deeper. Dams' water heats up in summer and cools in winter, so the temperature variation in water immediately below a dam can be greater than normal.

These criticisms of dams are why the rate of new dam building fell from 5,400 a year to only 2,000 in the 1990s, as the World Bank became increasingly reluctant to finance their construction. But there are many strong arguments in *favour* of dams.

Dams are vital to future survival of many emerging nations

The truth is that dams are vital to the future survival of many communities, providing huge amounts of fresh water for food and daily living, as well as clean, carbon-free power (once you allow for the emissions released during construction and for variable amounts of methane release).

If you have driven hundreds of miles across parts of Africa that have long periods of drought with intervals of heavy rain, you cannot avoid coming to the conclusion that dams are life-savers, food producers, power sources, wealth-creators, tourist attractions and insurance policies against climate change.

Dams also provide better control over water flow, and decrease the risk of flash flooding after torrential rain, capturing excess water safely. Dams are the only affordable means of generating large amounts electricity in many of the poorest regions, which have very little foreign currency to spend on oil or coal imports for power stations.

The World Health Organization estimates that 5.6 billion working days a year are lost because of ill health due to unsafe water. The World Bank estimates that every $1 invested in water projects gives a return of $2–5 in health, economic and social benefits.

Leaders in emerging nations that are short of water will not be dictated to by anti-dam, finger-wagging bureaucrats in the World Bank, or any other international agency, nor will they tolerate criticism by government leaders in developed nations. They know that water is a scarce resource that must be conserved and made to work for the community, and that it is impossible to do that fully without building many more dams – large and small.

Into the gap caused by this battle of words, Chinese companies are rapidly developing a global lead in dam building, after building many dams in China itself. China Exim Bank is now a major funder. As a result there has been pressure on companies and banks from developed nations to stop being so uncooperative about such projects. In any case, many of those who oppose financial support for building new dams in the poorest nations are themselves citizens of wealthy nations that have benefitted greatly from their *own* dams.

The future of dams in the United States

Take the United States, which has no less than 78,000 dams. Dams have played an important part in US prosperity for decades. The great Hoover and Glen Canyon dams provide more than 6 million people with power from the Colorado River.

But these dams are growing old: most were built between the 1940s and 1980s – 19,000 in the 1960s alone – and 25 per cent are more than 50 years old, rising to 85 per cent by 2020. A survey by the American Society of Civil Engineers found 3,300 dams to be unsafe and a large number of these are being demolished, usually because the cost of repairs is greater than their owners can afford. But at the same time, we are seeing many new dams under construction in the west of the United States, mainly to help with water shortages.

The inescapable fact is that all the arguments about dams damaging the environment are being rebalanced by the attraction of clean, free power, their very long lifespan and low maintenance.

Diverting rivers

Another way to try to solve water shortages is to divert large rivers into other rivers that are drying up. Rivers are nature's own water transport system and, by refilling them, the local ecosystem can be protected, aquifers start to refill and existing infrastructure comes back into use (water pumps and treatment plants, irrigation systems and so on).

China's water transfer project is designed to divert more than 40 billion cubic metres (10.5 trillion gallons) of water each year from China's longest river, the Yangtze, and its tributaries, partly to supply Beijing.[15] River diversions are also common in Russia. However, diversions can simply transfer a crisis from one river basin to another, especially if combined with the construction of dams. Bangladesh has blamed India for reducing parts of the country to near-desert by interfering with common rivers.[16]

Global desalination is growing fast

Energy and water are closely linked. Generating often uses large amounts of water for cooling, while the water industry uses power in pumping and processing. Water is converted to electricity by dams, and so on. But energy can also be used to make fresh water.

Our world already has enough desalination plants to supply 40 small cities – a total capacity of 55.4 million cubic metres a day.[17] There are two main ways to use energy to make fresh water from sea water. The first is to boil water – perhaps using waste heat from a process like smelting aluminium, which reduces the cost. The second is to force sea water through a membrane with pores so small that only water molecules pass through. Both methods are expensive – but membrane desalination costs are falling fast.

There will be a huge market in future for smaller desalination plants. GE is one of the world leaders in desalination – but many innovative companies are entering the market such as Veolia, Consolidated Water and Tetra Tech.

More efficient membranes require less pressure. An alternative may be filters made from carbon nanotubes, which could lower costs by 30 per cent. IBM's membranes are resistant to damage by chemicals such as chlorine, and remove 99.8 per cent of arsenic contamination from borehole water or industrial water waste. Such research is part of IBM's Big Green Innovations, backed by $100 million of funding.

If scientists can find ways to greatly reduce the cost of electricity from renewable or nuclear power, then in the longer term, desalination could become a viable option to supply entire cities or even nations (with the exception of large-scale agriculture). Desalination is already a commercially viable method of supplying cities with some of their water – but not yet in most cases to supply farms, where much larger quantities of water are needed, at much lower cost.

So, we have seen that up to 4.5 billion people could be short of water by 2050 unless things change. The good news is that we can expect rapid business and farming innovations to help solve many future shortages, enabling most of humankind to live with enough fresh water for daily activity, for growing food and for manufacturing.

Why dirty water makes people sick

Water may look clean, but can be dangerous, and dirty water is one of the greatest killers of children under 3 years old. Their greatest risk is contamination by human faeces, in which a single gram can contain 10 million viruses, 1 million bacteria, 1,000 parasite cysts and 100 parasite eggs. Common water-borne diseases include viruses such as infectious hepatitis and polio; bacteria, eg cholera and typhoid; protozoa, eg dysentery and giardiasis; helminths (parasitic worms), eg bilharzia, guinea worm and hookworm infections.

Large populations may be increasingly vulnerable to drought over the next 50 years, especially either side of the Sahara desert, stretching right across the Middle East to Pakistan and beyond. Even slight changes in climate are likely to hit these communities much harder than people in developed nations. One of the main reasons for global efforts to reduce the speed and severity of climate change is that the impact on these communities will be so hard to cope with. How can you move 100 million people? Where would they go? How will they be sustained where they are, if the world warms by 2°C?

Lack of rainfall could destabilize some of the poorest nations, triggering large-scale migrations, international tension and future regional wars. Many local communities will need a huge amount of support to survive and to maintain even the most basic standard of living.

Pure water using light

One of the world's greatest challenges is the lack of clean water. Wallenius has developed a way to purify water instantly without using any chemicals, killing all bacteria and viruses. It can work for public water supplies, swimming pools or in any other situation. The secret is ultraviolet light shining into the water as it passes over a specially treated metal plate.

ACTION

Business action

Do a water audit in your business as part of your manufacturing or property review and set tough targets for reducing consumption. Remember that water saving also reduces your carbon footprint because water use takes energy. If you are in a country that experiences regular water shortages, take steps to prove your corporation as a careful user. Improve water management in your properties – consider things like rainwater collection for irrigation, planting less water-hungry shrubs and trees, or no longer using mains water for your fountain (yes some companies still do it).

Consumer action

Request a water meter and monitor how much you use. Set targets for reduction but be clear why: cost reduction, saving energy, or actual water conservation or a combination. Water the garden less – lawns usually recover when the rains return, plant less thirsty species, and use water from roofs for plant watering. Get rid of tubs on patios and plant deep into the ground. Use mulch of grass cuttings or bark, or compost to reduce evaporation. Plant densely so that shade from leaves protects earth from being baked. Only use washing machines and dishwashers with full loads and buy low-water models. Use a shower rather than a bath. Fit aero taps that mix air into water – they are more efficient when washing directly under a flowing tap and in showerheads. Install a dual-flush toilet. Wash the car with a bucket and a quick hose down at the end.

So, we have looked at water conservation, but what about protecting forests – as preventing deforestation can be one of the most important and cost-effective ways to spend money in reducing emissions.

CHAPTER NINE
PROTECTING AND MANAGING FORESTS

They came just before dawn. Local forest dwellers were woken by the angry growl of powerful truck engines. Twenty huge timber lorries and 50 men, grinding up the road through rainforest from the frontier town of Satipo in Peru, right on the edge of the central Amazon at the border with Brazil.

One by one, the long convoy took a sharp left turn off the new road, lurching across open forest land that they had destroyed by logging just two weeks before. The men shouted to each other from the backs of the trucks as they passed near village homes. And then it started.

A small group of forest children soon gathered to watch from a distance, hiding in the undergrowth. They saw all the men carrying chain saws, in the early morning light. They heard the familiar whining roar as each saw began to bite into the trunks of tall mahogany trees. They waited a few minutes and then watched each majestic tree begin to fall.

Only last week, the same men turned up in their village and threatened to kill their fathers. Then they had shaken hands and given the village some money and food. In the next village, all the elders were beaten up a couple of months ago because they had been sending warning messages to the police in Satipo about the logging. However, no one from Satipo came to see what was happening. Bribes and threats had stopped that.

Deforestation is the third largest source of greenhouse gases, responsible for up to 23 per cent of total emissions from human activity[1] – more than all the cars, trucks, trains, aircraft and ships combined.[2] That includes not only the CO_2 released, but also nitrous oxide, methane, aerosols and other particles, and the impact of changes in reflectivity of the earth's surface. Around 13 million hectares of tropical forest are destroyed each year – one acre per second.[3] An area nearly three times as large as the whole of France was cleared between 1990 and 1995.[4]

> Ancient Bristlecone pines in the western United States are growing faster than in previous centuries because of global warming and increased CO_2 levels.[5]

It is hard to calculate these things exactly. Another study published in *Science Journal* estimated the total emissions from burning to only around 20 per cent. We may debate the figures but the message is clear: forest protection *must* be at the heart of any strategy for sustainable living.[6]

The good news is that it may cost only around $5 to save each ton of CO_2 from forest burning – a quarter of the price at which it is trading on the EU market. Forests that exist today are storing the equivalent of 40 times the world's annual carbon emissions.[7]

Planting new forests can restore damage rapidly

Human activity has a major impact on whether rain is useful or destructive. Take Rio de Janeiro, which is one of the most spectacular cities in the world, with 70 miles of beach, arranged in a series of bays and inlets. Most of the 10 million inhabitants live within walking distance of the sea. But the most unusual feature of Rio is a tropical rainforest in the heart of the city, which covers a large mountain.

Most tourists have no idea that those same mountain slopes were stripped bare in the early 19th century to build the city, for fuel, and to grow coffee. Tropical rains soon stripped away the soil, leaching nutrients out of what remained, leading to bare earth, serious flooding – and drought.

The virgin forest had been like a big sponge, absorbing heavy rains and releasing water into streams and rivers in drier periods. The entire ecosystem was destroyed. Yet just 50 years after replanting began in 1865, the slopes were again a rainforest, home to many thousands of exotic, native species. The city became cooler once more, rivers and streams more constant, and floods and small landslides stopped. What is more, Rio regained its crown, and with it became an attractive tourist destination. Re-colonization is often a swift process – bacteria, fungi, yeasts, insects, small reptiles and mammals, birds, amphibians, fish and plants of a hundred thousand varieties – all find their natural place.

> Every day, deforestation releases more CO_2 than 8 million people flying from London to New York.[8]

Soil matters as well as forests

Taking better care of soil in farming and forestry can also help trap more carbon. The earth's soil contains about 1,600 billion tons of carbon – more than plants (610 billion tons) and the atmosphere (750 billion tons):

- Carbon content in soil on US farmland fell by over 50 per cent from the 1890s to 1940, mostly due to soil erosion from ploughing.

- Uptake of carbon by trees and plants, and release by forests and soils, is around 120 billion tons a year, compared with global human emissions of 7 billion tons of carbon (as both CO_2 numbers are large).

- Humus in healthy soils contains up to 58 per cent carbon, unhealthy soils 20 per cent or less.

Aprovecho Research Center (ARC) based in Oregon, and Shengzhou Stove Manufacturer (SSM) produce portable, cheap and efficient fuel-wood stoves in high volumes for global distribution. Since 2008, 60,000 stoves have been sold, with production capacity now at 50,000 stoves per month.

Restoring topsoil can increase agricultural productivity and prevent soil erosion. Topsoil helps stop valuable phosphorus and nitrates being washed away.

Forests are growing in many regions

The amount of woodland has increased in 22 of the world's 50 most forested nations. Asia gained a million hectares between 2000 and 2005, El Salvador's forests grew by more than 20 per cent between 1992 and 2001, and China's by 47 million hectares since 1970. Only 12 per cent of China was forest in 1988, but now it is 16.5 per cent.[9]

A quarter of the world's forests are in Europe, mainly in Russian-speaking nations, and European forests are growing by around 1 million hectares every year, equivalent to the total forest land in Slovenia, mainly through active planting of new forests, plus some natural expansion into abandoned farming land.[10] Forests cover 44 per cent of Europe, around a billion hectares, storing 53 gigatons of carbon. There are more than 11 million different private owners of forest land in Europe, and their industry exports 100 million cubic metres of wood a year, employing 4.3 million people.[11]

One study projects that global forests could increase by 10 per cent (an area the size of India) by 2050.[12] It depends partly on whether forestry becomes an integrated part of carbon trading and management worldwide. The figure could turn out to be a significant underestimate if our world really committed to protection and enlargement of forests. The point is that reforestation is possible, and is probably one of the most cost-effective ways to help the planet.

Protecting forests will not be easy and we do not have much time

The reasons for deforestation vary with each nation but there are common elements:

- Forest land produces little or no income for the owner.

- No market for important functions of forests.

- Low financial incentives for protecting forests.

- Very low incomes of those living in or near forests can lead to deforestation to survive – eg for food, cooking or construction of homes.

- Economic development can mean more mechanization, better roads and larger companies – so trees are cut down and used more rapidly.

> Tropical rainforests are diverse ecosystems. We are losing 137 plant, animal and insect species every single day due to rainforest deforestation, 50,000 species a year.[13]

- Population growth and urbanization.

- Pressure for economic growth in lower income countries.

- Ownership of the forest – land rights – may be unclear or hard to enforce.

There are certainly many challenges:

- Loss of habitat and biodiversity.

- Loss of carbon capture.

- Deforestation may increase water run-off, soil erosion and degradation – especially in rainforests where soil may be very thin.

- Impact on local climate – eg reduced rainfall, rise in air temperature.

- Displacement of indigenous people.

- Lack of environmental controls and monitoring.

- Corruption of government departments.

One basic step is to make it more difficult to sell timber from tropical trees to developed nations. At present, less than 2 per cent of the world's tropical forest is certified as sustainable and most imported tropical timber is illegally harvested.

In 2008, the United States passed a Bill banning the import or purchase of illegal timber and the EU is taking similar steps. In the meantime, many retailers and manufacturers have been making great efforts to source their wood ethically. However, one block of wood is impossible to tell apart from another, and whatever laws are passed, we will continue to see smuggling and evasion on a large scale. So we need to find additional ways to protect trees.

Deforestation comes from:[14]

cattle ranching	5%
over-heavy logging	19%
palm oil plantations	22%
slash and burn farming	54%

In the past, most trees were cut by local villagers for fuel or to grow food. Today a growing threat is large-scale mining, logging and farming. However, the owners of these enterprises are relatively few in number and easier to target than millions of farmers.

Corporations – for example global soy, palm oil and timber industries – are being shamed into action.[15]

Make sure forests are worth more alive than dead

The first step to protect forest land is to give it far greater commercial value, close to the value that the same land would have for grazing, fuel, mining and so on.

Novo Aripuana is part of the Brazilian state of Amazonas, where illegal logging is destroying rainforest. The Juma Sustainable Development Reserve is an area of 1.2 million acres where local people are being paid to prevent trees from being cut down. Each family is allocated their own trees to protect. As long as their trees remain, each family gets $28 a month added to a special debit card. The funds come from carbon trading – as part of REDD. Investment is also made into schools, hospitals, transport, communications and skills training.[16]

Reducing Emissions from Deforestation and Forest Degradation, or REDD, is a global scheme to allow people to sell CO_2 locked inside trees in rainforests, creating carbon credits simply by protecting trees.[17] If the global carbon market grows to around $150 billion a year, and 10 per cent of it is spent protecting forests, the amount available for REDD schemes will be around $15 billion a year. But it could easily go a lot higher – to more than $50 billion a year. These credits are sold in the global market, as easily as oil or gold, to companies that need those credits to offset against their own output of CO_2.[18] Another term for these kinds of efforts is 'avoided deforestation'. The UN, World Bank, Australia, the UK and Norway have already provided $800 million in 2008–09 to get REDD projects going.

Does it work? Deforestation in the Upper Parana Atlantic Forest of Paraguay slowed down by more than 85 per cent after the Zero Deforestation Law came into force in December 2004. Before this, Paraguay had the second highest deforestation rate in the world. Soybean production has not been affected – it is the world's fourth largest exporter. The World Wildlife Fund used satellite images to track what was happening.[19]

A similar scheme is now helping to protect Madagascar's Makira forest. Independent experts warned the government that unless action was taken, deforestation would release more than 9.5 million tons of CO_2 by 2040. The Wildlife Conservation Society (WCS) and Madagascar's government formed a partnership to sell the carbon in the remaining trees. Half the money goes direct to the local community, while the rest is spent on conservation, government, overheads and monitoring.

The Gaia Association has provided ethanol-fuelled stoves to 1,780 refugee families in Ethiopia. Fuel is made from local waste such as molasses left over from sugar production. Fewer trees are cut down and health improves (no smoke and low carbon monoxide gas). Women are also safer, no longer spending long hours collecting wood outside refugee camps where they are often attacked.

CleanCook stoves were developed by a Swedish inventor 30 years ago and sold in developed world markets by Dometic AB. The stoves produce 1.5 kW per burner, close to the output of propane gas or LPG burners.

Carbon credits are also being created through the protection of 750,000 hectares of rainforest in Aceh Province, Indonesia, preventing 100 million tonnes of CO_2 emissions over 30 years. The project will provide income to local communities around Ulu Masen as an incentive to protect the forest.[20]

Venture capital funds are starting to buy these living carbon stores as investments to trade in future, as part of a global conservation effort. Canopy Capital, a private equity firm, has signed a deal to protect 371,000 hectares of rainforest in Guyana, South America. It secured rights to market the value of the forest for such things as biodiversity maintenance and carbon storage, giving 80 per cent of the proceeds back to Guyana. The agreement includes funding a major part of a $1.2 million research and conservation programme each year. The company thinks that each area of rainforest could have a different value, depending on factors such as presence of endangered species, or vulnerable indigenous people, potential for tourism or for harvesting sustainable products, or whether local people benefit from the conservation arrangements. It is developing a formal rating system.

One concern is that once forests start gaining value, there will be a land grab in countries where forest ownership is hard to prove. Another is that satellite images are only a general picture of what is happening on the ground. For example, there is some evidence that natural recovery of forest may be happening in some places faster than first thought. Monitoring is a real challenge with all these schemes, as is proving the real levels of protection, and being sure how long that protection will be in place. Satellite pictures can certainly help dissuade loggers from wantonly destroying whole areas of forest.

Online shopping plants a new forest

Treehoo.com is a new search engine, owned by a Swedish company that gives 50 per cent of profits to plant trees in developing nations. (NASA estimates our world needs 130 billion more trees in addition to the 400 billion on earth today to capture CO_2 emitted by human activity since the 1800s.) This year's global revenues from all online search, online advertising and e-shopping is around $350 billion, which means that if all searches and shopping were done through the site, 130 billion more trees could be paid for in a year. After only a few weeks, the site was already one of the 1,000 busiest in Europe.

How much carbon can forests store?

Trees remove CO_2 as they grow, but when the tree dies and decays, or is cut and burned, the carbon is released back into the atmosphere. The balance between storage and release of carbon by a mature forest can change depending on conditions.

A fully mature forest can only store more carbon than it releases if some of the carbon it fixes each year is permanently stored underground, for example in acid bog, which prevents decay. Forests can also increase carbon storage if trees are harvested in a sustainable way, and some of that wood is turned into long-term products. So long as more wood is kept in existing products than is destroyed by burning old products, the amount of carbon kept out of the atmosphere will grow.

In areas where 'slash-and-burn' is practised, switching to 'slash-and-char' can prevent rapid deforestation and subsequent degradation of soils. Charcoal is a stable form of carbon, produced by the slow burning of wood with only limited access to air. When mixed with biomass it creates terra preta, one of the richest soils on the planet. Such biochar stimulates microbial activity and retains moisture and nutrients. It is possible that the carbon may remain in the soil for over 1,000 years.

Biochar may become a new carbon-traded product, made by local farmers to improve their own soil and earn carbon credits. But if it is produced on an industrial scale, biochar furnaces may start driving a destructive new market, forcing up the prices of biowaste, which could end up with less food being grown (see pages 52–56 on biowaste pricing and the impact on food growing).

> At Aarstidernes farm in Barritskov, Denmark, is a pyrolysis Sterling engine, powered by wood-chips, which produces 250 kW electricity and heat per hour – and 3.5 cubic metres of charcoal a day. This biochar is used at the farm to improve soil fertility and to put carbon into the soil. If farmers were able to sell carbon trapped in biochar as a carbon credit, the machine would pay for itself in a few years.

Genetically-modified trees can grow faster

Trees vary in the amount of carbon that they capture each year. Eucalyptus and pine are faster growing species – pines store carbon twice as fast as beech trees, depending on growing conditions.[21] That means forest owners can influence the amount of carbon they can trade in their forests, depending on what species they replant in areas which are being logged in a sustainable way.

There are also opportunities to develop faster growing trees. American chestnut, for example, can produce up to three times more wood above ground than similar forest trees. Researchers at Purdue University in the United States have rescued this almost-extinct species, which was wiped out by a fungal attack, and combined its genes with 4 per cent of genes from the Chinese chestnut to make a resistant version. Because the tree also produces a hard wood, it is more likely to be used to make wooden products, tying up carbon longer than if used for paper or cardboard.[22]

Kampala Jellitone Suppliers in Uganda produces biomass briquettes made from agricultural waste. The 130 tonnes of briquettes sold every month reduce deforestation and save about 6.1 tonnes of CO_2 per tonne of briquettes used.

We could go further and alter the genetic code of existing trees in more radical ways to produce super-breeds, but need to be sure that we are not unleashing new life-forms in uncontrolled forest environments.

Paper and cardboard packaging industry – friend or enemy of forests?

Here is an issue that disturbs many people: does the paper and board industry result in deforestation, or does it provide a valuable market for wood, so increasing the land area that is growing trees? The answer varies with country and type of forest.

Let us take a forest that until now has not been actively managed. Such forests are full of dead and decaying wood, and are usually very diverse ecosystems. Harvesting dead trees in such places has zero impact on global warming. They could be burned or turned into products, which eventually end up in landfill. If dead wood is left in the forest, it will be used as carbon-based fuel by fungi, microbes, insects and other creatures, releasing CO_2, except a tiny proportion permanently locked into the forest floor (this is rare unless decomposition is halted in some way, so the wood is permanently preserved).

If living trees are cut from such a forest, then a clearing is made in the canopy in which very little carbon will be captured for the next few years. Undergrowth will flourish, together with small tree saplings, but the total amount of carbon fixed will be less than if that large tree had carried on growing.

Most carbon fixed by each tree is captured only in the last few years of its life, so allowing trees to reach large sizes is vital to efficient forest management, not only in growing more wood faster, but also in carbon capture. By shortening the natural life of forest trees, logging in virgin forest by definition means that carbon capture is less for a while, until those logged spaces recover. But in a regularly logged forest, we soon reach a steady state, where new growing trees are balanced by old trees being harvested. And regular clearance, which increases spaces between trees, will also accelerate growth of trees nearby.

Wood and pulp industry can help give value to growing trees

The biggest contribution of the wood and pulp industry is that it creates a market for new trees, encouraging people to grow more of them in regions where forestry is tightly controlled. If the value of those trees is higher than the land owner can get from grazing poor quality pastures, then old pasture soon gets planted to make new forest. That is the main reason why the amount of forest in Europe has increased by 15 per cent over the last 15 years (by an area the size of Greece), with added incentives from government grants.[23]

The pulp and paper industry is a huge consumer of wood, especially in countries like the United States, Canada, the Nordic countries and Asia-Pacific countries like Japan or Australia – Australia alone has an industry of AU$9 billion a year. The industry is also the fourth highest emitter of CO_2 in the United States.

It takes 40 gigajoules of energy to create a metric ton of finished paper, emitting around 7.3 tons of CO_2. But

Chemrec in Sweden is building a pilot plant to convert black liquor (waste) from the paper industry to produce a biofuel, which could be used to save up to 25 per cent of the country's gasoline and diesel consumption if used in every pulp mill, saving 10 per cent of national CO_2 emissions.

up to 66 per cent of the energy can be recovered in the most efficient mills. The industry has made great strides in reducing carbon use, using wood waste as fuel for boiler heating or for electricity generation, and selling bark for manufacturing into products or as an energy source.

Paper use globally will continue to grow fast

While demand for newsprint and some paper products is declining in many developed nations as a result of the online revolution (loss of readers and advertising revenue), in emerging nations, newspapers and the use of paper are booming. In India, for example, sales of newspapers and magazines are growing by over 12 million a year – a reflection of the rapid growth of India's middle class, itself a result of economic growth of more than 6 per cent a year, even in the 2008/09 global downturn.

China's consumption of all wood-related products has been increasing at an average of 8 per cent a year for many years (mostly paper and cardboard), and India by 11 per cent a year (half is paper and cardboard).[24] In comparison, use of paper in developed nations fell by 6 per cent from 2000 to 2005. However, that was from a very high

Our world uses 60 trillion pieces of paper a year – 5 per cent or 3 trillion is printed in homes or offices.

figure compared to emerging economies: Americans still use 300 kilograms of paper every year, compared to only 4 kilograms in India (and less than 1 kilogram a year per person in 20 African nations).

Paper use has *increased* in the United States and parts of Europe, not decreased, over the last five years, despite the proliferation of e-mails. One reason is reading speed and poor screen contrast or resolution. The human eye can process over 3,000 million pieces of information a second, including changes in colour tone, but a computer screen delivers a tiny fraction of this. Most people can scan printed paper (books, magazines, large reports or newspapers) up to 10 times faster than they can wade through long documents online. That is one reason why sales of books in the United States increased 2.5 per cent from 2002 to 2008. Electronic book readers will not wipe out the paper book industry any time soon.

You can make notes in paper copies of large reports, they are easier to refer to in meetings, and you can tear pages out for later use. All of these features mean that the paper industry will continue to grow globally, especially when you consider the paper 'famine' that exists in most African countries, even in schools.

The average business spends £300–£1,000 a year per person printing documents – energy, paper (80 per cent of the cost) and waste (including cartridges). That's around 1 to 3 per cent of the entire earnings of many companies, but only one in three large organizations have any idea how much they print.

e-Paper is often talked about: flexible, thin, low cost, high resolution. We still have far to go. In the meantime, expect a flurry of e-readers. Plastic Logic has a device the size of an 8.5 × 11 inch pad of paper, less than 1/3 inch thick, which weighs less than many periodicals. Future e-readers or e-books will allow freehand annotation, search and online access. But they will all have to compete with every other electronic display, including smart phones and pocket computers.

On balance, across the world we can expect a 2 per cent growth of the paper industry each year from now to beyond 2020. Much of that growth will be met by rapid expansion of paper and board exports from South America, Russia and China, which will increase pressure on their own forests, while European paper production will remain more stable or decline.

The publishing industry has led the way in recycling – newsprint reuse is well established in many nations, and new processes have enabled the proportion of recycled paper to be increased in high quality products. For example, the English editions of *Harry Potter and the Deathly Hallows* were made from 30 per cent recycled paper and 65 per cent from forests that are managed in a socially and environmentally responsible way. This saved 197,685 trees and 22 million pounds of paper, and a huge amount of energy as well as water use.

Cardboard packaging will grow fast

Cardboard use is also going to grow fast, as plastic packaging falls from favour around the world, whether this is plastic bags or containers that pollute streets and landfill. Plastics almost always use up carbon from oil, and can last thousands of years, buried in the earth. However, the plastics industry has hit back, pointing out that plastic locks carbon away almost forever, unless burned, and so dumping plastic in landfill is a form of long-term carbon storage. It has also developed better ways to print onto plastic bottles for example, and has redesigned bottle shapes using less plastic, to try to push back against companies like Tetrapak, which has 70 per cent of the market for cardboard-containing containers of liquid foods such as fruit juice and milk.

Newer kinds of plastics have been made from starch (food), which decompose in landfill over three years. But biodegradable plastics not only increase competition for food in global markets, potentially increasing food prices in the same way as biofuels from food, but also release their carbon back into the atmosphere.

Even biodegradable plastic will not reverse the trend to more paper and board packaging, and cardboard will continue to dominate packaging for all dry products that are transported around the world. Cardboard is convenient, strong and cheap, and cartons fold down to a compact size when not in use. We can also expect more re-useable cartons, which have smart features built into their walls using RFID chips so that packages can be tracked and located.

'Lexmark is a $4.5 billion print company serving many of the world's largest companies. It aims to save corporation print costs by 40 per cent and to reduce the environmental impact of that printing by 65 per cent, by reducing energy use, 100 per cent recycled cartridges and recycling more paper.'[25]

Chris Baker, UK and Ireland Sales Director, Lexmark

Cooking stoves

Malawi lost 75 per cent of its forests between 1972 and 1992 and continues to lose 2.8 per cent a year, much of the wood being used in cooking. This usually produces emissions inside homes, estimated to cause 1.6 million premature deaths a year, half among children under 5 years old, according to the World Health Organization. Cooking stoves will be responsible for a significant proportion of the 83 million Chinese citizens who will die from lung cancer and respiratory disease over the next 25 years (Harvard University research). Cooking stoves increase the risk of pneumonia, cataracts and tuberculosis (University of California, Berkeley).

The first wave of innovation in stove design was to reduce deforestation by allowing fuel to burn more slowly and efficiently. For example, Hestion stoves reduce the amount of wood needed for cooking by 80 per cent compared to an open fire. The next step is to make the home smoke-free. Envirofit stoves (sponsored by the Shell Foundation) draw air in a precise way to burn fuel more completely at higher temperatures. The Oorja stove developed by BP and the Indian Institute of Science does the same thing using an integrated, battery-powered fan to direct air onto wood pellets.

Both fail to deal with smokeless polluting gases. One way to do that is to vent them outside, or use propane gas or pellets, or solar radiation onto a cooking vessel – but most villagers in rural areas in places like Africa cook their main meal as the sun starts to go down.

Stoves need to be designed for local cooking methods and foods. For example, the dough for assida, eaten in Darfur, requires very vigorous pot stirring, during which some of the new pot designs fall over. In Darfur two-thirds of the fuel was being used to make sauces by frying onions, while designers had made stoves mainly for boiling water. Oorja's stove is not hot enough to cook traditional Indian breads, and just 3 per cent of chimneys in one Indian project were actually being used (*Economist*, 6 December 2008).

ACTION

Business action

Make sure you are able to trace the origins of the wood you use in manufacturing, especially hard woods. Make a commitment to further reduce waste by 20 per cent over the next two years, and to recycle or use wood chips as well as off-cuts, perhaps in your own biowaste boiler. Get a member of your team to do a paper/print audit and include it in your internal reporting. Set a target for reducing internal printing, and also for a major reduction in costs per sheet, with energy efficient printers, 100 per cent recycled cartridges, 100 per cent recycled paper for day-to-day internal use and so on. However, remind people that reading and commenting on long documents can be very inefficient on-screen – use common sense.

Consumer action

Recycle all newspapers and other paper. Reduce the amount of printer paper you buy – put yourself on a ration and reload paper printed only on one side. Burn waste wood from garden trees in a stove or boiler (use a clean air stove in cities). Do all you can to reduce the amount of wood going into landfill. Recycle all cardboard boxes and packaging.

We have seen how water and forests are both vital to our planet's future, and both are linked to food production – or rather food production can result in burnt forests and dried-up rivers. So how can we grow enough food to feed our growing population?

CHAPTER TEN
FEEDING THE WHOLE WORLD

Every day they gather under the trees during the school lunch break: 430 children in Sudan, waiting for the women to stir the hot porridge they have cooked on an open wood fire in a huge old oil drum. The children silently form long lines, holding their own metal plates that they bring each day from home. For many this will be their only meal of the day. Some have walked up to three hours through the bush in bare feet to get there, and will walk another three hours home before the sun goes down.

In a nearby village we found Kima: it was hard for us to tell just by looking if he was starving or not. His legs were thin, his tummy large but there can be other reasons for both. Just another nine-year-old AIDS orphan in the African bush, being looked after by a grandmother with little food. But he was certainly very hungry.

Perhaps the greatest moral challenge in our world today is the fact that over 1 billion people do not have enough to eat. Most are hungry. Many are losing weight. With weakened bodies, these people are vulnerable to infection and have little energy to work the land. Their children are born with health and mental problems because they were poorly nourished in the womb, and after birth they lack enough milk to thrive.

If this is the situation today, what about tomorrow? How do we feed an additional 3 billion people by 2050? And how do we do it all without destroying the remaining rainforests in the process of creating new farmland?

Population growth will fall

Here is some good news on population growth. While global population is likely to reach 9 billion by 2050, it is expected to fall slowly after that, so our food challenges will stabilize. Seventy nations already have fertility rates at or lower than replacement levels. Children per couple in Europe have halved from 2.7 during the baby boom to 1.4 today. Average family size in developing nations also fell from six to three children from 1950 to 2000. Bangladesh family size has halved in 20 years. In Iran it fell from seven in 1984 to 1.9 by 2006.[1]

Wealth is the reason: fertility drops fast when people start earning between $1,000 and $2,000 and usually reaches replacement levels at $4,000 to $10,000 a year.[2] In the poorest communities there is no social security, no pension and no protection in a crisis. Protection comes from many children. And as fertility falls, ageing becomes a serious issue, as in China which is old compared to India because of the one-child policy.

> One in five of all humans that have ever been born are alive today.

Contraception as a climate change strategy

Contraception may be five times cheaper than any green tech in preventing climate change.[3] A London School of Economics report suggests that every £4 spent on family planning over the next 40 years would reduce emissions of CO_2 by a ton, while green tech investment of £19 would be needed to do the same. The UN estimates that up to 40 per cent of births are unplanned. If all these family planning needs were met, it would save nearly six times the emissions of the United States or almost 60 times the emissions of the UK. UN data suggests that a large investment in family planning would reduce peak global population to 8.64 billion by 2050, from more than 9 billion.

Food and farming

Food production neglected for 30 years

Food production has been a neglected area for 30 years. Development aid to improve farming fell from 17 to 3.8 per cent between 1980 and 2006.[4]

Developing nations themselves have been investing only around 5 per cent of public revenues in farming.[5]

Up to 50 per cent of grain harvested in the poorest rural communities is eaten by mice and rats.

That is why crop yields have been rising recently by only 1–2 per cent a year (not at all in many of the poorest nations) compared to the 1960s 'green revolution' when yields grew annually by 3–6 per cent.[6] However, the food price shock of 2007–08 made governments realize how much momentum had been lost, while populations continue to grow. Basic agriculture is running at full capacity: 2008 crops were the largest ever and almost all global farming land is being cultivated. After a short fall, prices rose again by 10 per cent in the first 10 months of 2009.

Hunger is a hidden problem: unless someone is on the edge of starvation there is little to see. A young child or mother may be thin but that is easily blamed on other health problems. Only in the final stages of serious and prolonged starvation do we see children or adults with swollen bellies. In any case, there is far more to nutrition than weight: a child may look fine, but lack enough protein, minerals or vitamins to encourage brain development. A whole generation of children can grow up permanently damaged by a couple of years of failed harvests.

USAID buys surplus US food to give to relief agencies fighting hunger, but this 'food dumping' can reduce the incomes of local farmers. USAID is now trying to help farmers in recipient countries to harvest, store and sell more of their own food.

Almost all the worst impacts of climate changes will fall on the poorest of the poor, mainly because of hunger or thirst or both. We have already seen how water supplies can be better managed; that almost all water used today is for growing food. But there is more to feeding the whole world than managing water.

When food runs out and your children are hungry

People living in the poorest urban communities spend up to 80 per cent of their daily income on food, just to survive. When food prices double, parents cannot feed their children. They sell their furniture and other equipment to buy food. When they have sold even the utensils they use for cooking, what happens then? History shows that people often take to the streets in rage and frustration. Large-scale riots can develop within hours in such situations with very little organization, as we saw around the world in 2008, in countries from Haiti to Bangladesh.[7]

Since 2007 there have been food riots in more than 60 nations. Food riots toppled the Haitian government and destabilized other nations, from Senegal to Mexico, while the government of Madagascar was overthrown in a coup after agreeing in 2008 to lease half of the nation's entire arable land to South Korea.[8]

As Hilary Clinton, US Secretary of State, said recently:

> Massive hunger poses a threat to the stability of governments, societies and borders. Food security is not just about food. But it is about all security – economic security, environmental security, even national security.[9]

That is why military strategists are now employing food experts to help them anticipate future flashpoints around the world. High food prices can encourage extremist groups and lower thresholds for city riots.

UK consumers throw away up to £10 billion of food every year.[10]

Nations trading huge areas of farmland with other nations

Concerns about security are why some nations are buying up huge chunks of farmland in other countries. Over the last two years an area equal to all the farmland in France has been handed over for $20–30 billion to nations such as Saudi Arabia, Kuwait and China. The sellers are some of the world's poorest nations: Sudan, Ethiopia, Congo and Pakistan, nations which themselves at times have huge problems with feeding their own people. These mega-land deals are government to government, but may end with many small farmers forced off the land, with little or no land rights.[11]

The only purpose for these deals is to secure future food for wealthy nations. But those food supplies will be most useful at times of global shortages, when prices are highest: the very time when Sudan, Ethiopia and other land-traders may most need their own food to prevent hunger in their own people.

So countries that pay for these land deals are taking a big gamble. How are they going to be able to drive big containers of grain *out* of a country where every night the world sees their starving children on the TV news, and international food aid going in? They risk either such food containers being officially seized by the government or being attacked and looted by local people, or the legal agreements being torn up. And how would such agreements be enforced? Trade sanctions or countries declaring was?

The world can feed 9 billion people if farmed better

Food production touches on complex and interwoven issues. For example, in the earlier chapter on water use we have seen how companies can manage their own water supplies by trading 'virtual water' in food exports or imports (page 129).

Here are some of the ways that we can increase food production:

- *New ways to grow farmed fish* – without fishing for their food. Feeding wild fish to farmed fish is very destructive to limited marine resources. We can also develop new breeds of fish through conventional means or by genetic engineering which grow faster on less food (though there are risks that escaped fish interbreed in uncontrolled ways or compete for food).

- *Better ways to produce meat* – vegetarian substitute 'meat', or breeding more efficient cattle, sheep, pigs and chickens.

- *Better distribution* – reduce waste from rotten food. Most food grown in poorer nations is lost before it has a chance to be consumed. Depending on the crop, up to 50 per cent may be lost in the field, eaten by animals or spoiled. Up to 15 per cent is damaged during processing, transport and storage.¹³

- *Encouraging less food waste at home* – 30 per cent of US food, worth $48.3 billion, is thrown away each year.¹⁴ Every year the average UK household throws away food worth £424, mostly into landfill where it releases methane. Retailers should stop '2 for 1' offers, which encourage over-buying, change 'best-by' dates to 'safe-use-by', and sterilize food using techniques such as food irradiation, which is much safer than many fear.

- *End damaging and uncompetitive food subsidies*, eg by the EU. One of the fastest ways to help food production in the poorest nations is to cut the 40 per cent of the EU budget that is given in subsidies to farmers or fisheries – a total of €48 billion or 0.3 per cent of the entire EU economy.¹⁵ The poorest nations cannot compete with such EU farmers, either when trying to export to the EU, or in competition in other markets with EU produce. This damages their agricultural investment and prevents them earning currency from one of the main parts of their economies. To make matters worse, the EU charges variable import taxes on food.

Huge jump in farming yields in some nations

Most developing nations have stepped up support for their own farmers, building better roads to market, subsidizing seeds and fertilizers and providing safety nets to the poorest growers:[16]

- The Philippines set up a seed bank to improve seed quality and provide a reserve when crops are wrecked by typhoons.

- Lesotho and Uganda created 'seed fairs' to increase the varieties used.

- Tanzania and Mali are subsidizing the use of better grain and fertilizers.

- Nepal and Jamaica provided low cost water pumps for small-scale irrigation.

- Malawi is spending 4.2 per cent of GDP on low cost fertilizers to farmers. In 2005 the country imported 40 per cent of food, but in 2009 exported 50 per cent of what it grew, trebling maize harvests in four years.

- Brazil provided credit for 14,000 tractors in 12 months and a guaranteed purchase by the state of $800 of food a year (for reserves and to feed children at school).

- India guaranteed 100 days of minimum-wage labour to every rural household that asks, and introduced agricultural debt waivers for 40 million farmers, following the failed monsoon of 2009. Despite huge economic growth, India remains home to 33 per cent of the world's undernourished children.[18]

> Maize yields are growing twice as fast as rice and wheat, because new strains of maize are developed mainly by private companies with $1.5 billion investment a year, while wheat and rice development is mainly in government labs with only $350 million.[17]

Meat eating uses up more food

Over 30 per cent of the world's cereal harvest and 90 per cent of soy harvest is eaten by farmed animals; some cows need up to 16 kilograms of grain for every kilogram of meat they produce.[19] Every year our world now slaughters 55 billion animals – up from only 10 billion in 1965 – as incomes and populations rise.[20]

> Stonyfield Farm sells more than $300 million worth of yogurt – 7 per cent of the US market. It uses edible cups, 100 per cent renewable energy and a nutrition programme to reduce carbon emissions from its cows.

Eating less meat, or cutting out meat entirely, is one of the most important choices we can make to reduce our personal carbon emissions. Cattle grazing is one of the most powerful forces driving the destruction of rainforests, together with more land being needed to grow animal feed.

All this is going to create huge demand for phosphate to make fertilizer, but known reserves could run out in 100 years. Most comes from Morocco/Western Sahara, China, the United States, South Africa and Jordan. Expect many steps to improve nutrient management in agriculture, and in recovery of nutrients from waste (water) or manure/human excretions.

Is genetically modified food safe?

Genetically modified food is made by putting genes from one organism into another to try to improve yields, resistance to disease or drought, and so on. There are three main issues with GM crops: the first is human safety, the second is biodiversity and the third is the wider environmental risk. Human safety has been a big concern since the first GM food trials, but is becoming less worrying to food regulators as we become more familiar with the changes that have been made.

Genetic modification can be used in all kinds of ways. Unilever created a creamy and healthy ice-cream by adding the genes for an ice-structuring protein in Arctic fish to create a new kind of baker's yeast. The yeast makes the protein, which keeps ice-cream softer when frozen at low temperatures, while keeping fat content lower than it would otherwise have to be.

Some crops have been engineered to be completely resistant to a specific brand of very effective weed-killer. This means that farmers can plant a crop and then totally destroy all other plant life in the field on a regular basis. Biodiversity falls, and stresses increase on wildlife. The seeds are sterile so every year the farmers have to go back to the weed-killer and seed manufacturers, which is not a sustainable solution for those in the poorest nations who expect to grow each year from last year's harvest.

Wider environmental risk could arise if genetically modified plants fertilize natural plants, producing new hybrids in an uncontrolled way. The danger is that some new type of plant will arise with unexpected consequences, becoming a real nuisance as a weed. We know that pollen from GM crops can travel a surprising distance, which is also a concern for organic farmers who want none of such material on their land.

Solar greenhouses mean more food. GERES has helped villagers in the Himalayan region of India grow more food by helping them grow vegetables in passive solar greenhouses (Ashden Awards, 2009 winner).

For these reasons, and others, GM crops remain controversial, touted by some as one of the main answers to global food shortages, and attacked by others as a real danger to the environment. Consumers in the United States are much more relaxed about eating GM food than many Europeans. For example, US farmers are allowed to inject their cows with artificial growth hormone to increase their milk yield. In Europe such practices are regarded as unethical (suffering for the cow) as well as possibly unhealthy.

Reducing methane in agriculture

Genetic engineering of cows and sheep could create animals that absorb more carbon from their diet, producing less methane. Animal production creates 100 million tons of methane gas a year; 80 per cent is from decomposing waste but 20 per cent is from the bowels of cows and sheep. Cows produce more methane when given cheap, low-quality grain-based feed.[21]

Allowing cows to graze on pasture is healthier, for cows and humans, reduces the need for cultivation and transport of feed, as well as storage and spreading of manure, all of which use fossil fuels. Ten per cent of agricultural methane comes from the wet fields where rice is grown.

Thirty-three per cent of all human-linked greenhouse gas emissions are from food production, transport, packaging and cooking.

Factory farms produce more food but animals and workers suffer

While countries like the UK are moving away from factory farming, with strict controls on the rearing of pigs, for example, many of the poorest nations are only just discovering how much more food they can grow by enclosing animals in tiny spaces.

Animals often suffer in these conditions, and human health can also be affected with the spread of bacteria like salmonella among chickens for example. There is also the risk from dusty conditions for workers: up to 70 per cent develop acute bronchitis, of whom a third develop chronic bronchitis.[22]

Reducing food miles – shorter distance to market

Food can travel further than most shoppers realize, which wastes resources. However, it is easy also to over-react, in buying only local produce, which can wipe out the incomes of the poorest farmers in developing nations.

Here are some ways to reduce food miles. Researchers at Rutgers University estimated that supplying the State of New Jersey with tomatoes from other States was using up enough diesel each year to drive a large truck around the world 249 times.[23] Fish caught off the coast of Maine are flash frozen, shipped to China for processing into filets, and shipped back to the United States. In 2007, the United States exported 1.4 billion pounds of beef and veal (5.4 per cent of total beef production), and imported 3 billion pounds of the same.[24]

Multi-storey greenhouses

Most people live in cities but most food is grown in rural areas – often thousands of miles away. Plantagon has a vision to develop multi-storey greenhouses in cities. These structures will grow four times as much food per acre as normal greenhouses, and can be built up to 150 metres high. A spiral conveyor belt carries new plants in a continuous circle around and up the sides of the building to be harvested at the top. These iconic structures could become tourist attractions, as well as providing healthy, local food in a sustainable way.

Fair trade products for sustainable farming

Over 4,500 brands of sustainable coffee, tea, fruit, flowers and clothes are now part of the Fair Trade scheme. Sales were $4 billion in 2008, increasing by more than 20 per cent a year (40 per cent in UK, from 2007 to 2008), representing 1–20 per cent of all trade in some categories in the United States and the EU.[25] Growers are given a higher price as well as investment in their local communities. Seven and a half million farmers and their families are already benefiting from Fair Trade-funded infrastructure, technical assistance and community development projects.[26]

Biodiversity matters in plant and animal breeding

As farmers focus on higher yields, more of them are cultivating a small group of super-performing breeds of crops and animals. As a result, our world is losing an average of two domestic animal breeds each week, and half of all European farm animal breeds that existed in 1900 are now extinct.

Over 300 out of 6,000 breeds worldwide have died out in 15 years, with 1,350 in danger. Almost 96 per cent of vegetable types farmed in 1903 have been lost. More than 1,500 local rice varieties in Indonesia are extinct.[28] Ninety per cent of all animal-derived foods come from only 14 breeds. Twelve plant crops account for more than 75 per cent of the food grown in the world, while 75 per cent of all rice, wheat and maize come from only 12 plant species.[29]

> Green and Blacks chocolate is all Fair Trade and organic and has been a runaway success, becoming a global brand in just a few years, before being bought by Cadbury. Cadbury then converted all its Dairy Milk Bars to Fair Trade chocolate from Ghana.
>
> Starbucks buys 175,000 tons of coffee a year – 75 per cent of which is Fair Trade certified, supporting 1 million growers and their families. It is aiming for 100 per cent Fair Trade by 2015.[27]

The trouble with super-breeds is that they are all 'built' in the same way with similar patterns of resistance and vulnerability to infection. Farmers across whole nations become exposed to a risk of 'plague'. In 1970, US farmers lost $1 billion worth of crops after a disease killed a small number of types of corn. There was a huge outbreak of citrus canker in Florida in 1984 and in Brazil in 1991. During the 1840s, more than half the population of Ireland was growing a single variety of the potato. One fungus destroyed the entire potato crop, causing the Irish Potato Famine.[30]

Sustainable farming must mean greater diversity, making sure we do not hold the world hostage to a deep vulnerability inside a genetically modified super-breed.

The future of the sea and fishing

Melting glaciers and ice sheets on land are causing a rise in sea levels, probably an average of 2 mm a year over the last 40 years,[31] but it is hard to measure these things because the changes are small so far, and entire land masses are also moving slowly up and down on different tectonic plates. For instance, London is sinking into the sea while the west of the UK is rising.

Sea levels really do matter, as 10 per cent of the world population lives within 10 km of the coast, over half within 100 km (62 miles).[32]

Some scientists fear that sea levels may rise at least 80 centimetres this century, while the Intergovernmental Panel on Climate Change forecast 18–59 cm this century. Warmth causes water to expand, contributing to perhaps 10–20 cms of that total.[33]

If half the west Antarctic and Greenland ice sheets melt, sea levels will rise by 7 metres. The Arctic has lost over 40 per cent of its year-round ice since 1985, 14 per cent in 2004–5 alone, but these things vary from year to year. The winter of 2009 was very cold, but it is the longer trend that matters. West Antarctica lost ice 75 per cent faster in 2006 than in 1996.[34] In 2008 the Wilkins shelf in Antarctica lost 2,000 square kilometres of ice in six months. Greenland lost 1,500 cubic kilometres of ice from 2000 to 2008, making it responsible for a sixth of recent global seal level rises of 3 mm a year.[35] As ice melts, it reveals darker sea, which in turn absorbs more sunlight.[36]

A third of all CO_2 emissions are absorbed by oceans, forming carbonic acid, and the sea is already 30 per cent more acidic than 250 years ago. Eventually clams, mussels and other creatures with shells of calcium carbonate may find their protective covering starts to dissolve, while corals could fall apart.[37]

Ninety-five per cent of coral reefs have been damaged, 25 per cent have been lost, and all are vulnerable to global warming.[38] We are also seeing explosions of toxic algae, or red tides, fed by nitrogen-rich river water, polluted by fertilizers. Toxic algae kill fish and damage the entire ecosystem.

Cleanfish connects small-scale fish suppliers with distributors to get sustainable seafood to restaurant kitchens and supermarkets. 'Cleanfish Evangelists' educate chefs and consumers about how they source fish. Their 24 artisan fish producers have doubled sales each year for the last three years, now more than $20 million a year.

Future of fishing

Millions of square miles of sea beds have been turned into a marine desert by trawlers with huge nets, which scrape up every living creature of significant size, throwing huge quantities back dead. Shoals of fish have no chance against digital technology, and even the smallest vessels can locate whatever is below.

Ninety per cent of large predatory fish such as tuna, swordfish and sharks have gone and 85 per cent of large whales have disappeared from coastal waters.[39] A third of US fish stocks are overfished.[40] In the 1970s, from the West Coast of the United States boats were landing 11,000 tons of boccaccio a year – which fell to 214 tons in 2001. It could take 90 years for stocks to fully recover. If fishing is not controlled globally, most species currently fished will have almost disappeared by 2048.[41]

Yet despite all this, UK fishing boats still landed 750,000 tons of Atlantic fish in 2006, 66 per cent of the 1951 total catch. Worldwide, the total tonnage caught was over 93 million in 2006, compare with just 19 million in 1950. One reason was better technology to target shoals.[42]

One million tons of edible fish are thrown back dead every year, by EU boats that have accidentally caught fish that are already 'overfished' and outside their legal quotas for that year.[43] Between 40 per cent and 60 per cent of all fish caught by trawlers in the North Sea is dumped back into the ocean – a monumental waste of marine life.[44] Best quality cod, haddock and other prime fish are among them.

It would be best to abandon such a mad quota system and, if necessary call a temporary halt to *all* fishing in certain areas, to allow every type of fish to recover, since the fishing industry is incapable of targeting one type of fish without massacring other vulnerable stocks of similar size and habits. The trouble is that dumping happens in secret: records are impossible to keep without continuously policing every boat.

Traditional patterns of 'wild fishing' are unsustainable. Expect marine zones to be introduced globally by 2020, with 'sea maps' showing what activities are permitted where – whether drilling and mining, or fishing. The United States alone controls 4.4 million square miles of ocean, 25 per cent more than its land area.[45]

Fish farming must be major part of the answer

Future generations will think it as bizarre to watch huge fishing boats, with nets up to 5 miles long, motoring out to sea, as we do today thinking about cowboys in the mid-west United States shooting 280,000 wild buffalo a year in the last century. The reason that farmers in the United States began large beef farms is because easy kills of wild buffalo and other game had come to an end.

Fish farming could be a sustainable way to feed hundreds of millions of people with low-fat protein. Around half of all fish we eat in the EU already comes from fish farms – up from 34 per cent or 48 billion tons in 2007, worth around $71 billion. Cod, crayfish, bream, halibut, mussels, salmon and sturgeon are all farmed, and 70 per cent of the world's farmed fish are grown in China.

Fish farms are ideal for small local communities in low income countries to run, whether in lakes, dams or sheltered sea inlets. They are easy to build with a few nets on floats attached to a landing platform. Harvesting is straight-forward, and so long as the fish are fed regularly, the water is suitable, and fish are not too densely packed, the result can be a steady form of additional income alongside subsistence farming.

However, farmed fish are vulnerable to parasites and other infectious diseases, and are often treated with drugs, which can add to water pollution. Infections can also jump into wild fish stock. Farmed fish can escape when nets are faulty, competing with local fish for food, damaging food chains, and interbreeding in harmful ways.[46]

There is a more fundamental problem that needs to be solved before fish farming can become a truly sustainable means of feeding the world on a large scale: most fish we like to eat are predators, so they need to be fed fish themselves. It takes 1 kilo of fish meal to add 1 kilo to a farmed fish. In one sense that is good news: fish are much more efficient in converting their food into growth than cows, kilo for kilo. But it takes more than one kilo of fish to produce a kilo of fish meal.

Fish meal is usually made from anchovies, menhaden or sardines, which together account for almost a fifth of all catches annually, while another fifth of such marine harvesting goes to pigs and chickens. As these tiny fish become less plentiful, there are pressures to catch the next sizes up, further damaging food chains and the wider ecology. Young fish that should have been fished when older get caught up in the system, and sea birds go hungry.

One answer is to create genetically modified fish that thrive on a vegetarian diet – but the risk is that they will escape, with unknown consequences. And of course, the grain would still need to be sourced from somewhere.

In summary, food is a fundamental human need together with clean water, shelter, basic health, education and security. We already have all the technol-ogy and breeds we need to feed today's population. It is a scandal that a billion still go hungry at a time when a quarter of the world eats too much, and where wasted food alone could supply all the spare food we need. Such food shortages cause intolerable human suffering, and are a great moral stain on our world, for which we deserve to be judged harshly by future generations. The shortages also produce serious instability in nations.

Innovation at every step in the food process will deliver a new agricultural revolution, with healthier diets at reasonable cost. This revolution will require commitment from governments to end food import bans from poorer nations, and agricultural subsidies, as well as a commitment to ban food from biofuel factories.

In some parts of the world, where land is already semi-desert, we need to think of other ways to feed people than expecting them to go on growing all their own food. We need to look at new livelihoods that will allow them to continue living in dry countries, earning enough to buy their food from elsewhere. These adjustments, which will include rapid urbanization, will take more than two decades and will be painful for many of those living in such regions, who will need ongoing support during the transition in order to survive.

ACTION

Business action

Food companies are at the centre of change in consumer lifestyle choices. There are huge opportunities for farmers, manufacturers and retailers to gain market share by telling an attractive story about how their food is grown and reaches the table. Openness, transparency, healthy living – all these will be increasingly important. Look again at the formulation of every product and how you can innovate to reduce the resources used, increase nutritional value and increase shelf-life. Look for opportunities to get involved in Fair Trade or to extend the same idea with your own food supplies.

Consumer action

Chose Fair Trade products, and buy local fruit and vegetables if you can. Ignore 'best by' dates that are often far ahead of the date when food becomes unsafe and use your common sense to reduce the amount of food thrown away. Try not to over-buy and use the freezer more to keep your food longer. Remember that almost all the water you use is in the food you eat, and almost all the grain you eat is eaten by the animals whose meat you eat. Consider eating less meat to save food and reduce methane emissions. Choose fish from renewable sources.

So, we have seen how green tech innovation is transforming power generation, travel, cities and manufacturing. We have also seen how innovation can help protect forests, conserve water and will provide enough food to feed the whole world. We now need to look at how all this will be financed, and also at how we can encourage agility and innovation in business.

CHAPTER ELEVEN
FUNDING
GREEN TECH

Offsetting and taxes

In Chapter 1 we saw that all the technology we need for a sustainable future is already here, and that most of it repays its own costs in energy savings alone over a relatively short period. Throughout the rest of the book we have seen a huge number of examples of how green tech investment saves cost, improves profitability, creates better products, feeds the world, protects forests, provides water, helps business to win new customers and survive in the future. But raising the capital to make those initial investments is often a major challenge, especially in the aftermath of the credit crunch, when bank loans have been harder than usual to obtain.

While many governments have tried to fill the gap with a wide range of grants and other incentives, the fastest growing source of funding for green tech is from offsetting and carbon trading.

How to get funding for your green innovation

Ask four hard questions – all venture capitalists will do the same:

1 Do people really need this product 'by yesterday' – ie, is it an urgent and important need? Too many products are created for tiny markets or needs that do not exist (at that price).

2 Does market research confirm there are enough of these potential customers to fund a growing business?

3 What competitors are there, and at what price?

4 Can you make a list of very happy customers to make recommendations?

Most entrepreneurs fail a simple test, which is to be able to convince an investor or customer in a minute or two why their product or service is worth looking at further.

> Most *inventors* focus on the technology rather than the market. Most *investors* focus on the market rather than the technology.

Offsetting – a source for green funding

The greatest source of new funding for green tech will possibly be from off-setting or carbon trading – hundreds of billions of dollars.

Offsetting is a vitally important but controversial way to tackle climate change. It creates a carbon credit that can then be traded. Offsetting could be our most powerful weapon to control carbon emissions. Most important, offsetting could create one of the largest funds our world has ever seen, to help finance sustainable innovation, where the costs do not quite stack up commercially.

Offsetting is in effect a voluntary tax, where all funds raised have to be used in tackling climate change. While it may usually be preferable to invest first in direct energy saving, offsetting creates a great opportunity to go further.

Offsetting is a fast growing area: $7 billion was spent in 2002–07 investing in carbon-reducing schemes as companies began the offsetting stampede. That figure had jumped to $126 billion a year by 2009, representing 2.2 billion tons of CO_2. The Commodity Futures Trading Commission expects carbon trading to hit $2 trillion by 2015, most of which will be the same carbon savings being traded over and over again.[1]

Businesses and governments are spending many millions trying to cancel out their own CO_2 emissions by buying carbon credits, investing in carbon-saving projects around the world. Travel agents and airlines are offering carbon offsets when selling tickets and holidays. Marks & Spencer is aiming to become the first UK retailer to be carbon neutral, and Eurostar has offset the entire carbon use of its high speed rail including energy used in preparing food and drink for passengers and in printing tickets.

We live in a world of great extremes – in wages, wealth and so on. Saving an additional ton of carbon in a country like the United States can cost 5–10 times more than for the same amount in India or China. Offsetting allows companies to shop around globally for the fastest and cheapest way to have the greatest impact.

HSBC carbon free

In 2005 HSBC became a carbon-neutral bank, employing over 200,000 people. HSBC offsets all carbon used in its banking services. In 2007 KLM airline announced that it would offset all growth in carbon use. On current trends that means the airline will offset most flights by 2020. Both companies say they are offsetting because it is the right thing to do – but also believe that it will enhance their corporate image and help their businesses growth.

For example, there could be hundreds of thousands of carbon-saving innovations that are almost commercially viable, but not quite, depending of course on the oil price. Funds raised from buying offsets can be used to turn many of these innovations into reality.

Carbon trading will provide vast new funds for investment in low-carbon technologies, but it could also lead to one of the greatest financial frauds the world has ever seen: super-criminals trading non-existent virtual assets on carbon-saving exchanges. Governments will be slow to prosecute, sometimes compromised by their own fraudulent claims for high carbon use in the past compared to false data on carbon savings today, or by the difficulties of taking action.

Most people accept that offsetting is a good idea once they understand what it actually means. Companies need to explain exactly what they are doing and why, take great care in choosing reliable offset partners, and strictly audit what they do. Larger corporations will create their own offsetting schemes.

If there is no offsetting, companies will only be able to tackle their own emissions, spending huge amounts for small benefit, while outstanding carbon-saving projects in emerging nations collapse for lack of income.

The difference offsetting makes

Offsetting can mean more than 20 times the impact for the same price. Just compare the costs of do-it-yourself climate action with offsetting.

Do-it-yourself

Install solar cell panels on the factory or office roof: every watt of energy produced means less coal, oil or gas is burnt at a power station. Spending £10,000 on installing solar cells will save 40 tons of carbon over the next 15 years.

Cost per ton of carbon saved: £250.

Offset 1

Invest £10,000 in contributing to a carbon offset scheme – maybe part of the costs of a small hydroelectric dam on a river in a rural area where local people are burning oil for central heating for their homes, for hot water and cooking. The dam needs a 25 per cent grant from offsetting to be commercially viable, but the payback is huge. Over the next 15 years the scheme will save around 700 tons of carbon for every £10,000 of offset grant.

Cost per ton of carbon saved: £15.

Offset 2

Provide subsistence farmers in Africa with simple metal cookers that use only 25 per cent of the charcoal normally needed to boil water or cook a meal. Prevent deforestation around villages, towns and cities to make charcoal.

Cost per ton of carbon saved: £12.

Offsetting benefits often arise because they allow small businesses to combine resources, creating economies of scale. For example, you could buy a small wind turbine for the roof of your office, but it would be relatively inefficient compared to a large commercial turbine on a hill top. If a number of small companies combine what they would have spent on roof turbines to invest in a borderline non-viable commercial wind farm, they could have far more impact on carbon reduction.

Every business should consider offsetting as an integral part of its strategy and responsibility.

US: individual states go further than national government

The Regional Greenhouse Gas Initiative developed independently of Federal Government in North East United States, through emissions caps and trading of allowances. It will govern emissions from most power utilities that use more than 50 per cent fossil fuel. The trading scheme extends to older systems for trading air and water pollution.[2]

Why controversial?

There are many challenges, not least in proving rapid, genuine benefit. Some offsetting methods are hotly debated and should be avoided. However, offsetting has a vital part to play in fighting global warming, and will be used by most large companies.

Carbon trading has been attacked by many campaigning groups such as Friends of the Earth, which thinks that it can be a lazy way out for companies that should reduce energy use instead, and that the funds raised may be wasted on useless projects. Even something as simple as large-scale tree planting can have consequences if not carefully planned – such as a loss of biodiversity, people displacement and social disruption.

Friends of the Earth is campaigning instead for direct taxation on all forms of carbon use and regulation of emission production.[3] It argues that this would be easier to police, and countries that refuse to participate could have a carbon tax imposed on all the imports of their goods into participating countries. However, the big question is, what would happen to all that tax revenue? Ideally it would all go into a ring-fenced fund to provide financing for green tech initiatives. In practice it could be lost among all other government spending, which would mean that such a 'carbon tax' would lose half its impact. The stick would be there but the carrot would be missing. Nevertheless, carbon taxes may turn out to be what our world needs, if we continue to find problems in making carbon trades work.

Companies in developed nations are worried that severe restrictions on carbon use will make their products more expensive than those imported from low-regulation emerging nations. Some have called for carbon taxes to be imposed on all imports to the EU from such places. If carbon restrictions in the EU mean more products are imported which are made using carbon wastefully, some fear that the net result could be that the same amount of carbon is used, at a cost to EU companies and with zero benefit to the environment.

The reality is likely to be different. Even if the EU acted alone to halve emissions by 2050 compared to 2005, emission growth in other parts of the world would cancel out only 12 per cent of the EU restrictions. If all industrialized nations took action to reduce emissions by 50 per cent, the 'leakage' rate would fall to only 2 per cent.[4]

The fact remains that however carbon trading is set up the system can be open to abuse. For example, the UN suspended all funding for Chinese wind farms in December 2009, with worries that the government had deliberately cut state subsidies so that many projects would not be viable without UN support, thus qualifying for carbon-related funding. China had won over $1 billion of carbon credits under the Clean Development Mechanism.[5]

The first phase of carbon trading hit problems

The first phase of the European Emissions Trading System, from 2007 to 2009, was not a success, and the current phase, which lasts till 2012, has been filled with problems:

- Carbon price is too low to be useful.

- Incentives to increase emissions in the short term to qualify for extra allowances when set.

- Difficult to verify offsetting actions and impacts.

- Filling pockets of banks, investors and others.

- Destabilization of global economy with vast derivatives trading and use of other complex financial products relating to carbon trades.

- Shifting pollution from developed to developing nations (leakage).

The International Energy Authority has warned that the price of carbon credits will need to more than double to around $50 per ton of CO_2 by 2020 and $110 by 2030 in industrialized nations, to drive green tech fast enough if catastrophic climate change is to be avoided. In developing nations the price will need to be at least $30 a ton by 2020 and $50 by 2030.[6] Carbon was still trading at only $21 at the end of 2009 in the EU, and the United States still has no carbon trading scheme. The Senate has discussed a bill that sets $48 as the ceiling before 2020 and $90 by 2030.[7]

How offsetting can work

An airline has already invested in a new fleet of energy-saving planes, is packing more customers onto every flight and has cut energy in other areas. Its carbon output per passenger per mile flown is now far less than a decade ago. The airline now wishes to offset all remaining fuel use. It forms a partnership with an offsetting company that provides large grants for different energy-saving schemes, and alternative power generation projects, one of which is a series of small hydropower projects on rivers in India. The Indian power company could not make the projects work without a grant from the airline, which covers 30 per cent of construction costs.

What offsetting will cost your business

First we need to calculate the total energy consumption of your company. A complete audit should include an estimate of carbon use in making components or materials for products or processes. Here are some guidelines:

- 1 ton of carbon emitted as CO_2 = £10–15 to offset;
- concrete = 1 ton of carbon per ton of product;
- short-haul return flight = up 0.6 ton;
- executive car driven 12,000 miles = 4 tons;
- gas bill of £550 = 1 ton;
- electricity bill of £1350 = 1 ton.

You can find a carbon calculator at http://www.carbonfootprint.com/calculator.aspx.

Some organizations start by partial offsetting – offsetting conferences, for example.

How offsetting benefits business

As with all 'green' action, offsetting can strengthen corporate image and brand awareness, increase customer loyalty, and help win market share in a highly competitive market where products and services increasingly look almost identical in price and quality. When companies take their responsibilities to the community and environment seriously, it not only attracts customers but also the best talent. People want to work for great companies – not just profitable ones.

A single half-page newspaper advertisement can cost over £25,000, but a half-page of positive editorial coverage can be worth 5–10 times as much in swaying public opinion. Equally, a half-page of negative editorial can be hugely damaging. If a business is one of the first to fully offset, it can expect significant positive media coverage, with help from a skilled media department. So, in free promotion alone the benefits can be significant – more likely if combined with consistent messaging and values.

Belu bottled water

Belu's bottles are made of biodegradable 'plastic' starch made from corn. All carbon used in collecting, bottling, transporting and distributing the bottles is fully offset. For every bottle sold the company promises to provide someone in need with clean water for a month.

Business potential for offsetting companies

Many businesses will sell their carbon savings to others – or be involved in relatively informal carbon trading.

Consider a small business that sells wood-burning boilers to schools and local authorities. Fuel is low-cost waste from nearby wood cutting operations. Each new boiler saves 10 tons of carbon in heating oil each year for 15 years. Each ton saved will be sold online to another business as an offset credit for £15 each. The amount raised is used to lower prices on new boilers by £2,250, boosting sales.

Smaller companies can buy offsets online; see the comparison site: http://www.carboncatalog.org/providers.

ACTION

Business action

The rule is simple: take aggressive steps to reduce your carbon footprint, following the Business Actions at the end of earlier chapters. But when you have done so, offset all the rest. As we have seen this is unlikely to cost you a significant element of your turnover, but it will enable you to make a bold statement that your company is seeking to be carbon neutral. Be a carbon-neutral bus company, airline, food company or management consultancy – but do keep hammering away at reducing your carbon footprint, aiming to cut the amount you offset every year per unit of production or per employee.

Consumer action

Use a carbon calculator to work out the entire carbon consumption of your household, including heating, holidays, commuting and meals out. Then use the Consumer Actions in an earlier chapter to think about ways to reduce it. When you have done so, consider offsetting all the rest. It may cost you less than you think. You will then be on the first step to living in a carbon-neutral way. Each year, review your carbon use and see if you can manage using a smaller offset than the year before.

Both business and consumer action

Do choose carefully where you buy your offsets. You will get greatest value (lower overheads) by choosing a well established company with a strong track record and plenty of great reviews, which arranges private offsetting, rather than one that is UN/EU accredited. Make sure you tell the offsetter to use your money only for funding renewable energy such as wind power, and not schemes like tree planting, which will take some decades to capture most of the carbon promised.

Private funding is growing for green tech

Specialist green tech funds are growing in size but are still very small compared to the rest of the market. For example, Ludgate Environmental Fund invests in clean-tech and environmental companies. An early success was Ceres Power, in which it invested in 2001 and brought to market in 2004, with the share price rising tenfold, enabling the Fund to raise another €20 million.

Another example is Low Carbon Accelerator, the UK's first publicly listed venture capital fund dedicated to eco-companies. The fund went public in

2006, raising €50 million. It focuses on clean energy, energy efficiency, green buildings and greener transport.

Three-quarters of the wealth of countries like the UK is owned by those over the age of 65, and a big proportion of that is held by pension funds. These funds are bound by their own investment policies, and often find it hard to assess the potential of green tech and related businesses. Since 2004, Sustainable Finance has advised more than 50 international financial institutions about investing in sustainability as an industry. It developed the Equator Principles, as an industry standard for environmental and social diligence, used by 60 banks to assess and manage environmental and social risks in projects of €80 million or more. Banks agree only to lend where borrowers can prove that their projects will not harm society or the environment.

In future we can expect a significant proportion of finance for very small green tech businesses to come from microfinance. Hand in Hand is an example of a microfinance agency. It has supported 64,000 small businesses in India – growing by 4,000 a month. All 1,300 staff are Indian and backed by 5,500 volunteers. Loans average $125 and default rates are less than 0.5 per cent. Central administration costs are less than 3 per cent. Hand in Hand was founded by Percy Barnevik, former Chairman of ABB and of AstraZeneca. His aim is to help create 1.3 million new jobs in 250,000 new businesses in Tamil Nadu state alone, and 50 million new jobs worldwide over a decade.

Microfinance International was a start-up in 2003, providing financial services to Latin American workers living in the United States, who send over $69 billion home every year, often paying huge charges. MFI helps with remittances, cheque cashing, microloans and other services, which enable low-income workers to build financial knowledge and a credit history. It serves 70,000 people with a staff of 80, generating around $10 million in revenues.

These kinds of organizations promote small-scale economic development, and many social enterprises are started in this way.

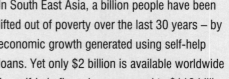

In South East Asia, a billion people have been lifted out of poverty over the last 30 years – by economic growth generated using self-help loans. Yet only $2 billion is available worldwide for self-help financing compared to $110 billion a year in development aid.

So, we have looked at hundreds of green tech innovations, and also at how they can be funded. But how do companies stay agile and innovative in this rapidly changing situation? How can we harness the creative energies of all our people to stay ahead as a dynamic, forward thinking and successful company?

CHAPTER TWELVE
BUSINESS AGILITY AND INNOVATION

Entrepreneurs will lead the way

If you're not failing every now and again, it's a sign you're not doing anything very innovative.

Woody Allen, actor and film producer

As we have seen in the previous chapters, many thousands of new green tech entrepreneurs are driving many new products to market. Some are working inside other people's companies, but the great majority have left to start their own.

Entrepreneurs are the life-blood of all societies and agents of change: they take risks and break through barriers. They have unstoppable self-belief and energy, engage investors, create new companies, form tribes of committed followers and kill old methods. They create wealth out of change, and new business out of crises.

These green tech entrepreneurs are both trend-spotters and trend-makers. Some of these entrepreneurs also work inside larger companies, keeping them agile, open to new thinking, on the edge.

The more agile you are, the better your vision needs to be

Agility is vital: being able to adapt and survive. Life is too fast to have only one strategy. Agility means having contingencies, being ready for different options, anticipating sudden changes in strategy by competitors, and being prepared for a quick purchase of a company that is short of cash and undervalued.

However, agility brings its own risks. The more agile and responsive you are, the more foresight you need, as well as depth of understanding of the wider market. Otherwise your agility may lead to rash decisions, taken too fast.

The puzzle of innovation

So, how do we encourage agility and innovation in response to all these changes? How do you keep your most agile, innovative and entrepreneurial people from leaving to start their own businesses or to work for a more dynamic competitor? And if you do manage to keep them, how do you harness their potential?

Here is a strange paradox: many CEOs complain about lack of innovation, but their own workers often say their leaders are hostile to new ideas. That's why innovation workshops are often electrifying, as they unleash all this frustrated creative power.

The first thing to do is change your culture by the way you behave as a leader or manager. For example, always reward those whose ideas are used, honour them publicly, give them ongoing profile, show them why their innovation has made such a difference to many people's daily lives, and before long you are likely to see more innovations.

Give them a clear vision and focus on the problem

When people have a clear vision of where you are going, and are passionate about making it a reality, you can't *stop* innovation and you also encourage agility: great ideas, concrete solutions, practical down-to-earth immediate actions to get great results. You are also more likely to get great cooperation, rapid agreement, solid effort, readiness to change and astonishing progress.

Give people space, allocate time as a team, encourage wild unusual thinking, think the 'unthinkable', don't interfere, be slow to criticize an early idea, use every suggestion as a learning opportunity, expect answers to come from unusual approaches – they often do – and *have fun!*

Innovative combinations

- Someone put a trolley and a suitcase together and got a suitcase with wheels.
- Someone put an igloo with a hotel and got an ice palace (a winter hotel made of ice, in Sweden).
- Someone put a copier and a telephone together and got a fax machine.
- Someone put a bell and a clock together and got an alarm clock.

People often don't bother because they don't understand the bigger picture, think the benefit is likely to be small, that someone else will do it, that there will be no demand for the idea, or because they are worried about failure and being blamed for trying something 'stupid'. So do make really sure your mission is clear and that people know *why* their work is really important.

CEOs behave differently in agile and innovative organizations. For example they may promise to respond to every e-mailed idea from anyone at any level in the organization. Anyone whose idea is used should be regarded as a hero. It takes courage to get out there and market a new idea, risking a mistake or having some people think you a fool.

Innovation – focus, focus, focus

Successful global companies that grow organically rather than by buying other companies, do so by devoting most of their energies to refining what they are already doing and to developing a small number of breakthrough ideas.

Only 80 of Fortune's Global 500 companies managed annual average growth of 5 per cent from growing their own sales, rather than through buying up competitors. Organic growth champions such as GE, BMW, Nestlé and Samsung gave their shareholders almost double the financial return of other Global 500 companies.[1]

Concurrent innovation has been a common feature in such companies. Progress in one area triggers changes elsewhere, and provides new resources for a third area. For example, when Peter Brabeck-Letmathe became CEO of Nestlé in 1997, he focused first on making the company more efficient. He then used the money he saved to double research and development. One of the results was Nespresso, which created a new market for portioned-coffee systems, with average sales growth of 30 per cent over eight years – $2.2 billion by 2009.

When GE launched Ecomagination in 2004, the first task was to cut the number of new initiatives in GE Global Research from more than 2,000 to just 80 – but each of them had potential for at least $100 million sales over three years. GE sends new ideas to a review board, which includes CEO Jeffrey Immelt, to assess potential and the investment needed to take each one to the next stage. Usually only 8 to 10 are in the pipeline at any time, each sponsored by top managers and defended fiercely against budget cuts. Half the new projects are usually to change how existing products are produced and delivered – for example combining 44 commercial finance sales teams into one. Ecomagination revenues and orders now exceed $17 billion.[3] GE is investing $1.5 billion a year.

> A major group of institutional investors, managing $31 trillion, formed the Carbon Disclosure Project, requesting large corporations to send data about their carbon-related risks every year. The volume of responses is increasing rapidly, year on year, as corporations wake up to the fact that they are being judged now on every aspect of their sustainability strategies.[2]

In the same way, Procter and Gamble focuses research and development on just 8 to 10 key areas, and Nestlé supports only the 10 most promising innovations, with progress personally tracked by its CEO.

Open innovation – share ideas faster

All great business innovation is about doing things differently to serve customers better. Innovations often come from unique combinations of ideas, from unrelated disciplines. Cross-fertilization is vital, yet most innovators work only with people inside their own companies, and are fiercely protective of their ideas. They may be secretive, not sharing their ideas even *inside* their own organization, maybe in competition with other departments or business units.

So-called 'open innovation' is a radically different approach, linking different groups together in a less formal way to solve complex problems faster. We see many examples of open innovation in the online

> 'Complexity of products is increasing, in terms of the breadth and number of technologies they include. Cars send maintenance data wirelessly to dealerships; sneakers contain silicon chips to fine-tune their fit. It just isn't possible for one firm to master all these skills, let alone house them under one roof.'
>
> Alan D MacCormack, Harvard Business School, *Best Practices of Global Innovators*

world. For example, Wikipedia is an open encyclopaedia, written and improved by hundreds of thousands of contributors, who give away their knowledge in order to be part of something truly great. Anyone in the world can change any sentence in a few seconds on almost any page.

Google has been using open innovation to help solve complex global challenges. It recently put out a call for 'ideas to change the world by helping as many people as possible'. Thousands of people from more than 170 countries submitted more than 150,000 ideas, from general investment suggestions to specific implementation proposals. Google noticed common elements in the responses, which it wove together into innovative approaches to solving some very pressing problems.

Online communities are agile, rapidly evolving and open to influence. For them, open innovation is as natural as the air they breathe. They communicate 24 hours a day at the speed of light, forming and re-forming new specialist networks and interest groups, sharing common problems and finding answers together in a form of 'collective intelligence'.

This new generation of digital natives is already creating huge pressures on companies and governments. They trust the opinion of strangers who are part of their community far more than politicians, CEOs or marketing claims. They are punishing companies online for cover-ups, secrecy, deception, antisocial behaviour, careless acts or wrecking the environment.

'Open source' software is an example of open innovation. Anyone is able to read the computer code and to make improvements, which they can share with their wider community. The Linux operating system and Joomla website database software were developed this way.

Most innovative manufacturers are using open innovation to some degree, whether they fully understand what they are doing or not. Life is too short to try to find answers to complex manufacturing or research problems if someone else has already developed an answer and is willing to cooperate with your company to develop it rapidly.

Faster innovation through wider networks

Many companies get their own scientists and engineers to develop all new products from research to strategy, only contracting out very small parts of the process (if at all). In theory, such a strategy is very efficient. However, it has led to tens of thousands of 'me-too' products, mere extensions of existing products. Radical breakthroughs are rare.

Take the pharmaceutical industry. The top 10 companies have research and development budgets that are as large as the combined GDP of 130 nations, yet 70 per cent of ground-breaking new products over the last five years have been developed *outside* of big pharma teams, by some of the world's 4,000 small biotech companies. As a result, large pharma companies are now spending much of their research budgets buying up or licensing other people's innovations. They each had a choice: innovate more openly or die.

Pfizer used a collaborative model in its deal over the blockbuster Lipitor. The drug's creator, Warner-Lambert, partnered with Pfizer to turn a good product into a huge success, using Pfizer's strong marketing and sales teams (Pfizer later merged with Warner-Lambert).

Likewise, GE has developed open innovation in partnerships with universities. For example, it has developed a pathology scanner to digitize slide images in partnership with the University of Pittsburgh Medical Center. GE is also collaborating with Eli Lilly and the Memorial Sloan-Kettering Cancer Centre to develop new data analysis tools.

> 'It is better to have enough ideas for some of them to be wrong, than to be always right by having no ideas at all.'
>
> Edward de Bono, originator of lateral thinking

IBM is also a major supporter of open innovation, working with universities, but at the same time collecting more patents each year, for its own use, than any other company. Many IBM innovations have their origins in some kind of collaboration.

Procter and Gamble is well known as a champion of open innovation and as a result it often gets to hear about innovations before its competitors. A key aim of open innovation is to position yourself as the partner of choice when a smaller company is looking to sell or license an innovation or to work in partnership.

Deutsche Telekom has spun off several new start-ups, backed by venture capital, since adopting open innovation in 2004, when it set up Deutsche Telekom Laboratories as a research institute affiliated to Berlin Technical University. Similar partnerships developed with Ben-Gurion University, Israel, and in Silicon Valley, and the number of researchers and scientists doubled to 300.

Apple has a closed innovation programme for hardware and basic operating of devices like the iPhone, but encourages open innovation in development of applications. Google has opened up the Android operating system to thousands of collaborators and is also encouraging open innovation in the development of applications. Google is one of the most innovative companies in the world. Every employee is given a free day every week to innovate, which does not have to be confined to their own business unit.

> ## Roche Pharmaceuticals – want-find-get-manage
>
> *Want:*   Scan what is going on outside the company, and match with wish list of what is needed, bottlenecks for innovation, key technology needed urgently.
>
> *Find:*   Network with universities, start-ups and so on, especially in places like China, Japan or Russia where discoveries may race ahead of what is in patent offices.
>
> *Get:*   Many innovations are redundant in 18 months so move fast. Look at objectives for each company, boundaries of agreements, market models, intellectual property, termination, and who will oversee the contract and enforce it.
>
> *Manage:* Making these relationships work can be a challenge. Who makes decisions? Who presents to investors? How do we respect each partner and value their different contributions?
>
> Intellectual property rights can be complex. For example, if you sell a licence to another company on one innovation, be sure that another part of your business is not selling a global package deal to someone else.
>
> Gene Slowinski, *The Strongest Link* – adapted

Procter and Gamble has a strategy to harness the talents of 1.5 million scientists with relevant research who are outside the corporation, combined with the intellectual fire-power of their own 8,600 research team.

Open innovation does not always save money. It shifts the costs of innovation from internal research and development to legal and intellectual property teams and to business development teams.

So what about *sustainable* innovation?

Open innovation allows other companies to exploit ideas that they cannot exploit, in ways that benefit everyone. It prevents wasted effort 'reinventing wheels'. Most large corporations own huge numbers of patents that they will never use. Maybe they do not fit current priorities; maybe they have been overlooked; maybe they are more suited to another kind of business.

IBM has given away the patents on a recyclable cardboard packaging insert that needs less fuel to make and transport than those commonly used today. DuPont has given away a technology that detects pollution in soil, air or water by using a microbe that changes colour when exposed. Xerox has donated a way to remove toxic waste from groundwater.

Sharing patents can have a huge impact. Nike shared its own water-based adhesive technology with different shoemakers that supply the company. As a result, the average level of harmful solvents used by Nike suppliers have fallen to less than 15 grams – from 350 grams a decade ago. The patents are all gathered in one place, which can easily be searched through a webpage. Eleven companies have already donated 100 patents. Platforms like Green Xchange allow companies to charge a fixed annual licence fee if they wish, and can also restrict licensing by rivals or for any use that might compete.

Companies will still want to protect their best ideas and innovations, but often the only way to realize their true value is to share that knowledge with others. When it comes to social entrepreneurs, using green tech to help save the world, the motivation to work in collaboration rather than competition is often very high.

It can be hard to give technology away. If not done correctly, a company that uses a donated technology could find itself infringing another company's patent. And deciding which patents can be given to others may mean time-consuming discussions internally with legal teams, research and development, business units and the corporate responsibility department.

Eco-Patent Commons was started in 2008 by IBM, Nokia, Pitney Bowes and Sony working with the World Business Council for Sustainable Development. Companies give environmental patents to the Commons community and any member can use them – for free. It works because many companies have developed and patented innovations to help them help the environment, but which are not their core business and will never make it as commercial products inside their own organization. They do not have the will or capacity to try to sell those patents to specialist companies, and so chose to give the knowledge away as part of their commitment to being responsible corporate citizens.

A key issue in accelerating green tech in the poorest nations is technology transfer, which is often held back by ownership issues. Initiatives like Eco-Patent Commons can assist that process. The Carbon Trust has proposed setting up a global network of Climate Innovation Centres to further encourage this.

Crowd-sourcing for sustainable innovation

'Crowd-sourcing' is when you push a problem out into a large innovative community to solve rapidly. InnoCentive Inc is a world leader in crowd-sourcing and prize-based innovation. It has created a global community of 180,000 Solvers – people committed to helping find practical answers to problems.

Cities have been invited to launch their own challenges to the community – for example on ways to become more carbon efficient, make it easier to recycle or to save energy in schools. Cities just have to put up the prize for the winning Solver. Chicago Chamber of Commerce was the first major metropolitan organization to post a challenge. It was solved after more than 125 ideas were proposed to increase the numbers of people using mass transportation to 1 billion rides a year. A Chicago-based urban affairs writer won the $5,000 prize. Wayne Spradlin, CEO of InnoCentive says: 'We are providing cities with a new resource: the collective brain power of their most active community members and the rest of the world.'

Kiva is a microfinance organization that blends funding with crowdsourcing. Kiva connects entrepreneurs to lenders, who have lent over $100 million in four years to help new businesses in poverty-stricken countries. Kiva uses social networks such as blogging communities, together with iPhone applications. It keeps more than 100,000 people updated on Twitter daily, and more than 5,000 through Facebook.

Habitat for Humanity helps people build homes. It encourages people on social networks to shape the content of their online pages with comments, photos, links and more. It has more than 22,000 Facebook fans. People can become involved even if they aren't able to help build a home, and stay connected with updates and stories from those they're supporting.

Hewlett Packard runs a crowd-sourcing contest every year, inviting grant proposals from universities worldwide. The company lists eight key areas where it is seeking help with innovation, and scientists suggest research projects to match. The HP grants are around $75,000 a year, often for three years. The aim is to tap the collective intelligence of leading academics.

Isolate or integrate innovation teams?

In some ways the opposite of open innovation is the black box or skunkworks approach, where an innovation team is working in isolation from the main business, protected by support from very senior leaders.

The benefit is that rapid innovation can take place without opposition from those in other business units whose very existence may be threatened if the project takes off. However, it can be hard for the rest of the organization to feel any sense of ownership if the project does take off, which can create huge problems later on.

Summary

So, we have seen that the world's greatest sustainability challenges can be solved by rolling out globally some of today's technologies, that innovation will not only reduce prices but will also open up huge numbers of better ways of achieving the same things. We have seen the impact of open innovation, and how a new generation of digital natives are going to seize the initiative in green tech innovation.

We have also seen a recurring lesson: only the smartest, most innovative and most agile will survive the green tech revolution. This radical shift in our world will affect all companies in all sectors of all sizes, to one degree or another. For many it may require only minor adjustments to save costs and refit themselves for a sustainability-minded future. For others it will require fundamental changes to how they do business.

For those who understand the future of sustainagility, it will open up huge new market opportunities with breath-taking potential: new income streams that will develop with a velocity rarely seen over the last hundred years.

AFTERWORD: TEN STEPS TO PROFITABLE SUSTAINABILITY

Some companies are slow to act on sustainability. They think it is a waste of time and money, while others are using green innovation to win competitive advantage, increase profitability and improve their brand. This is the truth: companies that waste resources and damage the environment are likely to waste money, alienate their customers, worry their investors and lose market share.

New consumers for a green tech world

Watch out for social consumers who are making decisions based on environmental image. This is leading investors to discount shares of firms they think are badly positioned for a warmer future.[1]

The economic meltdown raised fundamental questions about what kind of world we want or need in future. The elusive search for happiness is attracting more attention than ever. Consumers are thinking more about *personal* sustainability: things that really matter to them and to those they care about. The economic crash made us all think again about the mad chase for ever-faster economic growth.[2]

Managers who buy products or services from other businesses are also influenced by the same values that they are using in their personal lives, when they have to choose between almost identical companies. Which company do I believe in? Which is the company I am most proud to be working with?

Here are questions to ask in developing your business strategy, related to sustainability and climate change:[3]

- How are *customers changing in how they think and feel* about their own lives?
- How will changes in demand affect our *pricing*?
- What percentage of *climate change costs* can we pass to customers?
- How can we generate *new revenue streams* from low-carbon products?
- What *new forms of income* will there be, eg carbon credits?
- What threats are there from *low-carbon competitors*?
- What could *changed weather patterns* do to our business?
- How will *new regulations* affect our costs, eg emissions allowances?
- Will our *emissions* be taxed in some nations?
- What *capital* do we need to spend to reduce emissions?
- How will low-carbon targets affect our *raw material costs*?
- How much will our *energy costs* rise?
- How will our *risk profile* affect our insurance premiums?
- How will our *customers* view our *green credentials*?

Myths that stop action

In many companies there are a number of myths that stop leaders from taking action. Here are eight of the most serious ones.

MYTH 1 'We can't afford it right now'

Your strategy on sustainability may be the deciding factor in whether your business survives or dies. When times are tough, small differences between corporations become huge. As Richard Goode, Director of Sustainability at Alcatel-Lucent says: 'In good times, sustainability can be a competitive differentiator, in lean times,

'To conserve energy and improve profitability, we need to move more things with fewer resources. That's why we continue to invest in efficient equipment and processes.'

Frederick W Smith, Chairman, President and Chief Executive Officer, Fedex[4]

it's a defensive strategy, and in really hard times, it can determine your survival.' Xerox CEO Ann Mulcahey believes that being 'a good corporate citizen' saved the company from bankruptcy.[5]

MYTH 2 'It requires lots of staff'

Sustainability teams only need to be small – four people or less, even in multinationals as large as AT&T. Sustainability is about a mindset, not a massive new department. One or two key individuals may be needed to keep provoking change, but sustainable agendas should be part of every business leader's job – for example saving energy costs, reducing carbon emissions, conserving water, reducing toxic waste. It is the *right* thing to do.

MYTH 3 'There's no money to be made from sustainability'

As we have seen, our world will spend $40 trillion in the 'green tech, boom', not including huge new expenditures on water, food, cleaner manufacturing and so on – plus hundreds of millions on consultancy. Either your business grabs some of this action, or your competitors will.

Every business is in the green tech business, because every business is now expected to act in a more responsible way. Start by turning off the office lights and computers at night, recycle more of your waste and encourage your customers to do similar things. Sustainability actions are an insurance policy: you may not see immediate gain, but they protect you from risks to your brand.

Thousands of new companies and brands have been created that are entirely green-focused, such as Seventh Generation, Clorox's GreenWorks, and Motorola's Renew mobile phones. Not only are these brands bringing in millions in revenues, they are also enhancing the brand image of their parent companies. Procter and Gamble expects to generate $50 billion in cumulative sales from 'sustainable innovation products' in the five-year period ending in 2012.

Seventy-one per cent of UK graduates would rather work for a company with strong ethical values, and 76 per cent would consider leaving a company because of weak corporate social responsibility (CSR).[6]

Many companies have even found they can resell used products and materials that were considered waste. Verizon now generates $27 million a year by sorting and selling recyclable materials from its waste, also saving a million dollars in waste removal.

Johnson & Johnson has undertaken 80 sustainability projects since 2005 and achieved $187 million in savings with a return on investment of 19 per cent. Coca-Cola has made a 20 per cent return on its energy saving investments. Diversey, global provider of commercial cleaning solutions, expects to save $2 for every $1 it invests in green tech within five years.

MYTH 4 'It's just for big companies'

Companies of every shape and size are making money out of sustainability – ones as small as Numi Organic Tea ($15 million a year) or as large as Hewlett-Packard ($110 billion a year).

It is often easier for smaller companies to be agile, innovative, lean and resourceful when it comes to green innovation.

Bigger companies do have an advantage in being able to put pressure on their suppliers to be greener (Wal-Mart and Procter and Gamble are prime examples). They are also well placed to influence government policy, but smaller companies can be just as effective, or more so, at almost everything else.

> Numi Organic Tea uses 100 per cent biodegradable or recyclable packaging materials, and has won the WRAP award (Waste Reduction Award Program) in four out of the last five years from the state of California. It was recognized as one of the top five companies in the State for the waste-reduction initiatives. Sustainability is integrated in every decision made.

MYTH 5 'It's mostly for business-to-consumer companies rather than companies selling to other companies'

It is absurd to say that because customers are other business buyers, and not consumers, that going green does not matter. You are probably throwing profits down the drain – for example in higher fuel costs. Danny Wong, Director of Sustainability at Avery Dennison (selling to other businesses), found that energy savings alone justified its investment – 'a pleasant surprise'.

A growing number of business buyers are choosing to buy from companies they really believe in. If you are pitching against competitors at a similar price and specification, do not be surprised if those with the better image on sustainability win more business. A major telecom manufacturer found that the number of buyers from large corporations asking about its sustainability policies had risen from one in eight to 50 per cent in just three years.[7]

MYTH 6 'If we make claims about sustainability, we'll be accused of greenwashing – just hyping things up to make a sale'

While some companies no doubt exaggerate their green credentials, you will be safe so long as you are open about the efforts you are trying to make and the challenges you face in reaching your goals. Partnering with NGOs can help build credibility about your efforts.

MYTH 7 'NGOs are our adversaries'

Many companies steer away from environmental organizations because they fear attacks in the media. This is a missed opportunity. Many of these organizations are now looking to develop strong partnerships with corporations they might have attacked in the past, because they have come to realize that this is often the most effective way to change things. Organizations like Friends of the Earth, Greenpeace, the World Wide Fund for Nature/World Wildlife Fund and Conservation International are working with companies in this way.

For example, Coca-Cola is working with the World Wide Fund for Nature/ World Wildlife Fund to help the company meet its water needs without reducing or damaging local supplies. Hewlett-Packard partners with several NGOs. Suzanne Apple, Vice President and Managing Director, Business and Industry, at the World Wide Fund for Nature/World Wildlife Fund regards such partnerships as a 'win–win' opportunity.[8]

MYTH 8 'We don't have to worry because we don't make things'

Wal-Mart is a prime example of a company that doesn't make things, yet is working with suppliers to measure the carbon impact of every item it sells – 88 per cent of the company's footprint is in its supply chain, and only 12 per cent is under its direct control. So if the company is going to achieve carbon neutrality, it has to work hard with its suppliers to reduce carbon in the products it buys.[9] Every company has opportunities to save costs, make more money and improve their green image.

Ten steps for your company

Throughout this book we have listed Business Actions; here are some more:

1 Make 'sustainability' a central part of your strategy.

2 Look at the resources you use – directly or in products you buy.

3 Take steps to reduce carbon use and other resources.

4 Tell your own 'sustainability' story better than your competitors.

5 Link every sale to a benefit, eg 'every bottle of water sold pays for clean water for an adult for a month'.

6 Partner with environmental groups and other experienced people who can advise you – gain insight, improve product and process design and help the cause.

7 It must be profitable – which means pricing right and controlling costs.

8 Make sure you work closely with experienced people who can advise you.

9 Remember that a billion raindrops form a huge river – small things add up and do count.

10 Encourage your suppliers and customers to think greener.

Ten steps for governments

More important than any list of government actions is to show bold, clear leadership on issues relating to sustainability. Keep the issues in the media by including them in public announcements and speeches. Back up the general commitment by rigorous actions taken within every government department:

1 Reduce your own carbon footprint with a sustainability audit of different departments, and practical action, eg new heating and cooling systems.

2 Take radical steps to ramp up alternative energy production and to support local manufacturers to deliver what your country needs.

3 Be bold in making big decisions where arguing has gone on far too long – eg, deciding whether a wind farm will go ahead or not, or about carbon capture.

4 Pass regulations forcing adoption of new technologies where the cost to end-users will be low, because regulations create a mass market, and will lower unit cost. Example: requiring 20 per cent of the roof area of new buildings to be covered with solar cells.

5 Create focused incentives for technology use – eg, attractive tariffs for home owners who sell electricity to the national grid.

6 Agree mechanisms for carbon trading – or tax carbon – but do it quickly, and monitor carefully so you can adjust the policy to be most effective.

7 Link technology and finance in international negotiations – eg, grants from developed nations used to meet the cost of feed-in tariffs or for carbon capture at power stations.

8 Increase venture capital for green-tech start-ups.

9 Encourage collaboration and cooperation between green tech research centres.

10 Agree international action on a wide range of environmental measures to prevent companies switching operations to countries with more relaxed standards.

Finally... 12 things we can all do as a consumer

There are thousands of small actions that each of us can take that together can have a massive impact. It is easy to feel overwhelmed by the problem, but a hundred small actions a month, taken by 7 billion people, will create almost a trillion small impacts. Here are just a few, most of which will cost you little or nothing so long as you can borrow the capital for a short while, or will even save you money:

1 Improve insulation in your home.

2 Replace your old, inefficient boiler and old central heating controls.

3 Get a smart meter and start monitoring your power use – your bills will probably fall.

4 Change your car to a hybrid or electric vehicle – and help provoke the government or utility companies to develop greener power to recharge it.

5 Walk and cycle more.

6 Work from home more.

7 Buy local food and from local shops.

8 Eat less meat and make cotton and wool clothes last longer (water and land use).

9 Recycle more.

10 Repair more things instead of throwing them away.

11 Turn down the heating, or adjust the air conditioning thermostat – adjusting one degree closer to the outside temperature will save 10 per cent fuel.

12 Buy an offset for all carbon you cannot avoid using.

Take hold of the future – or the future will take hold of you.

FURTHER INFORMATION

Global Change Ltd

Global Change Ltd was founded by Dr Patrick Dixon in 1996 as a global trends and consulting company, working with multinationals to provide consumer and industry trends forecasting, including green tech and sustainability, as well as help with strategy, innovation and the development of agile leadership.

Clients include:

- *IT, Telecom and Distribution:* Google, Hewlett Packard, IBM, Infosys, Microsoft, NCR, Philips, SAP, Siemens Group, Fujitsu Siemens, Toshiba, Unisys AT&T, Belgacom, BT, Danish Post Office, DHL, Fedex, Mobilcom, MTN, Nokia, O2, Swedish Poste, British Post Office, Times of India, Qualcomm, Vodafone.

- *Travel:* Air France, Automobile Recycling Netherlands (ARN), Automobile Association, Dassault Falcon, Dubai Ports Authority, EADS/Airbus, Ford, KLM, Portuguese Tourist Board, Stagecoach, Swiss airline, Tourism in Ireland, Virgin Atlantic.

- *Energy, Chemical industry, Mining:* BASF, BP, ExxonMobil, General Electric, Hindalco, SHV Gas, Sulzer, Vattenfall, Veitch.

- *Financial services:* Allianz, Aviva, Bank of Ireland, Barclays Bank, BNP Paribas, Credit Suisse, Deutsche Bank, HSBC, Macquarie Bank,

Minsheng Bank, Morgan Stanley, Munich Re, Prudential, RBS, RMB, Saga, SEB, Skandia, Swiss Re, Swiss Stock Exchange, UBS, Zurich Financial Services.

- *Food and Drink/Packaging, Health:* Carlsberg, Diageo, Kraft Jacobs Suchard, Nutreco, Rexam, RPC, Sara Lee, Schwan's Frozen Foods, Tetrapak, Unilever, 3M, Avon, BUPA, Genentech, Gillette, GSK, Johnson and Johnson, NHS (UK), Roche, Novartis, Siemens Medical, Smith and Nephew, Wyeth Pharmaceuticals.

- *Government and UN:* World Bank, UNIDO, UNAIDS, EU; government departments in the United States, the UK, Ireland, South Korea, UAE, Kazakhstan, Lithuania, Portugal.

- *Marketing, Advertising and Design:* Belgium Marketing Federation, Marketing Forum Turkey, Finland Marketing Federation, Macann Erikson.

Contact details and Sustainagility resources

http://www.globalchange.com – 12 million unique visitors and 2 million video views (presentations).
Dr Patrick Dixon: patrickdixon@globalchange.com; Tel: +44 7768 511 390.
http://www.twitter.com/patrickdixon – 27,000 followers – join the conversation.

Globe Forum – Innovation Market Place

Globe Forum was founded by Johan Gorecki in 2003 to promote sustainable innovation.

We are a matchmaker between innovators, entrepreneurs and investors as well as between corporations, the public sector, cities and regions. We arrange prestigious and first class conference events in major cities around the world. We focus on business innovation, sustainability and fast growth markets. We create a productive environment for projects and ideas within the sustainability area to help them become reality. We offer a permanent platform for interaction through our online community.

Globe Awards are made each year to outstanding entrepreneurs, multinationals, cities and other groups in the area of sustainable innovation.

Our mission is to bring sustainable innovations to market. An important part of Globe Forum is the online community:

- Find decision makers and experts fast.
- Help innovations with fundraising.
- Open doors to thousands of companies.
- See your contacts' contacts.
- Market yourself in a professional context.
- Open up new sales channel.
- Let other people find you.
- Manage and expand your network.

Globe Forum Partners include:

SAS – Scandinavian Airlines; Öhrlings PricewaterhouseCoopers, SIDA – Swedish International Cooperation Agency; NIB – Nordic Investment Bank; DHL; HP – Hewlett-Packard; *International Herald Tribune*; Bird & Bird International Law Firm; First Card; First Light; Audi; Grey Stockholm; The City of Gdansk; HRG; Finnair; Lotus Travel; MindTree; The Pomorskie Voivodeship; The City of Poznań; Premiere Global Services; Scandic; Sustainia; Tricorona; Veckans Affärer; Volvo Cars; Swedbank; Wielkopolska Region.

Contact details and Sustainagility resources

Globe Forum, Humlegårdsgatan 14, SE-114 46 Stockholm.
http://www.gfbn.com.
+46 (0)8 586 199 00
info@globeforum.com.

NOTES

Chapter 1

1   See Chapter 10
2   Reuters, 9 November 2009
3   Future of Energy, *Financial Times*, 4 November 2009
4   National Ice Data Centre, 2009
5   Catlin Arctic Survey, *Financial Times*, 15 October 2009
6   Stern Review on the Economics of Climate Change, 30 October 2006
7   The World Bank: World Development Indicators database, Gross domestic product (2008), World Bank, 1 July 2009
8   *The Age* (Australia), 23 October 2006 and *The Guardian*, 8 June 2009
9   OECD World Energy Report, November 2009
10   *Independent*, 18 November 2009, quoting research by Professor Corinne Le Quere and others in *Nature Geoscience*
11   See Chapter 2 and Professor Mark Jacobson, Stanford University and Mark Delucchi, Research Scientist, Institute of Transportation Studies, University of California, *Scientific American*, November 2009
12   See Chapter 2 and *Proceedings of the National Academy of Sciences*, June 2009, study by Professor Michael McElroy at Harvard University
13   *Scientific American*, March 2009
14   World Nuclear Association, *Financial Times*, 4 November 2009
15   See Chapter 3
16   Catlin Arctic Survey, *Financial Times*, 15 October 2009
17   See Chapter 4, and 'Uranium recovery from Seawater', Japan Atomic Energy Research Institute. 1999-08-23, www.jaea.go.jp/jaeri/english/ff/ff43/topics.html; full text of research paper: www.npc.sarov.ru/english/digest/132004/appendix8.html
18   See Chapter 4
19   World Nuclear Association, *Financial Times*, 4 November 2009
20   *Financial Times*, 7 December 2009
21   Intergovernmental Panel on Climate Change
22   See Chapter 9 and *Linking Reduced Deforestation and a Global Carbon Market: Impacts on Costs, Financial Flows, and Technological Innovation*, FEEM Working Paper No. 56, 2009, CMCC Research Paper No. 66
23   See Chapter 9
24   *Financial Times*, 10 November 2009
25   www.reuk.co.uk/Feed-in-Tariff.htm
26   See Chapter 6
27   *The Guardian*, 5 February 2009
28   DEFRA, published 13 March 2007
29   Bloomberg report, 8 July 2009
30   Competitive advantage on a warming planet, *Harvard Business Review*, by Jonathan Lash and Fred Wellington, 2007

31 Competitive advantage on a warming planet, *Harvard Business Review*, by Jonathan Lash and Fred Wellington, 2007

32 *Financial Times*, 11 November 2009, quoting World Energy Outlook Report by International Energy Agency

33 *The Guardian*, 10 June 2009

34 Former US Secretary of State for Defence, James Schlesinger, addressing US Senate Committee, http://www.energybulletin.net/node/11014

35 *China People Daily*, 19 November 2002; www.english.peopledaily.com.cn/200211/19/eng20021119_107043.shtml

36 *Sunday Times*, 6 December 2009

37 *Economist*, 21 June 2008

38 *Economist*, 5 December 2009

39 *Economist*, 21 June 2008

40 BBC News, 15 September 2009

41 *Daily Telegraph*, 6 November 2009

42 *Financial Times*, 11 November 2009, quoting World Energy Outlook Report by International Energy Agency

43 Competitive advantage on a warming planet, *Harvard Business Review*, Jonathan Lash and Fred Wellington, 2007

44 Andrew Ager, head of emissions trading at Bache Commodities in London, quoted in *The Guardian*, 29 November 2009

45 Cleantech Group

46 Szalay, A and Gray, J, Science in an exponential world, *Nature*, **440**, 23 March 2006

47 Source: B Lab

Chapter 2

1 eSolar estimate: www.esolar.com/news/video_sierra

2 OECD World Energy Report, November 2009

3 *Financial Times*, 11 November 2009, quoting World Energy Outlook Report by International Energy Agency

4 OECD World Energy Report, November 2009

5 REN21 2007 report, *Financial Times*, 4 November 2009, and OECD World Energy Outlook, November 2009

6 Evaluation of Global Wind Power, Christina Archer and Mark Jacobson, *Journal of Geophysical Research – Atmospheres*, 110, D12110; 30 June 2005

7 UN report 2008: www.euroasiaindustry.com/page/366/The-Power-of-Renewables

8 *New Scientist*, 6 December 2009

9 M Z Jacobson and M A Delucchi, A Path to Sustainable Energy by 2030, *Scientific American*, 2009

10 US Energy Information Administration

11 *Scientific American*, November 2009

12 M Z Jacobson and M A Delucchi, A Path to Sustainable Energy by 2030, *Scientific American*, 2009

13 Professor Mark Jacobson, Stanford University and Mark Delucchi, Research Scientist, Institute of Transportation Studies, University of California, *Scientific American*, November 2009

14 Professor Mark Jacobson, Stanford University and Mark Delucchi, Research Scientist, Institute of Transportation Studies, University of California, *Scientific American*, November 2009

15 To produce 16.9 terawatt hours a year, from coal-fired power stations like Drax, which is 40 per cent efficient, with average fuel cost over 20 years of around 4 cents per kilowatt hour = $676 billion a year in fuel

16 *New Scientist*, 6 December 2009

17 eSolar estimates: www.esolar.com/news/video_sierra

18 If you average out the impact of cloud cover and distance from the equator

19 The upper atmosphere receives around 1.4 kilowatts per square metre during daylight, but by the time this passes through the air we breathe, it falls to 1 kilowatt at sea level when the sun is directly overhead. Physikalisch-Meteorolisches Observatorium Davos, World Radiation Centre calculations. See also discussion: http://en.wikipedia.org/wiki/Insolationhttp://www.pmodwrc.ch/pmod.php?topic=tsi/composite/SolarConstant

20 REN21 2007 report, *Financial Times*, 4 November 2009

21 US Department of Energy estimates – enough power to electricity currently used but not enough to replace all fossil fuel used in heating, transport and so on.

22 US Department of Energy estimates – enough power to electricity currently used but not enough to replace all fossil fuel used in heating, transport and so on.

23 *Scientific American*, March 2009

24 *Sustainability Investment News*, 3 March 2009

25 *Economist*, 5 December 2009

26 *Scientific American*, December 2009

27 *New Scientist*, 6 December 2009

28 *Scientific American*, March 2009

29 www.esolar.com/esolar_brochure.pdf

30 German Aerospace Centre estimates

31 www.enviromission.com.au/

32 Pictures of the Future, Siemens, Autumn 2009

33 REN21 2007 report, *Financial Times*, 4 November 2009

34 *Daily Telegraph*, 24 January 2010

35 *Economist*, 6 December 2008

36 *Economist*, 6 December 2008

37 *Economist*, 6 December 2008

38 *Economist*, 6 December 2008

39 Proceedings of the National Academy of Sciences, June 2009, study by Professor Michael McElroy at Harvard University

40 Professor Mark Jacobson, Stanford University and Mark Delucchi, Research Scientist, Institute of Transportation Studies, University of California, *Scientific American*, November 2009

41 REN21 2007 report, *Financial Times*, 4 November 2009

42 REN21 2007 report, *Financial Times*, 4 November 2009

43 ASD Reports, 2008

44 KTH, Royal Institute of Technology, 9 November 2009

45 Proceedings of the National Academy of Sciences, June 2009, study by Professor Michael McElroy at Harvard University

46 Pictures of the Future, Siemens, Autumn 2009

47 Pictures of the Future, Siemens, Autumn 2009

48 Proceedings of the National Academy of Sciences, June 2009, study by Professor Michael McElroy at Harvard University

49 British Wind Energy Association

50 *Scientific American*, December 2009
51 US Energy Department figures
52 US Energy Department figures
53 *Scientific American*, March 2009
54 *Economist*, 21 June 2008
55 Pictures of the Future, Siemens, Autumn 2009
56 *Financial Times*, 11 November 2009
57 www.statkraft.se/presscenter/nyheter/varldens-forsta-saltkraftver-har-slagit-uppdorrarna!.aspx
58 REN21 2007 report, *Financial Times*, 4 November 2009
59 The World Factbook, CIA, 2008
60 MIT estimates
61 *Scientific American*, March 2009
62 REN21 2007 report, *Financial Times*, 4 November 2009
63 www.swissinfo.ch/eng/front/detail/Man_made_tremor_shakes_Basel.html?siteSect=105&sid=7334248&cKey=1165839658000

Chapter 3

1   www.icjt.org/plants/uni/a/uni342a.html
2   Pictures of the Future, Siemens, Autumn 2009
3   Pictures of the Future, Siemens, Autumn 2009
4   Speech by Prime Minister Fredrik Reinfeldt: Taking on the Challenge: The Swedish Presidency of the European Union, 9 June 2009: www.sweden.gov.se/sb/d/11741/a/128014
5   *Daily Telegraph*, 10 November 2009
6   World Nuclear Association, *Financial Times*, 4 November 2009
7   *New Scientist*, 12 September 2009
8   *Economist*, 3 January 2009
9   *New Scientist*, 26 February 2009
10 UK Department of Trade and Industry, *The Energy* Challenge: www.berr.gov.uk/files/file32014.pdf
11 *New Scientist*, 10 January 2009
12 US Energy Information Administration: www.eia.doe.gove/pub/oil_gas/petroleum/analysis_publications/oil_market_basics/demand_text.htm#U.S. Consumption by sector
13 *Financial Times*, 11 November 2009, quoting World Energy Outlook Report by International Energy Agency
14 *Scientific American*, October 2009
15 *Scientific American*, October 2009
16 *New Scientist*, 28 June 2008
17 UK Department of Environment, 2009: www.eia.doe.gov/emeu/international/reserves.html
18 UN figures: www.unctad.org/infocomm/anglais/gas/market.htm
19 *Scientific American*, December 2009, Russian scientists estimates for methane hydrates under the Siberian shelf alone
20 *New Scientist*, 27 June 2009
21 *New Scientist*, 27 June 2009
22 *New Scientist*, 27 June 2009
23 *New Scientist*, 27 June 2009

24 *New Scientist*, 27 June 2009
25 *New Scientist*, 27 June 2009
26 US Department of Agriculture figures for 2009. Biofuel use of grain, and calculation by Friends of the Earth, based on average global food consumption, *The Guardian*, 23 January 2010
27 Future of Energy, *Financial Times*, 4 November 2009
28 *Scientific American*, March 2009
29 REN21 2007 report, *Financial Times*, 4 November 2009
30 REN21 2007 report, *Financial Times*, 4 November 2009
31 REN21 2007 report, *Financial Times*, 4 November 2009
32 Scottish Association for Marine Science Report: 'Potential of marine biomass for anaerobic biogas production', Maeve Kelly and Symon Dworjanyn
33 Reports from Colorado State University's Engines and Energy Conservation Laboratory and University of New Hampshire
34 *Scientific American*, December 2009
35 *Economist*, 18 July 2009
36 *Economist*, 18 July 2009

Chapter 4

1 *Daily Telegraph*, 1 December 2009
2 Johnson Controls, personal communication 2008
3 Pictures of the Future, Siemens, Autumn 2009
4 *Economist*, 10 October 2009
5 *Economist*, 10 October 2009
6 Pictures of the Future, Siemens, Autumn 2009
7 US Electric Power Research Institute
8 *Economist*, 10 October 2009
9 Pictures of the Future, Siemens, Autumn 2009
10 *Economist*, 10 October 2009
11 *Economist*, 10 October 2009
12 *Economist*, 10 October 2009
13 Pictures of the Future, Siemens, Autumn, 2009
14 *Economist*, 21 June 2008
15 Pictures of the Future, Siemens, Autumn, 2009
16 Eurostat, August 2009
17 *Scientific American*, March 2009
18 *Scientific American*, March 2009
19 Pictures of the Future, Siemens, Autumn, 2009
20 BBC News, 27 April 2007: news.bbc.co.uk/1/hi/world/europe/6597743.stm
21 *Daily Telegraph*, 6 November 2009
22 World Nuclear Association, *Financial Times*, 4 November 2009
23 *Daily Telegraph*, 10 November 2009
24 *Daily Telegraph*, 10 November 2009
25 *The Guardian*, 5 February 2009
26 www.bloomberg.com/apps/news?pid=20601100&sid=aQZtg3hJdMYA
27 www.bloomberg.com/apps/news?pid=20601100&sid=aQZtg3hJdMYA
28 www.bloomberg.com/apps/news?pid=20601100&sid=aQZtg3hJdMYA
29 *Economist*, 6 December 2008
30 *Economist*, 21 November 2009

31 John McCarthy, Professor of Computer Science at Stanford University, emeritus: http://www-formal.stanford.edu/jmc/progress/nuclear-faq.html

32 www.infomine.com/commodities/uranium.asp

33 World Nuclear Association, September 2009

34 World Nuclear Association, September 2009

35 John McCarthy, Professor of Computer Science at Stanford University, emeritus: www.formal.stanford.edu/jmc/progress/nuclear-faq.html

36 John McCarthy, Professor of Computer Science at Stanford University, emeritus: www.formal.stanford.edu/jmc/progress/nuclear-faq.htm

37 World Nuclear Association, September 2009

38 World Nuclear Association, September 2009

39 World Nuclear Association, September 2009

40 *Uranium 2005: Resources, Production and Demand*, jointly prepared by the OECD Nuclear Energy Agency (NEA) and the IAEA

41 World Nuclear Association, September 2009

42 www.news.softpedia.com/news/Global-Uranium-Reserves-Are-Running-Low-127213.shtml, 17 November 2009

43 World Nuclear Association, September 2009

44 World Nuclear Association, September 2009

45 *Uranium 2007: Resources, Production and Demand*, jointly prepared by the OECD Nuclear Energy Agency (NEA) and the IAEA

46 Uranium Recovery from Seawater, Japan Atomic Energy Research Institute, 23 August 1999: www.jaea.go.jp/jaeri/english/ff/ff43/topics.html; full text of the research paper: www.npc.sarov.ru/english/digest/132001/appendix8.html

47 www.nucleargreen.blogspot.com/2008/03/cost-of-recovering-uranium-from.html; see also *Desalination*, **232**, 1–3, 30 November 2008, pp 243–53 for similar work by Indian scientists

48 Cost Estimation of Uranium Recovery from Seawater with System of Braid Type Absorbent, Tamada Masao, Seko Noriaki, Kasai Noboru and Shimizu Takao (Central Research Institute of Electric Power Industries, Japan), *Transactions of the Atomic Energy Society of Japan*, 2006, **5** (4) pp 358–63

49 1983 estimates by Bernard Cohen, Professor Emeritus of Physics at Pittsburgh University, former president of the Health Physics Society, the main scientific society concerned with radiation safety. He has written several books on nuclear energy; see www.formal.stanford.edu/jmc/progress/cohen.html

50 Professor of Computer Science at Stanford University, emeritus www.formal.stanford.edu/jmc/progress/nuclear-faq.html

51 International Energy Agency, www.bloomberg.com/apps/news?pid=20601100&sid=aQZtg3hJdMYA

52 www.bloomberg.com/apps/news?pid=20601100&sid=aQZtg3hJdMYA

53 *New Scientist*, 9 October 2009

54 www.world-nuclear.org/info/inf66.html

55 *New Scientist*, 9 October 2009

56 *New Scientist*, 9 October 2009

57 *New Scientist*, 9 October 2009

58 *New Scientist*, 9 October 2009

59 *New Scientist*, 9 October 2009

60 *New Scientist*, 9 October 2009

Chapter 5

1 General Aviation Manufacturers Association, 2008
2 *Financial Times*, 4 November 2009
3 Competitive advantage on a warming planet, *Harvard Business Review*, by Jonathan Lash and Fred Wellington, 2007
4 Institute for Analysis of Global Security
5 *Economist*, 5 September 2009
6 *Financial Times*, 4 November 2009
7 California Energy Commission: www.consumerenergycenter.org/transportation/consumer_tips/vehicle_energy_losses.html
8 Electric Power Research Institute, California, study quoted in *New Scientist*, 20 September 2008
9 *Scientific American*, March 2009
10 *Financial Times*, 4 November 2009
11 Future of Energy, *Financial Times*, 4 November 2009
12 *Economist*, 4 July 2009
13 *Scientific American*, March 2009
14 *New Scientist*, 15 August 2009
15 Iveco figures
16 www.roadtransport.com/Articles/2009/07/22/134224/aero-trailers-get-boost-in-ricardo-report.html
17 www.roadtransport.com/Articles/2009/07/22/134224/aero-trailers-get-boost-in-ricardo-report.html
18 California Energy Commission: www.consumerenergycenter.org/transportation/consumer_tips/vehicle_energy_losses.html
19 www.discovery.org/a/6431
20 *Scientific American*, December 2009
21 news.cnet.com/8301-11128_3-10013303-54.html?part=rss&subj=news&tag=2547-1_3-0-5
22 California Energy Commission: www.consumerenergycenter.org/transportation/consumer_tips/vehicle_energy_losses.html
23 www.levantpower.com/technology.html
24 www.epa.gov/smartway/documents/drivertraining.pdf
25 www.epa.gov/smartway/documents/drivertraining.pdf
26 *Scientific American*, December 2009
27 *New Scientist*, 15 August 2009
28 *New Scientist*, 15 August 2009
29 www.roadtransport.com/Articles/2009/07/22/134224/aero-trailers-get-boost-in-ricardo-report.html
30 www.cta.ornl.gov/data/index.shtml
31 *Scientific American*, December 2009
32 *Le Figaro*, report, 26 November 2009
33 *The Guardian*, 28 November 2009
34 NAFTA Institute, June 2009: www.nmiba.com/nafta/presentations/08-victor-valdes.pdf
35 UK Prime Minister Gordon Brown, speech, 24 July 2009: www.energysavingtrust.org.uk/Resources/Daily-news/Climate-change2/1.1bn-investment-to-electrify-rail

36 *New York Times*, 12 August 2009, quoting Research by the University of California, Berkeley

37 US Department of Energy, *The Business Insider*, 4 May 2009, 'The True Cost of High Speed Rail for the US is More Than $500 Billion'

38 US Department of Energy, *The Business Insider*, 4 May 2009, 'The True Cost of High Speed Rail for the US is More Than $500 Billion'

39 www.guardian.co.uk/environment/2009/jan/22/greenwash-train-travel

40 Siemens mobility, *Evening Standard*, 23 November 2009

41 *The Scotsman*, 30 October 2009, £27 billion estimated for cost of 600 miles high speed track London to Scotland, for example

42 *Financial Times*, 11 November 2009

43 Fourbillion.com estimates

44 Intergovernmental Panel on Climate Change

45 CO_2 emissions for the average UK home: www.carbonfootprint.com/calculator. aspx and www.energysavingsecrets.co.uk/

46 *Sunday Times*, 29 December 2009, satellite study by UK Met Office

47 *Financial Times*, 4 November 2009

48 International Shipping Federation, 1 July 2009: www.marisec.org/

49 Calculations by BP and researchers at the Institute for Physics and Atmosphere in Wessling, Germany, *Guardian*, 3 March 2007

50 DHL figures

51 Reuters, 10 January 2008, and Operational Research Society, 1982: www.jstor.org/pss/2581518

52 *Economist*, 3 January 2009

53 www.worldcruise-network.com/features/feature687/

54 www.gcaptain.com/maritime/blog/ocean-kites-top-10-green-ship-designs/

55 DHL figures

56 Fedex Annual Report, 2008

57 DHL figures

58 *New Scientist*, 15 August 2009

59 From Competitive Advantage on a Warming Planet, *Harvard Business Review*, Jonathan Lash and Fred Wellington, 2007

60 Total percentage of EU freight in tons/kilometre

61 Road Freight Transport Vademecum, from the European Commission, March 2009

Chapter 6

1 Pictures of the Future, Siemens, Autumn 2009

2 Pictures of the Future, Siemens, Autumn 2009

3 *Scientific American*, December 2009; different estimates for CO_2 emissions from cement range from 5 to 7 per cent a year

4 *New York Times*, 31 March 2009

5 Energy Saving Trust, UK

6 *Which?* Reviews, UK

7 *Which?* Reviews, UK

8 Domestic Heating Market, UK 2009–2013, AMA Research, 1 February 2009

9 Greenpeace UK website

10 Greenpeace UK website

11 Greenpeace UK website

12 'Newsroom: Steam', ConEdison: www.coned.com/newsroom/energysystems_
    steam.asp, and Bevelhymer, C, 10 November 2003, 'Steam', *Gotham Gazette*:
    www.gothamgazette.com/article/issueoftheweek/20031110/200/674
13 *Scientific American*, March 2009
14 www.brw.cam.au/
15 US National Green Roof Congress
16 US National Green Roof Congress
17 Pictures of the future, Siemens, Autumn 2009

Chapter 7

1   Procter and Gamble website
2   *Daily Telegraph*, 6 November 2009
3   *Financial Times*, 29 November 2009
4   Pictures of the Future, Siemens, Autumn 2009
5   Co-operative Bank report, *The Guardian*, 30 December 2009
6   Pictures of the Future, Siemens, Autumn 2009
7   Pictures of the Future, Siemens, Autumn 2009
8   *The Guardian*, 28 November 2009
9   http://www.triflowconcepts.com
10 Cisco Systems Annual Report, September 2008

Chapter 8

1   *Sunday Times*, 8 November 2009
2   Stockholm International Water Institute, quoted in *Scientific American*, August
    2008
3   Stockholm International Water Institute, quoted in *Scientific American*, August 2008
4   BBC News, 10 January 1999: www.news.bbc.co.uk/1/hi/world/south_asia/252308.
    stm
5   *Economist*, 6 December 2008
6   1kg of wheat uses 1,000 litres in growing (the same as 1 ton, or 1 cubic metre of
    water); 1,000kgs = 1 ton, so a ton of wheat uses 1 million litres, or 1,000 cubic
    metres
7   Stockholm International Water Institute, quoted in *Scientific American*, August 2008
8   www.en.wikipedia.org/wiki/Environmental_impacts_of_dams
9   www.internationalrivers.org/en/way-forward/world-commission-dams/world-
    commission-dams-framework-brief-introduction
10 World Wide Fund for Nature/World Wildlife Fund
11 World Wide Fund for Nature/World Wildlife Fund
12 World Wide Fund for Nature/World Wildlife Fund
13 Freshwater Institute (Canada), estimate
14 World Wide Fund for Nature/World Wildlife Fund
15 *National Geographic News*, 28 February 2008
16 www.rediff.com/news/2005/mar/23river.htm
17 Global Water Intelligence report

Chapter 9

1   Intergovernmental Panel on Climate Change
2   *Daily Telegraph*, 28 November 2009

3 Butler, R and Laurance, W of the Smithsonian Tropical Research Institute in Panama, 'New Strategies for Conserving Tropical Forests', quoting UN figures, September 2008, *Trends in Ecology & Evolution:* www.bio-medicine.org/biology-news-1/The-drivers-of-tropical-deforestation-are-changing–say-scientists-4347-1/

4 United Nations Food and Agriculture Organization estimate

5 Proceedings of the National Academy of Sciences, DOI: 10.1073/pnas.0903029106

6 *Science Journal*, 23 April 2009, 22 authors of report including Thomas W Swetnam of the University of Arizona in Tucson

7 Lord Stern estimates, author of the Stern Report 2007, quoted in *Guardian*, 28 November 2009

8 www.independent.co.uk/environment/climate-change/deforestation-the-hidden-cause-of-global-warming-448734/html

9 Gittings, J, 2001, 'Battling China's deforestation', World News: www.guardian.co.uk/world/2001/mar/20/worlddispatch.china

10 www.europeanforestweek.org/48475/en/

11 www.europeanforestweek.org/48475/en/

12 Owen, J, 2006, 'World's Forests Rebounding, Study Suggests', *National Geographic News*: www.news.nationalgeographic.com/news/2006/11/061113-forests.html

13 Leakey, R and Lewin, R (1996) *The Sixth Extinction: Patterns of life and the future of humankind*, Anchor

14 Hance, J, 15 May 2009, Tropical deforestation is one of the worst crises since we came out of the cave, Mongabay.com, *A Place out of Time: Tropical rainforests and the perils they face*: www.news.mongabay.com/2008/0515-hance_myers.html

15 Butler, R and Laurance, W of the Smithsonian Tropical Research Institute in Panama, 'New Strategies for Conserving Tropical Forests', quoting UN figures, September 2008, *Trends in Ecology & Evolution*: www.bio-medicine.org/biology-news-1/The-drivers-of-tropical-deforestation-are-changing–say-scientists-4347-1/

16 *Economist*, 26 September 2009

17 www.papers.ssrn.com/sol3/papers.cfm?abstract_id=1444810, Linking Reduced Deforestation and a Global Carbon Market: Impacts on costs, financial flows, and Technological Innovation, *FEEM Working Paper No. 56*, 2009, *CMCC Research Paper No. 66*

18 www.papers.ssrn.com/sol3/papers.cfm?abstract_id=1444810 Linking Reduced Deforestation and a Global Carbon Market: Impacts on Costs, Financial Flows, and Technological Innovation *FEEM Working Paper No. 56.2009 CMCC Research Paper No. 66*

19 www.panda.org/what_we_do/successes/?79520/Deforestation-rates-slashed-in-Paraguay

20 www.fauna-flora.org/news_ulu_masen.php

21 Forum of Forests and Climate Change: www.fbycc.org/

22 Douglass Jacobs, Associate Professor of Forestry and Natural Resources, Purdue University Study, *Forest Ecology and Management*, June 2009: www.sustainablebusiness.com/index.cfm/go/news.display/id/18394

23 www.europeanforestweek.org/48475/en/

24 FAO figures 2007 for growth in paper and cardboard consumption 1985–2005; StatScan figures, May 2007, for growth in wood consumption 2000–2005

25 Lexmark presentation

Chapter 10

1 *Economist*, 31 October 2009
2 *Economist*, 31 October 2009
3 London School of Economics Report, Fewer emitters, lower emissions, *Daily Telegraph*, 10 September 2009
4 *Financial Times*, 10 November 2009
5 *Economist*, 21 November 2009, figure from 2005
6 *Economist*, 21 November 2009
7 *Financial Times*, 10 November 2009
8 *Financial Times*, 10 November 2009
9 *Financial Times*, 10 November 2009
10 *New Scientist*, 28 November 2009
11 *Economist*, 23 May 2009
12 Intergovernmental Panel on Climate Change, 2007
13 'Saving Water: From Field to Fork: Curbing Losses and Wastage in the Food Chain', brief authored by the Stockholm International Water Institute, the UN Food and Agriculture Organization, and the International Water Management Institute: www.siwi.org/documents/Resources/Policy_Briefs/PB_From_Field_to_fork_2008.pdf
14 'Saving Water: From Field to Fork: Curbing Losses and Wastage in the Food Chain', brief authored by the Stockholm International Water Institute, the UN Food and Agriculture Organization, and the International Water Management Institute: www.siwi.org/documents/Resources/Policy_Briefs/PB_From_Field_to_fork_2008.pdf
15 www.ec.europa.eu/budget/budget_glance/what_for_en.htm
16 *Economist*, 21 November 2009
17 *New Scientist*, 21 November 2009
18 *Financial Times*, 10 November 2009
19 www.sustainabletable.org/issues/climatechange/#fn7#fn7
20 www.sustainabletable.org/issues/climatechange/#fn7#fn7
21 EPA estimates, 2004: www.sustainabletable.org/issues/airpollution/#fn12#fn12
22 www.sustainabletable.org/issues/airpollution/#fn20#fn20
23 www.sustainabletable.org/issues/climatechange/#fn22#fn22
24 www.sustainabletable.org/issues/climatechange/#fn22#fn22
25 Fair Trade Labelling Organizations International, 2009
26 Fair Trade Labelling Organizations International, 2008, FLO International: Annual Report, 2007
27 *The Guardian*, 28 November 2009
28 United Nations Food and Agriculture Organization
29 United Nations Food and Agriculture Organization
30 United Nations Food and Agriculture Organization
31 *Economist*, 3 January 2009
32 *Economist*, 3 January 2009
33 *Economist*, 3 January 2009
34 *Economist*, 3 January 2009
35 *New Scientist*, 21 November 2009, research at Utrecht University
36 *Economist*, 3 January 2009
37 *Economist*, 3 January 2009
38 *Economist*, 3 January 2009

39 *Economist*, 3 January 2009
40 The Pew Oceans Commission, reported in 2003
41 *Economist*, 3 January 2009
42 *Economist*, 3 January 2009
43 *Daily Mail*, 21 September 2007
44 *The Guardian*, 30 August 2008, EU official estimates
45 *Scientific American*, December 2009
46 *Economist*, 3 January 2009

Chapter 11

1 *Daily Telegraph*, 6 November 2009
2 Competitive Advantage on a Warming Planet, *Harvard Business Review*, Jonathan Lash and Fred Wellington, 2007
3 *Daily Telegraph*, 6 November 2009
4 OECD Report, quoted in *Financial Times*, 5 November 2005
5 *Financial Times*, 2 December 2009
6 *Financial Times*, 11 November 2009, quoting the World Energy Outlook Report by the International Energy Agency
7 *Financial Times*, 11 November 2009

Chapter 12

1 Centre for Organizational Excellence, Switzerland
2 Competitive Advantage on a Warming Planet, *Harvard Business Review*, Jonathan Lash and Fred Wellington, 2007
3 Competitive Advantage on a Warming Planet, *Harvard Business Review*, Jonathan Lash and Fred Wellington, 2007

Afterword

1 Competitive advantage on a warming planet, *Harvard Business Review*, Jonathan Lash and Fred Wellington, 2007
2 Soper, K and Daly, H, Beyond Growth, *New Scientist*, 18 October 2009
3 Adapted from Competitive Advantage on a Warming Planet, *Harvard Business Review*, Jonathan Lash and Fred Wellington, 2007
4 Fedex Annual Report, 2008
5 Personal interviews, Globe Forum
6 PriceWaterhouseCoopers survey, *The Guardian*, 28 November 2009
7 Personal interview, Globe Forum
8 Personal interview, Globe Forum
9 Personal interview with Matt Kistler, Senior Vice President of Sustainability at Wal-Mart

INDEX

With over 42 years of publishing, more than 80 million people have succeeded in business with thanks to **Kogan Page**

www.koganpage.com

KoganPage